AZERBA

To Philip G. Kreyenbroek

AZERBAIJAN

Ethnicity and the Struggle for Power in Iran

TOURAJ ATABAKI

I.B.Tauris *Publishers*
LONDON • NEW YORK

Revised edition published in 2000 by I.B.Tauris & Co Ltd
Victoria House, Bloomsbury Square, London WC1B 4DZ
175 Fifth Avenue, New York NY 10010
Website: http:/www.ibtauris.com

In the United States and Canada distributed by St. Martin's Press
175 Fifth Avenue, New York NY 10010

First published in 1993 as *Azerbaijan: Ethnicity and Autonomy in
Twentieth-Century Iran* by British Academic Press
an imprint of I.B.Tauris & Co Ltd

ISBN   1   86064   554 2

A full CIP record for this book is available from the British Library
A full CIP record for this book is available from the Library of Congress

Library of Congress catalog card: available

Typeset by the Midlands Book Typesetting Company,
Loughborough
Printed and bound in Great Britain by MPG Books Ltd, Bodmin, Cornwall

Contents

List of Illustrations

1. Political activists attending the founding conference of the Democrat Party of Azerbaijan. Tabriz, September 1945

2. A memorial meeting for the Azerbaijani Constitutionalists. Tabriz, March 1946

3. Gholam Yahya Daneshiyan, Commander in Chief of the Armed forces of the Autonomous Government of Azerbaijan together with a group of Feda'iyan. Zanjan, April 1946

4. Members of the Tabriz Plenum Committee of the Democrat Party of Azerbaijan

List of Tables

List of Maps

Preface to the Second Edition

I certainly don't belong to that group of academics who enthusiastically accept the publisher's offer to reprint their books without even a modest editing. This is indeed more valid when a study is dealing with contemporary political as well as social issues. The research for this edition of this work was conducted and concluded when the Soviet rule was still prevalent over the Caucasus and Central Asia, regions neighbouring northern Iran. For the last two centuries, Iran was accustomed to having an expansionist, even most recently, the second world power as a neighbour on her northern borders. However, within the span of a few years, as an alternative to the vast Soviet empire, Iran came to enjoy a long common borders with three republics to each of which Iran is politically as well as economically superior. Nevertheless, each of these three republics, Azerbaijan, Armenia and Turkmenistan, accommodate a majority population whose corresponding ethno-linguistic groups live within Iranian territory. In the long run, Iranian Azerbaijan could not remain unresponsive to the socio-political changes, which have been occurring in the Caucasus since the fall of the Soviet Union. It was certainly necessary to deal with these changes in this study, however, due to some technical burdens, it was not possible for me to revise my work in full. As well as correcting errors in the text, I have therefore revised and updated the epilogue.

The first edition of this book attracted a broad attention not only in the West but also in Iran and the Republic of Azerbaijan. While in Iran Tus

Publishing House published the Persian translation, in the Republic of Azerbaijan, different chapters of it were translated and published in the local journals. Furthermore, the original English edition was reviewed in different academic journals. Although some of the reviewers, in their assessment failed to observe the required academic impartiality, nevertheless, I feel obliged to thank them at least for the time they allocated to reading this work. I am especially grateful to Rahim Reisnia an Azerbaijani expert from Iran, whose unbiased review of the Persian edition was enlightening to me. I could not conclude this note without expressing my gratitude to Iradj Bagherzade and Lester Crook at I.B.Tauris for their encouragement and trustworthy editorial assistance.

Touraj Atabaki

Preface

This work began as a study of the rise and fall of the autonomous government of Azerbaijan (1945-6). By focusing primarily on Iranian politics during the early 1940s and the post-World War II period, it was my intention to pursue an unconventional, non-partisan approach in examining the foundation of the autonomous government. In particular, I wished to follow an approach different from those scholars and historians whose only frame of reference with regard to the "Azerbaijan crisis" has been one based on international relations and the effects of Cold War developments. However, as the work progressed, I came to realize that relatively new notions of nationality and autonomy were of capital importance in bringing about the establishment of the autonomous government of Azerbaijan, and that the course of events throughout that period in Iran could only be adequately understood in the light of the growing antagonism between regionalism and centralism on the one hand, and, on the other hand, the decisive, new conceptual shifts affecting such notions as ethnicity, ethnic identity and nationality.

In Chapters 1 to 3, I present a more general historical overview of the origin of Azerbaijani ethnic identity. As a backdrop to political thought in Iranian Azerbaijan in the nineteenth century, I compare and contrast diverse forms of political discourse which were then current and influenced notions of ethnicity, nationality and citizenship in the Ottoman Empire, as well as in Iran. In Chapters 4 to 6, the primary focus is on the socio-political background of the autonomous government of Azerbaijan.

In this study, in addition to the official Iranian government sources, the Soviet Union archives, the British Foreign Office, and the United States National Washington Archive, I draw upon hitherto inaccessible or scarcely used source materials which originate with the Democrat Party of Azerbaijan and the autonomous government itself.

Iranian history being to a great extent unrecorded oral history, I have occasionally included in this study information based on interviews with leaders of the Democrat Party of Azerbaijan, former members of the autonomous government, and other contemporary politicians. These interviews, which were carried out in different cities of Europe, as well as in the republics of the former Soviet Union, have thrown light on a number of obscure points in the course of events and enabled me to check the validity of other primary and secondary sources.

The sources which I have drawn upon are from all camps involved with the events and belong to a category of primary source materials which have seldom been consulted. By making use of newspapers, books and proceedings of closed organizational meetings of both the Democrat Party of Azerbaijan and the autonomous government itself, memoirs of those active during the period and interviews, together with other contemporary Iranian journals and publications, it is my aim to present a balanced account of the events of the period, an account which does not neglect how the "other side" perceived the situation.

I would here like to take the opportunity to thank those who have given me assistance in the writing of this book: Ervand Abrahamian for his constant guidance and unflagging support, Frederick de Jong for his invaluable encouragement, John Gurney, Philip Kreyenbroek, Anna Enayat and Lester Crook for their constructive comments and criticism of earlier drafts of various chapters. And lastly, for his endless patience in editing the manuscript, I wish to express the great debt of gratitude which I feel I owe to John O'Kane. He has generously devoted much of his time to this task and given me his moral support throughout.

I would also like to thank Hedayat Matin Daftari, Naser Pakdaman and Jahanshahlu Afshar, who generously provided some materials and information which were in their possession. I am also grateful to the Controller, HM Stationery Office in Britain, as well as the staff in various archives in the former Soviet Union, for giving me permission to quote from their unpublished documents. Finally, I would like to thank my mother who never tired of sending me all the materials I requested from Iran, and my wife Sharareh and our baby daughter, Atossa, whose patience and understanding have created a happy home atmosphere, thus allowing me the peace of mind and concentration necessary to complete this book.

Needless to say, none of the above mentioned persons or institutions is responsible for any deficiencies contained in the book.

Touraj Atabaki

Note on Terms and Transliteration

The disintegration of the Soviet Union and the establishment of a series of new independent republics could occasion confusion in the employment of historical geographical terms. However, since for the most part references in the present work are to the historical period when those regions were contained within the territory of the Soviet Union, it seems only reasonable to retain the older familiar names rather than to adopt the newly invented ones. For example, the term "Soviet Azerbaijan" has been retained to designate Azerbaijan of the Caucasus in the Soviet period rather than the Republic of Azerbaijan.

The Azerbaijanis in Iran call their homeland *Azarbayjan* rather than Azerbaijan. However to conform to the more common English spelling the latter form is employed throughout this book.

Transliteration is always a thorny problem when one is dealing with several languages and alphabets at once. The system I have adopted in this work for Persian and Ottoman Turkish is a modified version of the system used by the *International Journal of Middle East Studies (IJMES)*; for the sake of convenience diacritical marks have been omitted, with the exception of *'ayn* (') and *hamzeh* (') for the Persian; and in representing the vowels for Ottoman Turkish. In the case of Azerbaijani terms, I have followed a modified Persian system except again in representing the vowels. Current English spelling of names such as Azerbaijan and Isfahan have been retained.

Glossary

ahali	people, citizen
akhund	low-ranking clergyman
anjoman	council, society
asnaf (singular: senf)	guild
dowlat	state
eblaghiyeh	proclamation
farman	royal decree
feda'i	fighter, devotee, armed volunteer
ferqeh	party
hezb	political party
hokumat/hükumat	government
iyalat	province
jahad/jihad	holy war
kafar/kafir	infidel
khan	chief
majles	parliament
maktab	traditional elementary school
mamlekat	kingdom, country
mardom	people
mellat/millat/millet	community; in modern times used for "nation"
mojahed	freedom fighter
mulla	low-ranking clergyman
ommat/ümmet	religious community
qowm (plural: aqvam)	ethnic group

qowmiyat	ethnicity
ra'iyat	common people, subject, peasant
roshanfekr	intelligentsia
seyyed	descendant of the Prophet
shora	council
tabaqeh (plural: tabaqat)	class, group
tayefeh (plural: tavayef)	clan
'ulama (singular: 'alem)	clergymen
vakil	representative, deputy
vaqf	religious endowment
vatan	homeland, fatherland
velayat	district

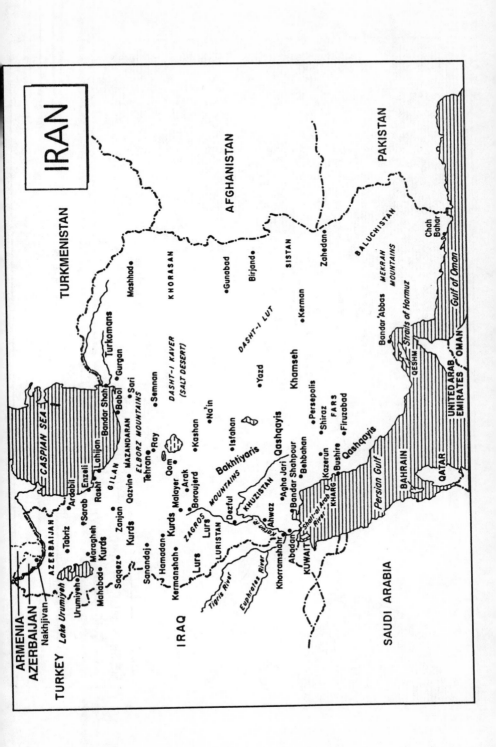

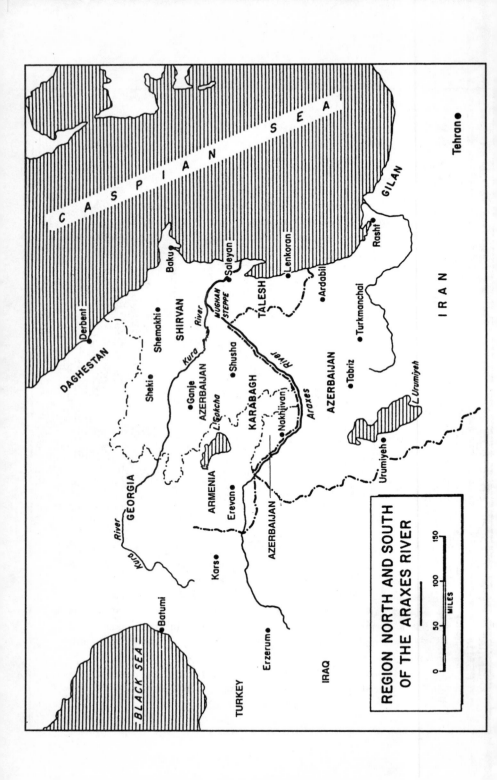

REGION NORTH AND SOUTH
OF THE ARAXES RIVER

Introduction

Traditional historiography frequently neglects the systematic investigation of power structures. If history is seen essentially as a complex of the clear and conscious plans and intentions of individual people or groups, the rivalries and petty jealousies of elites can easily appear as trivial background phenomena which are insignificant with regard to the course or 'interpretation' of history. Without sociological schooling both the difference between ideology and the actual distribution of power, and the function of ideologies as aspects of the actual distribution of power, do indeed remain unclear and undefinable.

N. Elias, *The Court Society*, p. 276

The twentieth century, in terms of political history, may well be distinguished, above all else, as a century of rampant nationalism, which witnessed an unprecedented proliferation of small-scale, sovereign nation-states. Moreover, founding such newly invented nation-states often entailed the invention of necessary historical traditions to justify and give coherence to the emerging state. Rewriting history became a major factor in bringing groups of people together and strengthening their sense of identity and political unity. In some cases the mere application of ancient, historically resonant names was enough to evoke a consensus of political legitimacy. To the Greeks the glorious name of Macedonia was – and still is – as important as Persia is for Iranians and Turan, to a lesser extent, is to some Turks. Consequently, the social connotations of certain key socio-political phrases, as well as geographic terms, became an important element in claiming political independence and legitimacy, and in reshaping the geographic boundaries of newly emerging sovereign states.

If the most striking political development at the beginning of the twentieth century was the collapse of two old empires, the Ottoman

1

Empire and that of Tsarist Russia, the end of the present century is marked by the dramatic collapse of a superpower, the Soviet Union. As a result of this disintegration, a number of newly founded sovereign states have been established, most of them in search of what they perceive to be their suppressed, historically authentic identity.

After World War I, when the old Russian Empire was replaced by the new revolutionary Soviet state, there were those who believed that the age of nationalism – at least in Europe – had come to an end and that a new era had dawned for humanity, an era in which class identity, it was assumed, would replace the old, nineteenth-century concept of national identity. Indeed, the Soviet Union itself by promoting this idea was pretending that on the soil of the old empire a new homeland had been founded which would be the breeding ground for the new "Soviet man". The main feature of this new homeland was supposed to be its inherent potential to transcend the identities of diverse ethnic groups. In accomplishing this "historical determinism", and paving the way for the new kind of individual, "Soviet man", an attempt was made to rewrite history, both on the regional level, and on the level of large international empires.

Conversely, in order to protect their own identity against the comprehensive, all-engulfing Soviet identity, within the same school of historiography a petty nationalistic trend gradually began to appear, introduced by local historians. The radical rewriting of the history of Soviet Azerbaijan (the present day Republic of Azerbaijan), which lies to the north of Iranian Azerbaijan, is a vivid example of this form of politically motivated historical revision.

In the histories of Azerbaijan,[1] which were written in the post-Stalin period to replace the earlier Stalinist version of the country's history, one has no difficulty identifying the attempt being made to emphasize the continuity of the history of the "Azerbaijani Turks". According to authors of this kind, from antiquity the region of Azerbaijan has been the homeland of particular Turkic tribes. Another example which demonstrates the attempt to exploit simple geographical terms in order to invent historical legitimacy is the use, in certain intellectual circles both in Iranian Azerbaijan and in the former Soviet Azerbaijan, of phrases such as *Shumali* (northern) and *Junubi* (southern) Azerbaijan, to designate the regions north and south of the Araxes River. It is obvious that what lies behind this choice of terminology is the desire to proclaim the cultural homogeneity in both geographical areas, with the implied call for unification of Iranian Azerbaijan with the present day Republic of Azerbaijan.

For Iranians in general, and Iranian Azerbaijanis in particular, the political connotations inherent in such concepts as ethnicity and nationality emerged in the years immediately following upon the Constitutional Revolution of 1905-9. The influence of nineteenth-century Western ideas with regard to nation, nationalism and national sovereignty, in conjunction with the spread of pan-Turkism in neighbouring Anatolia, made some circles of Iranian middle class intellectuals anxious about the consequences of the political changes which the region was undergoing at the beginning of the twentieth century. The main concern of these intellectuals was to protect Iran's sovereignty and to combat any tendencies for the country to break up into separate regional states.

Following the collapse of the Ottoman Empire, when the idea of a greater homeland for all Turks was propagated by Turkish nationalists, and some appeals were made for Iranian Azerbaijan to secede from Iran and to join the new pan-Turkic homeland, a small group of Iranian intellectuals based in Berlin became the most vociferous advocates of preserving Iranian identity and sovereignty. The members of this group of intellectuals, who later returned to Iran and held influential positions in the government, became the founders of a trend in Iranian historiography which is known above all for its emphasis on continuity in Iranian culture and for upholding the country's pre-Islamic values.

When World War I erupted, political chaos and confusion swept across Iran. The successive governments proved to be incapable of solving the country's escalating problems and implementing fundamental reforms. However, in the north of the country – in Azerbaijan, Gilan and Khorasan – there were reform-minded individuals who believed that if they succeeded in launching regional campaigns to initiate change and reform in their own region, the same reforms would gradually spread through the whole country. The agenda of these regional campaigns did not include the call for secession, but rather these efforts represented an attempt to establish stable political power in Iran, while considering the question of a fair division of powers between the central government and local authorities throughout Iran.

The concept of fully fledged autonomy, in the modern sense of the word, came to Iran only some years later and as a by-product of Marxism. In the Marxist literature written or translated by Iranian

Marxists, Iran was described as a "multi-national" land, where all nations, except the Persians, were subjected to tyranny by the latter. Moreover, in order to free themselves from "Persian chauvinism", the other "nations" were advised to adopt the Soviet model, i.e. to establish autonomous regions within Iran's political boundaries. On the other hand, there were times when, in their propaganda, the Iranian Marxists by-passed the idea of establishing the autonomous regions and proclaimed the early Bolsheviks' view of the right of nations to self-determination, the right to secede and form an independent state. However, being a clandestine political group, the Iranian Communists were unable to demonstrate whether they were capable of implementing either of these new models. During the reign of Reza Shah Pahlavi (1925–41), neither they, nor any other political party, had the opportunity to participate in political life.

For Iranians, the Anglo-Soviet invasion of Iran in August 1941 was more than simply the end of sixteen years of autocratic rule by Reza Shah. Despite the fact that the "open atmosphere" of political life in Iran which began with the invasion gradually disappeared after the fall of the autonomous government of Azerbaijan, the rapid politicization which took place from 1941 was unlike anything Iranian society had experienced since the Constitutional Revolution of 1905–9.

The emergence of political parties and trade unions in the big cities raised the level of people's political awareness and increased their class, as well as their ethnic, consciousness. There was a widespread feeling that the Iranian Parliament, which had been generally regarded as a "rubber stamp", would now play an active role in the country's decision-making, rather than obediently passing government-proposed bills.

Furthermore, in some provinces of Iran, Reza Shah's abdication in 1941 was seen as marking the end of a government policy which stressed the supremacy of the Persian-speaking part of the population. This policy had been promoted particularly during the previous ten years of Reza Shah's rule. Now, after 16 years of an official government policy of intolerance towards diverse ethnic groups, social grievances and ethnic sentiments suddenly had the chance to emerge into the open. Newspapers and books began to be published in languages other than Persian. Likewise, in some provinces, reinstating ethnic culture and stressing ethnic identity were considered not only as a reaction against the homogenizing policy of Reza Shah, but also as a means of exerting pressure on the government to pay more attention to the economic needs of the countryside.

Azerbaijan was one of the several geographical regions which had suffered in various ways from being economically neglected during the reign of Reza Shah. The local power vacuum which resulted from the invasion of north-western Iran by Soviet forces, together with the recent past of economic deprivation and a developing sense of ethnic identity, were factors which greatly contributed to the acceleration of social change. The time was ripe for new ideas, and there was a readiness to seize upon new theories to explain the nature of society and politics.

Taking advantage of the new international alignment, in September 1945 the newly founded Democrat Party of Azerbaijan convoked a National Assembly and subsequently set up the National Government of Azerbaijan. At the same time, the official army was disbanded and, as a substitute, a new paramilitary organization, known as the *Feda'iyan*, was founded. In the event, the Democrat Party of Azerbaijan managed to hold power for almost one year. The dramatic downfall of the National Government came in December 1946 when the Central Government sent an army into Azerbaijan and forcibly put an end to the rule of the autonomous government.

The main body of this book examines the development of ethnic identity in modern Iranian Azerbaijan, and the way that this sense of ethnic identity was transformed into direct political action which led to the establishment of autonomous government of Azerbaijan. In view of the importance of the autonomous government set up by Azerbaijanis as the first practical attempt at regional autonomy by an ethnic group in modern Iran, a more detailed account of its history is given. Moreover, in order to present a balanced account of the rise and fall of that government, it is of capital importance to consider earlier political developments in Iran and in particular the momentous events which took place during the period 1941–6, that is, the period beginning with the abdication of Reza Shah and the occupation of Iran by the Allied powers, and ending with the collapse of the short-lived autonomous government of Azerbaijan.

The years of the "crisis" of Azerbaijan and the policies of the autonomous government of Azerbaijan have been discussed in several books and a number of academic articles on the twentieth-century history of Iran as well as on the Soviet Union's relations with the West and Iran. In view of the exhaustive treatment which the subject has received, one might well assume that there is little need for yet another study in this area. The fact is, however, that the majority of these books and articles focus predominantly on international relations and the effect of Cold War developments on events and government policy in Azerbaijan. Moreover, many of these contributions unfortunately suffer from being politically biased and are based on incorrect or inaccurate information. As an example of a purely factual error, H. Thomas in his recent book on the Cold War confuses Pishevari (head of the autonomous government of Azerbaijan) with Sultanzadeh, the famous veteran Communist who disappeared in Stalin's 1935–8 purges.[2] Or again, Ladjevardi, in his admirable study of the labour union movement in Iran, when dealing with the Azerbaijan "crisis", erroneously refers to Truman as having given Stalin an "ultimatum" with regard to evacuating Soviet forces from Azerbaijan.[3]

The present book neither intends to cover the whole twentieth-century history of Iran nor pretends to solve every theoretical problem related to the concepts of ethnicity, nationality and citizenship in Iran's modern history. By focusing on Azerbaijan as a case study, this book hopes to throw more light both on the development of Azerbaijani ethnic identity and on its reciprocal relations with the wider question of Iranian national identity. The other major concern of this book is to highlight the problems which a modern nation-state faces when it is confronted with the question of regional autonomy. In my description of the course of events relevant to the rise and fall of the autonomous government of Azerbaijan, I have tried to bear in mind what the eminent Persian historian Abolfazl Beyhaqi remarked a thousand years ago when he presented his account of a recently deceased vezir: "Although I should confess that I despised the person, nevertheless, in writing this history I will avoid presenting any statement which might seem fanatical or vindictive, and thus the reader will not find fault with me."[4]

1

Origins of the Azerbaijanis

When 'Omar b. al-Khattab sought the advice of al-Hurmuzan, saying: "Shall we begin with Isfahan or Azerbaijan (Aturpatkan)?", al-Hurmuzan replied: "Isfahan is the head, and Azerbaijan the wing. Cut off the head, and the wings will fall off together with it."

Al-Baladhuri, *Kitab Futuh al-Buldan*, p. 472.

Turk, Azeri or Azerbaijani?

Azerbaijan, situated in the north-west of present day Iran, is a region with a population of 7,770,000 (out of the nation's total population of 49,765,000)[1] and has its own distinctive language which more than any other single factor accounts for its separate identity. The geographical term Azerbaijan, according to the distinguished Iranian historian, Ahmad Kasravi, most probably derives from the name of a local commander, who ruled over the region when Alexander the Great invaded Iran in 330 BC[2] Aturpat, whose name means Guardian of the Fire, and his descendants ruled over Aturpatkan (Azerbaijan) for centuries – a region where "the fire-temples were very common".[3]

The Islamization of Aturpatkan dates back to the seventh century when the Arab army, following its victories on the western frontier of Persia, marched towards the north and in 642 AD succeeded in conquering what was known, in accordance with Arabic pronunciation, as Azerbaijan. The Islamic geographers describe Azerbaijan as being

7

bounded to the south by Zanjan and to the east by Deylamistan, Tarom
and Gilan. To the west lay Varasan or Varadan, and the Araxes River
formed the northern limit of the region.[4]

As is evident from this description, the region lying north of the
Araxes River, which is today the area of the Republic of Azerbaijan
(former Soviet Socialist Republic of Azerbaijan), is not included within
the geographical boundaries of old Azerbaijan. The anonymous tenth-
century geographical work, *Hodud al-'Alam*,[5] refers to the region north
of the Araxes as Aran. The Araxes River is clearly taken to be the
northernmost limit of Azerbaijan. Likewise, Ibn Hawqal considers the
Araxes River to form the southernmost border of the region Aran.[6] To
this we may add the remark of another tenth-century traveller,
al-Muqaddasi, who divides the land of Iran into eight regions (including
Aran and Azerbaijan):

> Aran is a land somewhat like an island lying between the
> Caspian Sea and the Araxes River. Its capital city is
> Barda'a.[7]

And again, in the thirteenth century, we find that the geographer Yaqut
al-Hamavi also records that Azerbaijan was distinct from Aran:

> Between Azerbaijan and Aran lies the river called the
> Araxes. The region to the north and the west of this river is
> Aran, and whatever lies to the south is called Azerbaijan.[8]

Finally, the quasi-encyclopedic work entitled *Borhan-e Qate'*, which
was completed in 1652, explains the word Aras (Araxes) as:

> the name of a famous river which flows past Teflis and
> forms a boundary between Azerbaijan and Aran.[9]

Al-Istakhri, the early tenth-century traveller, refers to the language of
the Azerbaijanis as "Farsi and Arabic", but he adds that "the people of
the outlying districts of Barda'a speak Arani".[10] According to the
famous historian al-Mas'udi, also of the tenth century, the Persians are:

> a people whose borders are the Mahat Mountains and
> Azerbaijan up to Armenia and Aran, and Bayleqan up to

Darband, and Ray and Tabaristan and Masqat and Shabaran
and Jorjan and Abarshahr, and that is Nishabur, and Herat
and Marv and other places in the land of Khorasan, and
Sejistan and Kerman and Fars and Ahvaz ... All these lands
were once one kingdom with one sovereign and one language
... although the language differed slightly. The language,
however, is one, in that its letters are written the same way
and used the same way in composition. There are, then,
different languages such as Pahlavi, Dari, Azeri, as well as
other Persian languages.[11]

It is at least clear that the author considers Azeri as a member of the
Persian language family.

Even as late as the thirteenth century, six centuries after the conquest
of Azerbaijan by the Muslim Arabs, Azeri was still spoken in
Azerbaijan, as Yaqut al-Hamavi testifies:

Its [Azerbaijan's] inhabitants have beautiful faces and delicate
skin and speak a language which is called *Azeriyeh*, which no
one understands but they themselves.[12]

The Arrival of the Turks

The Turkic language entered the region of Azerbaijan as a result of the
great migration of Turks into Asia Minor in the eleventh century. "The
first group of Oghuz consisting of about 2,000 tents arrived in 1029 and
they were well received by Vahsudan ... Again in 1044, some 5,000
Turkmen returned to Azerbaijan from Mesopotamia through Diyarbakr
and Armenia and occupied the town of Khoy."[13] However, what may
be considered as the conclusive event took place in 1054 when Toghrel
Beg, the eminent Saljuq warlord, arrived in Azerbaijan and Aran to
receive the submission of the local rulers.[14]

The language which these newcomers brought with them was that of
the south-western (Oghuz) group of Turkic languages. The new
language, though strongly influenced by its close encounter with the
indigenous Azeri – the language spoken in Azerbaijan prior to the
Turkish invasion – gradually replaced the latter and came to be the

dominant language of Azerbaijan.

Following the advent of the Saljuqs, Azerbaijan was invaded once more, this time by the Mongols in the spring of 1221. Although the massive onslaught of Genghiz Khan was marked by bloodshed and devastation, in the years that followed Azerbaijan nevertheless slowly recovered and eventually entered on a period of peace and prosperity. Upon his return from the conquest of Baghdad in 1258, the Mongol ruler, Hülegü Khan, chose to reside in the city Maragheh which then became the capital of the Il-Khanid dominion in Persia. This was the beginning of an era of high cultural development. It was then that Nasir od-Din Tusi, the Grand Vezir, under the Mongol Khan's patronage erected the city's famous astronomical observatory. As with the case of Maragheh, Tabriz too enjoyed prosperity under the powerful Il-Khanids. Indeed, in 1265, when Hülegü's successor, Abaqa, ascended the throne, by way of innovation he moved the capital of the empire from Maragheh to Tabriz.[15]

In the fifteenth century, an era dominated by the descendants of Tamurlane, Azerbaijan was mainly ruled by the Qara Qoyunlu and Aq Qoyunlu Turkmen. Being the principal rival of the Timurids, the Turkmen repeatedly invaded Azerbaijan, and as a result the province often suffered extensive devastation. However, during this phase of its history, there were periods when the province enjoyed peace and prosperity, especially under the Qara Qoyunlu (1438–67), when Tabriz became the capital of the Black Sheep Turkmen, whose dominion at its peak stretched from Anatolia to Herat.[16]

The spread of Azerbaijani, the local form of this branch of Turkish, was so successful that by the beginning of the sixteenth century when Shah Isma'il established the dominion of the Safavid dynasty in this region, there was scarcely any trace of the old Azeri, and by then Azerbaijani was "the common language of the people of Azerbaijan".[17]

During the sixteenth and seventeenth centuries, the political history of the region is marked by competition, and on many occasions outright military confrontation, on the part of two great empires: the Ottomans in Anatolia, and the Safavids in Persia. By putting absolute emphasis on Shi'ite Islam in a geographical area which had been traditionally inhabited by Sunni Muslims, the Safavids were attempting to establish religious sanctions which would guarantee their sovereignty in the face of the Sunni Ottoman threat.

According to the sixteenth-century historian, Hasan Beg Rumlu, when

Shah Isma'il, the founder of the Safavid dynasty, took up his residence in Tabriz, he issued a decree to collect together all the available Shi'ite theological works. However, even in a big city like Tabriz only one such book could be found.[18] The anecdote, it would seem, is meant to illustrate the lack of formal Shi'ite learning in the region at that time.

During two centuries or more of Safavid rule, Azerbaijan was ravaged on several occasions by invading Ottoman armies. Undoubtedly, the most disastrous of these military episodes took place in 1635 when the Ottoman sultan Morad IV's forces occupied Tabriz and laid the city waste.

Through the first half of the eighteenth century, the Ottoman campaigns into Azerbaijan continued. Taking advantage of the political confusion in Persia at the end of the Safavid era, and justifying their military action on the basis of combatting the latter's "heresy", the Ottomans once more invaded Azerbaijan and Ardalan (Kurdistan). However, later, in the mid-eighteenth century, when Nadir Shah Afshar, a Sunni commander, gained power in Iran, the Ottomans reluctantly withdrew from the province.[19]

The well-established Ottoman policy of military expansion into Azerbaijan, coupled with the major religious conflict which only intensified throughout the centuries, goes a long way in explaining the hostile Azerbaijani attitude towards what came to be the modern Republic of Turkey. On the other hand, despite the uninterrupted Ottoman threat to Azerbaijan, which often caused instability in the province, one should mention the many intermittent periods of peace and prosperity when, as a result of its strategic position on the important trade route and line of communication between Trebizond and central Iran, Azerbaijan developed commercially.

The history of Azerbaijan in the nineteenth century is predominantly influenced by the impingement of a new empire on the Persian political scene. Being on the frontier with the Russian Empire, Azerbaijan gradually came to be under intense diplomatic, economic and military pressure from the Russians. Following upon the humiliating military defeats of 1813 and 1828, the Persian frontier with Russia was fixed by the Treaties of Golestan and Torkamanchay. As a result, Persia was forced against her will to abandon her eastern Caucasian provinces forever. Furthermore, under the terms of the treaties, Russia also exacted commercial as well as fiscal privileges throughout the country.

Consequently, the position of Azerbaijan as a passageway for Russian economic penetration into the rest of Persia came to assume a capital importance. In the Azerbaijan-centred Qajar Empire (1790–1925), Tabriz persisted as one of the main commercial centres of Persia, and the second politically most important city of the country, where the heir to the throne resided with his own court circle. Moreover, this was the period during which the city of Tabriz became characterized by greater openness to the outside world and proved to be more receptive to new ideas than other cities in Persia. This would eventually make Tabriz into the foremost breeding ground of progressive political thinkers and helps to explain why Azerbaijanis played so prominent a role in the Constitutional Movement in the early twentieth century.

Azerbaijanis, a Nation or an Ethnic Group?

Regarding Azerbaijanis as a *nation* or as an *ethnic group* implies that one has a working definition of both these socio-political terms. For the purpose of this study, the essential question will be how the notion of Azerbaijanis' being a *mellat* (nation) rather than merely a *qowm* (ethnic group) gained ground, at least among a fraction of the politically minded Azerbaijanis – which was to have important consequences for the autonomous movement in Azerbaijan.

The fall of two great empires in the early twentieth century, i.e. those of Tsarist Russia and the Ottomans, generally contributed to promoting the concept of the right of nations to self-determination. Later, in the post-World War II period, the concept was to take on even greater political importance in view of the rapid process of decolonization and the emergence of numerous new nation-states. The question of what constitutes a nation and what is the basis of the right to self-determination is, therefore, central throughout this period, particularly in those parts of the world where these political concepts only began to affect the thinking of ordinary people in relatively recent times. Could any group of people, by simply calling itself a nation, expect to enjoy the right to self-determination and proceed to set up an independent state? If not, then what were the necessary criteria which would justify the existence of a distinct and separate nation? And is there an essential difference between a nation and an ethnic group? If so, in what precisely does that difference consist?

In the sections which follow below, an attempt is made to find an

answer, at least in part, to these questions which were of great importance in shaping the new patterns of political thinking of Iranians as they
entered the modern world. The cases of Iran and the Ottoman Empire
will be considered and compared as two distinct national contexts with
regard to their similarities and differences. In both these empires, as we
shall see, along with other political developments in the late nineteenth
and early twentieth centuries, such key political concepts as ethnicity,
nationality and citizenship underwent significant modification and
transformation.

Nationality versus Ethnicity

To forestall an optimistic expectation that any clear, cut and dried,
scientific answers to this question can be found, let us bear in mind
Seton-Watson's statement:

> I am driven to the conclusion that no "scientific definition"
> of *nation* can be devised; yet the phenomenon has existed and
> exists.[20]

Perhaps one easy, make-shift answer to the question "What is a
nation?", could be as follows:

> Two men are of the same *nation* if, and only if, they share
> the same culture, where culture in turn means a system of
> ideas and signs and associations and ways of behaving and
> communicating.[21]

At first sight, this definition might appear adequate but it does not give
any weight to *consanguinity* or *common lineage* as a basis for bringing
people together in the framework of a nation. The etymology of the
word "nation" – from the Latin *nascere* (to be born) – reminds one that
there was originally a notion of kinship involved in the concept of a
nation.

The word *nation*, in its modern sense, was born in the European age
of enlightenment and revolution. Although the word can be traced back
to the thirteenth century in English literature, it had the "primary

connotation of blood related groups"[22] and did not include the other ties, besides those of blood, which could bind a specific group or people together. Therefore, the first task which the new concept of nation had to accomplish was demolishing the old accepted view of centralized, fixed blood descent and "destroying the legitimacy of the divinely ordained hierarchical dynastic realm".[23] The sovereignty and legitimacy claimed for itself by the new concept of nation undoubtedly goes back to the socio-political context of Europe in the seventeenth and eighteenth centuries.

> By the early seventeenth century, *nation* was also being used to describe the inhabitants of the country, regardless of that population's ethno-national composition, thereby becoming a substitute for less specific human categories such as the people or the citizenry.[24]

It is noteworthy that the word "nation" has never had one fixed meaning everywhere in Europe. Whereas "nationality" in English and French, for instance, came to mean citizenship, in German *nationalität* signifies a person's ethnic identity, nationality being translated as *staatsangehörigkeit* (literally, "belonging to a state"). The German usage of *nationalität* to mean ethnic group is particularly appropriate in the case of the Austro-Hungarian Empire, or, for that matter, the Russian and Spanish Empires, where ethnic diversity was the norm rather than the exception.

In 1917, when the Bolsheviks took control of the wide extent of territory previously ruled over by the Russian Empire, one of the main tasks they were faced with was how to bring together the heterogenous nationalities living in this vast land. In order to perform this task, an attempt was made by the early Bolsheviks to give a more "ordered" definition to the concept of nation. Stalin's definition has been current for many years and has been adopted by Communist theoreticians, especially in the Third World. According to Stalin, a nation is: "a historically evolved, stable community of people, formed on the basis of a common language, territory, economic life and psychological make-up manifested in a common culture".[25]

What is missing in Stalin's definition is the desire of a people who might possess some of these criteria – though not necessarily all of them – to be called and conceived of as a nation. Such an aspiration, which may even be concealed at times, is given prominence in the definition of a nation offered by Benedict Anderson:

> *Nation* is an imagined political community, and imagined as both inherently limited and sovereign.[26]

And he goes on to clarify what he means by imagined community:

> It is imagined because the members of even the smallest nation will never know most of their fellow members, meet them, or even hear of them, yet in the minds of each lives the image of their communion.[27]

Along with the term "nation", another word which usually presents special problems of definition in studying regional questions, is the adjective "ethnic" and its related noun "ethnicity". These latter words are frequently employed as if interchangeable with "national" and "nationality", while ethnic group is used as an equivalent of the word "nation". This ambiguous usage of the word "ethnic" and its derivatives usually carries specific political connotations when it is not merely the result of a simplistic approach to regional identity.

In a tribal society one may belong to a certain tribe but, at the same time, be a member of a larger group of people with whom one is linked by a "common destiny". The fact of being related to the other members of one's tribe by language, dialect or customs does not necessarily exclude having a basis for uniting with other neighbouring groups. We take as the foundation of a separate ethnic group those particular notions, sentiments and vital activities which distinguish it from other groups around it. In this sense, the group identity is "the image by which the group is identified and in terms of which the group can be recognized as reproducing itself in successive generations as distinct from other, usually neighbouring groups".[28]

In rounding off what has been said, it may be helpful in defining the difference between nation and nationality, on the one hand, and ethnic group and ethnicity on the other, to conclude that the former terms specifically refer to territorial boundaries, whereas the latter identity is based on cultural factors which have not necessarily led to territorial demarcations. Ethnicity, indeed, is a perception of ethnic identity, whereas ethnic identity may be based on any aspect of culture, i.e.

language, religion, etc., which a group of people exploits in order to differentiate itself from other groups. In doing so, it proclaims some sort of recognition within a political system or beyond it. The mobility concealed in this proclamation could soon evolve into a consciousness of group solidarity and leads to presenting a series of political demands, including some group rights. When this *mobilized* ethnic group succeeds in establishing a country with defined political boundaries of its own and with full sovereignty, it has become a *nation*.

Turks, a *Millet* or an *Ümmet*?

In the mid-nineteenth century, an Armenian from Istanbul who was entering Austria at Trieste was stopped by a civil servant and asked what nationality he held. "His unsophistical and prompt answer was "Catholic". The officer, somewhat puzzled at this novel nationality, reminded him that they were also all Catholic there, but called themselves Austrians or Italians. Now what is your nationality? Thereupon our worthy friend unflinchingly reiterated that he was a Catholic, nothing else but a Catholic, for they now had, through the interference of the French ambassador, a patriarch of their own, and were recognized as a nation!"[29] Our converted Armenian friend, by declaring himself to be a member of the so-called Catholic nation, was simply translating the word *millet* as "nation". Presumably, he was not aware of the nineteenth -century European interpretation of the term nation. For him nation meant *millet/mellat*, and therefore a member of a nation was the follower of a particular faith or religion.

The following lines from the *Zobdat al-Asrar*, a nineteenth-century poetic work by Safi 'Alishah, illustrate the exclusively religious significance of the term *mellat*:

> Oh Christian! since you are of the *mellat* of Jesus, You have
> no connection with the *mellat* of Islam.[30]

The Austrian officer might have avoided all this confusion if he had asked the bewildered Armenian whose subject he was, rather than what nation he belonged to. The term *ra'iyat* or *ra'iyeh* which can be loosely translated as subject, was a term commonly accepted by the people living within the territories controlled by the Ottoman Empire, irrespective of their language, their creed, or whether they were Muslims or non-Muslims. As long as a person fulfilled his duty by paying tax, he was entitled to consider himself as belonging to the *ra'iyeh*.

Besides *millet* and *ra'iyeh*, there was a third term current in the Ottoman Empire which designated a member of the Muslim community. Every Muslim, regardless of whether he was a Turk, a Kurd, or an Arab, or from the Balkan Peninsula, was considered to be a member of the *umma* or *ümmet*, the latter being the Turkish form of the Arabic word for "Islamic community". *Ümmet* was not only applied to Sunni Muslims but theoretically Shi'ites as well were included in the all-embracing term, despite the persecution which the latter suffered at the hands of the Ottoman administration.

According to Niyazi Berkes, it was the modern Turkish writer and reformer Ibrahim Shinasi (1824–71) who for the "first time used the word *millet* in the sense of nation".[31]

> In the first leading article of the *Tercüman-i Ahval*, published in 1860, Shinasi discusses the interest of the fatherland (*Vatan*) and remarks that while the non-Muslim subjects of the empire had their own newspapers, there were no 'truly Ottoman' newspapers, since hitherto no member of the 'dominant *millet*' had been willing to publish one.[32]

The Ottoman administration apparently found this new usage of the term *millet* quite convenient and began to make use of it, which provoked a reaction among another group of Ottoman intellectuals, namely the young Ottomans in exile. Namik Kemal, the patriotic writer, criticized the Porte in 1868 for using *millet* in the sense of nation, for which he specified *ümmet*. *Millet* he applied only to a religious community.[33]

What was causing a problem for the followers of Namik Kemal was the new idea, emanating from nineteenth-century Europe, of the territorial nation-state based on the single nation. On the other hand, to use the term *ümmet* in the old sense meant one would be including only Muslims, and the Young Turks were aware of the fact that Islam as a religion was not enough to unite the fisherman of the Black Sea and the peasant from the suburbs of Damascus within the framework of a nation. The most such disparate elements could expect was to be united as citizens. But beyond the problem of that sort of cultural diversity was the fact that using *ümmet* to cover citizenship would mean setting up a barrier against non-Muslims, who had always been differentiated by the term *millet*. The dilemma which was emerging over terminology came down to the embarrassing question: "What sort of citizenship is it that does not include all citizens?"

Unfortunately, the road back to the "good old values" was also blocked. The usage of *ra'iyeh* was not possible either, since, as mentioned above, *ra'iyeh* specifically designated anyone who paid taxes, whereas the ruling class and the *'askariyeh* (the military), being traditionally exempt from taxation, could not be included within the *ra'iyeh*. In principle, the late nineteenth-century concepts of nation and nationality, citizen and citizenship, were applicable to every individual, regardless of sex, class, and religion.

The dismantling of the Ottoman Empire and the birth of the new Republic of Turkey solved many of these difficulties. The obstacles and barriers which hindered the dominant group – the Turks – were all removed. The Republic of Turkey was based on the ideas expressed in the National Pact of 1919-1920. Anatolia came to be defined as the land "inhabited by the Ottoman Muslim majority united in religion, in race, and in aims". It was not long before Anatolia became Turkey, a new territorial state, which was considered to be the Fatherland of the nation known as the Turks: one country, one nation.

Iranians, an *Ommat*, a *Mellat* or *Ahali*?

The Iranians did not have so large an ethnically diverse population to cope with as did the Ottomans, and consequently they often employed the above mentioned terms with greater flexibility. One important difference with regard to ethnic considerations was that, during the nineteenth century, the Christian population in Iran was relatively small compared to the situation in the Ottoman Empire. Napoleon III was simply stating the obvious when he remarked in a letter to Naser od-Din Shah in which he compares Iran to the Ottoman Empire:

> The advantage of His Majesty's situation over that of the Sultan is that the latter is dealing with a minority of Muslims and a majority of Christians.[34]

Mohammad Shah, the father of Naser od-Din, in a famous manifesto publicized on 20 April 1840, referred to the Catholics as a *qowm*, not as a *mellat*. In this document, the Shah goes so far as to declare that Catholics will have the same rights as Muslims enjoyed:

> The Catholic *qowm*, with regard to following the dictates and the laws of its religion and the pursuit of prosperity, will enjoy the same provisions that His Majesty has deigned to concede to [all] servants of his Celestial Court.[35]

As mentioned above, in the Ottoman Empire, the terms *ümmet* and *millet* were commonly used to designate Muslims and Christians respectively. By contrast, the Iranians preferred to refer to the Muslim Ottomans not as belonging to the *ommat* but as a *mellat*. Mirza Hoseyn Khan Ajudanbashi who was Mohammad Shah's first ambassador to France in 1839, while passing through the Ottoman Empire *en route* to France, expressed his admiration for the *"mellat-e 'Osmaniyeh"* because of their upholding the principles of Islam. He remarked:

> In all fairness, the *mellat-e 'Osmaniyeh* endeavours to carry out the five duties of Islam with such commitment as exceeds description.[36]

Having reached France, he expresses his disappointment at what he takes to be the unstable relations existing between the king and the French nation:

> The intention of one group of the French *mellat* is, that having absolutely abolished the principle of sovereignty, they will place dominion in the hands of the mass of the people and the representatives of the *mellat*.[37]

As we see, for Hoseyn Khan Ajudanbashi, the French and the Muslim Ottomans are both considered to be a proper *mellat*. It is quite clear that when he applied the term *mellat* to the Muslim Ottomans, he was disregarding the important distinction which the Ottomans themselves retained in their use of *ümmet* and *millet*. Hoseyn Khan uses *"mellat-e 'Osmaniyeh"* in the sense of Ottoman nation.

Less than half a century later, in his well-known book on politics, *Resaleh-e Mosumeh beh Yek Kalemeh* (A Treatise Entitled "One Word"), Yusef Khan Mostashar od-Dowleh makes free and frequent use of the terms *mellat*, *ommat*, and *ahali*. Mostashar od-Dowleh, who was one of the outstanding enlightened reformists of the nineteenth century, wrote his *Resaleh-e Mosumeh beh Yek Kalameh* in Paris in 1870, where he was posted as the Iranian government's *chargé d'affaires*.[38] He was an Azerbaijani and the son of a merchant of Tabriz. It was Mostashar od-Dowleh who, for the first time, advocated and promoted the idea that: "The origin of the authority of the *dowlat* (state) is in the will of the *mellat*."[39] In his *Yek Kalemeh*, he puts stress on the importance of having a "written law" which must be approved by the *mellat* and which will define and control all aspects of the relationship between the *dowlat* and the *mellat*.[40] Further on in the same work, he uses the term *ahali* (people/ peoples) as synonymous with *mellat*:

> The *ahali* have great authority with regard to the legitimacy
> of government practices.[41]

His definition of *mellat* and *ahali* is such as to include every *citizen* of Iran ("*ahali-ye Iran*" or "*mellat-e Iran*"), irrespective of a person's religion, race, language, or class status: "The king and the beggar, the *ra'iyat* and the military" were all members of the *ahali* and the *mellat*.[42]

As is clear, Mostashar od-Dowleh is employing the term *ra'iyat* in the same sense as it has in contemporary Ottoman writings, i.e. all tax payers were considered to be *ra'iyat*, in distinction to a Persian *lashkari* or Ottoman *'askari* (member of the military class).

On the other hand, Mostashar od-Dowleh uses the word *ommat* with a meaning quite different from that current in Ottoman circles. Whereas the Ottomans employ *ümmet* to designate all Muslim inhabitants of the Ottoman Empire, the Iranians use *ommat* with the same meaning as *mellat*:

> When the *ahali* of France and the other civilized governments
> debate and discuss, through the intermediary of their
> representatives, what is right and wrong ... matters and policy
> which in most cases are able to become the cause of
> complaints, after the council of the *mellat's* representatives

has canvassed all opinions, what possible confusion and
tumult can still persist in the *dowlat* and the *ommat*? Besides
legislation, most administrative matters in *Farangestan* are
also implemented with the consent of the *mellat* and the
dowlat.[42]

It is interesting to note that, in the eyes of Mostashar od-Dowleh, the
French could also be described as an *ommat* or a *mellat*. The terms were
interchangeable for him and bore the same meaning.

In 1888, in a letter to the heir apparent, Mozaffar od-Din, Mostashar
od-Dowleh criticized the government's mismanagement and advocated
that "*kolliyeh-e ahali-ye mamlekat* (the entire *ahali* of the kingdom) be
granted equality before the law, since all the *tavayef* – *aqvam* (clans-
ethnic groups) who live in Iran should share in the good fortunes as well
as the misfortunes of the homeland".[44]

As is clear from this passage, Mostashar od-Dowleh conceives of the
mellat-e Iran or the *ahali-ye Iran* as consisting of all the diverse *tavayef*
or *aqvam* (plural of *tayefeh* and *qowm* respectively) which live within the
territory of Iran.

Like many another enlightened reformer, Mostashar od-Dowleh paid a
high price for his ideas and convictions. In the prison of Qazvin, he was
beaten over the head so violently with his book "*Yek Kalemeh*" that he
became blind. Shortly thereafter, in 1895, he died.[45]

The ideas of Mostashar od-Dowleh and others like him paved the
way for the Constitutional Revolution of 1905–9. Article Two of the
Constitutional Code, which was promulgated in 1906, defines
the *Majles* (Parliament) as the "representative of the whole *ahali* of the
mamlekat of Iran". Article Eleven requires every member of Parliament to
swear to defend the principles of monarchy and to uphold the rights of
the *mellat*, as well as to act only "in the interest and benefit of the *dowlat*
and the *mellat* of Iran".[46]

Neither in the Constitutional Code of 1906, nor in the supplement
which was added to it one year later, is there any reference to *qown* or
aqvam, and all Iranians are considered to be members of the *mellat* or the
ahali-ye Iran.

These terms are by no means confined in their usage to the
Constitutional Code. In a pamphlet published in 1907, Sani' od-Dowleh,
the head of the First Parliament, introduced his reform program by
warning:

> Should the pillars of government (politicians) and the
> individuals of the *mellat*, as of this day, not achieve their
> specific goals, then it will not be long before the gathering
> floods and contending winds shall tear up by the roots the
> stock of our *qowmiyat*.[47]

Here Sani' od-Dowleh uses the term *qowmiyat* to mean nationality,
instead of *melliyat*, which was and still is the standard term in Persian
dictionaries for nationality. The Ottomans had long since been employing the word *melliyat* and not *qowmiyat* to signify nationality.[48] The
explanation for Sani' od-Dowleh's idiosyncratic usage may have to do
with his educational background. He had studied Arabic after complet-
ing his primary education,[49] and was perhaps more in touch with
Arabic political terminology. In Arabic of modern times *qowmiyya* has
always been the term for nationality and not *milliyya*.

As an interesting illustration of how the Iranian intelligentsia was
generally adopting Ottoman usage rather than what was becoming
current in contemporary Arabic, we may cite the words of a little
known book entitled *Haqq-e Daf'-e Sharr va Qiyam bar Zedd-e Zolm*
(The Right to Ward Off Evil and Rise Up against Tyranny) which was
published anonymously a few years after the Constitutional Revolution.
After promoting and defending the right of the *mellat* to "stand up" and
fight against "cruelty and injustice", the author warns that if the *mellat*
does not do so, there will soon be no trace left of *melliyat* and *Iranigari*
(Iranianism).[50]

The years immediately following the Constitutional Revolution are
often referred to as the era of democracy, due to the lack of restrictions
on literary and political expression which characterized the period. By
this time, new connotations were accruing to the word *mellat*. Now
usages begin to occur which redefine *mellat* as the oppressed mass of
people in Iran. The upper class is perceived as living from the labour
and the produce of the peasants, workers and craftsmen. Since this
small elite does not work itself but merely exploits others in order to
maintain a life of ease, it has no right to be included within the *mellat*,
according to this new notion. In a *shab-nameh* (nocturnal leaflet) of
1909 entitled *Mellat Kist va Hoquqash Chist?* (Who Make Up the
Nation and What Are Their Rights?), the new definition appears in the
following form:

The *mellat* consists of the toiling inhabitants of a particular country. The *mellat* is made up of those people who acquire their livelihood by hard work and the sweat of their brow and consequently live in hardship and affliction. In other words, the *mellat* consists of those who, in the city, depend on mutual help and co-operation and work to procure one another's comfort. One person, for instance, is a shoemaker, so that others will not go without shoes. Another person is a blacksmith in order to meet the needs of the shoemaker and others in this area. In the same way, there is a grocer, a druggist, a seller of fodder, a tailor, a cloth merchant, and a farmer. Every one of these individuals from among the people – from the farmer to the merchants of every variety – all make up the *mellat*.

Furthermore, the leaflet goes on to exclude those social classes and groups which apparently could not be included in the *mellat*:

Only 'free-loaders' are not to be considered as belonging to the *mellat*, because they do not work for people's comfort and provide for their own needs. They are persons who, throughout the year, live a comfortable life at home or in pleasant places with attractive views, passing their time in ease. They do not contribute one iota to the work of the people. On the contrary, they merely expect that others will work and that they will be provided with their necessities and their luxuries from the fruits of others' labour. Therefore, this group of free-loaders and idlers cannot be called the *mellat*.[51]

One of the new political groups which clearly adopted this definition of *mellat* in its programme was the Iranian Social Revolutionaries, who preferred to be called "*Ejtema'iyun Enqelabiyan*". Their insignia, however, bore the inscription "*Jam'iyat-e Sosiyal Revolusiyoner-e Iran* (The Society of the Iranian Social Revolutionaries), *(Ahrar - Hov'al-Qader)*". In its official program, the *Jam'iyat-e Sosiyal Revolusiyoner-e Iran* after declaring its sympathy and concern for the "oppressed Iranian *mellat*" who have been "caught in the tyrannical claws of the internal and external wolves", calls upon the "*zare'* (farmers), *asnaf* (guild members), *tojjar* (merchants), *san'atgaran* (artisans), *ahl-e nezam* (the military)" and the students to co-ordinate their efforts to form a *melli* (national), sovereign government.[52]

It is particularly noteworthy that the *Ejtema'iyun Enqelabiyun* were the first political group to advocate the exclusive use of the Persian language as the "official language of the country", insisting that it must be employed not only in the national parliament, but in the provincial councils as well.[53]

It must be realized that throughout the period described above, the serious concern for defining words such as *mellat*, *ommat*, *qowm* and *ahali* was confined to small groups of Iranian intellectuals. Similarly, shifts in meaning or new definitions of words like *Turk*, *Azeri* or *Azerbaijani* occupied the attention of an even smaller number of the intelligentsia. The importance of these intellectual preoccupations becomes all the more clear when one realizes that, historically, there had not been a persistent strong, centralized state in Iran, or strong popular consensus on these matters. Consequently, the new meanings of the terms referred to throughout this chapter were considered by many political thinkers at the time to be potentially dangerous and divisive.

Azerbaijanis, a Nation in the Caucasus, an Ethnic Group in Iran

The downfall of the government of the Russian Empire prepared the ground for the emergence of an independent republic in Transcaucasia. In November 1917, a Transcaucasian Commissariat was established in Tiflis. The first official declaration which the commissariat issued in the name of the Transcaucasian Revolutionary Democracy emphasized the need to implement "the right of nations to self-determination which the Russian Revolution had proclaimed. And five months later, on 22 April 1918, the Georgian Mensheviks, the Armenian Dashnakists and the Muslim Musavatists, in a partially co-ordinated endeavour, announced the formation of the Transcaucasian Federative Republic.[54]

This manifestation of Transcaucasian unity proved to be short-lived. By 26 May 1918, during the final session of the conference held to reach a peace settlement with the Ottoman Empire, "the underlying animosities between the three members of the Transcaucasian

Federative Republic quickly came to light and co-operation soon broke down".[55] That same day, the Transcaucasian Assembly met in order to dissolve the ephemeral Federative Republic. Immediately thereafter, the Georgian National Council proclaimed an independent Georgian Republic and, within two days, the Armenians had followed suit and declared their own independent Republic.

Meanwhile, on 27 May, the Muslim National Council met in Tiflis and "resolved to declare the independence of *Azerbaijan*, a republic that was to encompass *southern and eastern Transcaucasia*".[56] On the following day, "the governing body of the Transcaucasian Tatars, now Azerbaijan, selected Ganja (later renamed Kirovabad) as the republic's temporary capital".[57]

Adopting the name of Azerbaijan for the area of southern and eastern Transcaucasia soon caused concern in Iran and Azerbaijan. Mohammad Amin Rasulzadeh, the founder of the Republic of Azerbaijan in Transcaucasia, understood – during these early days – the territory of this new Azerbaijan to consist of "the Baku and Elisavetpol *gubernias*, the southern districts of the Tiflis and Yerevan *gubernias*, and the country of Zakatal".[58] Later, when the republic had been toppled by the Bolsheviks and Rasulzadeh had been forced to seek asylum abroad, he admitted that this choice of a name for the new republic had been a mistake.

In an article which he wrote on the history of the short-lived Republic of Azerbaijan, Rasulzadeh acknowledges that: "Albania (the former Soviet Azerbaijan) is different from Azerbaijan (Iranian Azerbaijan)."[59] Moreover, in a letter to Taqizadeh, he declared his eagerness to do "whatever is in his power to avoid any further discontent among Iranians".[60]

However, if the Republic of Azerbaijan, was the name adopted by the Muslim Musavatists, when the Bolsheviks established their rule over the region, they did not hesitate to retain the same name. On 28 April 1920, the government of Musavatists was overthrown by the revolutionary Bolsheviks, and an independent Soviet Republic of Azerbaijan was proclaimed.[61]

By adopting the Soviet nationality's policy of building a series of nation-states and state-nations on the territory of the old Russian Empire, an Azerbaijani nation was defined. With their own distinctive language, they became the inhabitants of a region in the south Caucasus, later known as the Soviet Socialist Republic of Azerbaijan.[62]

Contrary to the political developments in the southern Caucasus, in Iran the province of Azerbaijan remained an integrated part of the country. Furthermore, during the years which followed, when a modern nation-state was established in Iran under Reza Shah, the Azerbaijanis were considered to be an ethnic group, while the term Iranian was applied to them as members of a nation.

2

Genesis of the Autonomous Movement in Azerbaijan

Our Shah is somewhat lacking in common sense ... He doesn't think about what he will do if the people, having lost all patience, rise up with one heart and one purpose and abandon obedience and reserve ... These people have not and will not act in this manner out of sheer barbarism but rather because there is no other remedy. What they undertook by way of humility, supplication, and appeals for justice went completely unheeded and consequently they eventually reached this stage.

"Those Who Have Awakened in the Country", a nocturnal leaflet distributed on 21 April 1906, in Tehran, in: M. M. Sharif Kashani, *Vaqe'at-e Ettefaqiyyeh dar Ruzegar*, vol. 1, p. 21.

The Constitutional Revolution

During the events of the Constitutional Revolution of 1905–9, there was no trace of aspirations for regional autonomy among the Constitutionalists. What one finds in contemporary writings in Iran is the widespread conviction that the path to social and political improvement lies in a firmly established, centralized government based on law and order. For at least a decade after the Revolution, such political aspirations were the chief characteristics which distinguished the

Constitutionalists from their conservative opponents, "the champions of despotism".

In the Constitutional Revolution, like-minded Azerbaijanis, Persians, Bakhtiyaris and Gilanis fought alongside one another against those forces who supported "lawlessness" and the absolute arbitrary power of the monarchy. They were united in their opposition to the *dowlat* (state) retaining its monopoly on decision-making. Their objective was not to divide this power among the different ethnic groupings in the country in order to establish separate independent states based on ethnic identity. Although, in their view, the Revolution was supposed to change the old power structure which was centralized, arbitrary and despotic, the new government would still be centralized. Now, however, it would be rational and function on the basis of a written constitution.

The *Qanun-e Asasi* (Constitutional Code) of 1906 was drafted in great haste and, as a result, overlooked or did not adequately provide for many essential aspects of a constitutional government. As one of the members of the royal court wrote at a later date, the Qajar monarch was known to be at death's door and everyone was in an unsettled state. There were those who went as far as to "ask the monarch's doctor to postpone his death for at least one week, until the laws would be ready".[1] It was hoped that the king would be able to give his ratification of the final draft of the constitution before he died. In the event, the king did give his official approval to the Constitutional Code (in December) and then died ten days afterwards.

The deputies of the *Majles*, who could hold office only if they belonged to certain social classes and professions,[2] soon realized the shortcomings of the early form of the Constitutional Code and therefore appointed a commission of six members to draft additional laws which came to be known the *Motammam-e Qanun-e Asasi* (Supplement to the Constitutional Code).[3]

The chief flaw of the Constitutional Code was its failure to provide for a division between the legislative, executive and judicial branches of power. The ministers, for instance, were directly accountable to the king, rather than to the *Majles*. Furthermore, fundamental democratic principles which would guarantee the people's sovereignty were blatantly absent from the practical workings of the government.

Shortcomings such as these were so obvious and the conflicts between the *Majles* and the government became so acute that on one occasion a particular deputy is recorded as having complained:

> Don't we have a constitutional government? And if so, why does it not fulfil the basic requirements of constitutionalism?

The prime minister, Moshir od-Dowleh, promptly retorted:

> No! Here there is no constitutional government. The Shah has granted you an assembly which convenes for the purpose of being consulted with regard to the laws of the country.[4]

In view of perceived deficiencies in the constitution, the appointed commission proposed a Supplementary Code which was finally ratified in October 1907, after months of contention between the Constitutionalists and the newly crowned Shah, the latter being supported by a group from among the clergy.[5]

One important subject which the Supplementary Code dealt with was the right of the people in the provinces to have their own provincial councils. According to Articles 90–93 of the Supplementary Code, every city and every province would have a council whose primary functions, as representative of the central government, would be to supervise local affairs and to collect and allocate the taxes of the region in question.

The role which the Azerbaijanis played in urging the *Majles* to adopt the idea of provincial councils cannot be overestimated. The Tabrizis were pioneers in establishing their own councils even months before the Supplementary Code was ratified.

The Council of Tabriz

Anjoman-e Tabriz (the Council of Tabriz) was founded in September 1906. Although its original function was to elect and nominate deputies for the *Majles*,[6] it soon turned into a regional parliament in its own right.[7] Some foreign observers went as far as to compare it with the soviets which were formed during the Russian Revolution of 1905,[8] and suspected that the latter had exercised an influence on the Council.[9]

The *Anjoman* published its own newspaper called the *Jarideh-e Melli* (The National Newspaper), the first issue of which appeared in October

1906. After thirty-seven issues, this bi-weekly changed its name to
Anjoman. It is noteworthy that the newspaper, under both its names,
was written in Persian. In addition to publishing news about the Council
itself and the minutes of its various meetings, the newspaper *Anjoman*
published national news and especially news relating to the *Majles*. In
some issues, there were long didactic editorials dealing with the
fundamental principles of constitutionalism and such topics as "the true
meaning of *Liberté, Égalité, and Fraternité*".[10]

In the early days, the Tabriz Constitutionalists referred to the Council
as the *Majles-e Melli* (the National Assembly) in their lectures and
publications. Indeed, in the first issue of the *Jarideh-e Melli* there is an
editorial article which gives full coverage to the founding of "the
Majles-e Melli".[11] In Tehran there was immediate concern expressed
over the use of such a title. Some deputies in the *Majles* in Tehran
accused the Tabrizis of overstepping their functions and assuming the
status of a *Dar osh-Showra-ye Markazi* (Central Grand Assembly)
rather than that of a provincial council.[12]

The Azerbaijani deputies on hand in Tehran reacted promptly by
denying that members of the local Council had any such intentions.
Meanwhile, the newspaper *Anjoman* (no. 41, 9 February 1907)
confirmed what the Azerbaijani deputies had said in the *Majles*. They
emphasized that the *Anjoman-e Tabriz* was a provincial council and not
a national parliament. From then on, the Tabrizi Constitutionalists were
more punctilious in employing one of the following two titles for their
council: *Anjoman-e Tabriz* (Council of Tabriz), or *Anjoman-e Iyalati-ye
Azerbaijan* (Provincial Council of Azerbaijan).

Some historians overestimate the influence which the Russian
Revolution of 1905 exercised on the Constitutional Revolution in Iran.
The Iranian historian Homa Nateq, for instance, believes that the actual
term *anjoman* which the Tabrizis adopted for their council was a
translation of the Russian word "soviet". To support her argument, she
refers to a book on the Russian revolution of 1905 (*Tarikh-e Enqelab-e
Rusiyeh*) by Dr Khalil Beg Lobnani. In the Persian translation of this
work, the translator, Seyyed Abdolhoseyn Razavi, translated the phrase
"Petersburg Soviet" as "*Anjoman-e Petersburg*".[13] However, this
translation was only published in July 1908, after which time it was
quickly banned by the government, though it appeared in a second
edition in October 1909.[14] In any case, the translation itself was

published too late to have been an influence on the founders of the *Anjoman-e Tabriz*.

The Council of Tabriz, besides attending to regional affairs and functioning as a court of justice which dealt with numerous complaints from all over the province, exerted pressure, directly or indirectly, on the *Majles* in the capital. The Azerbaijani deputies in Tehran were in close contact with Tabriz and, on many occasions, they consulted with the Council of Tabriz about parliamentary matters.[15] And there were times when the Council of Tabriz did not hesitate to put direct pressure on the *Majles* and the government in order to achieve its goals. For instance, when the newly crowned Shah, Mohammad 'Ali Mirza, began to behave as if he did not recognize the existence of the *Majles* and the constitution, the Council of Tabriz sent a telegram to the *Majles* presenting seven demands, including that the Shah give written confirmation that the Iranian government was a fully constitutional government and that every city and province had the right to a regional council.[16] Later, too, when the Shah revealed his opposition to the *Majles* by publishing a declaration entitled "*Rah-e Nejat va Omidvari-ye Mellat*" (The Road to Salvation and the Hope of the Nation)[17], the Council of Tabriz immediately dispatched a telegram to the provincial councils of Khorasan, Fars, Kerman and Isfahan, accusing the Shah of "having broken his promises". In the same telegram, the Shah was referred to as "a traitor to the country and to the nation", and the cry was raised for "all Iranian brothers to stand up and safeguard the Grand Assembly and the Constitution".[18]

Mohammad 'Ali Mirza had, indeed, broken his promises. He eventually presented the *Majles* with an ultimatum and three days later, on 23 June 1908, he issued the order to bombard the premises of the *Majles* and thus began a whole new chapter of the Iranian Constitutional Revolution.[19] At a later date in a letter to the prime minister, Moshir os-Saltaneh, the Shah justified his actions by blaming unauthorized "Councils" whose "interference in government affairs had unleashed chaos in the country and forced him to liquidate the *Majles*". He promised that the "suspension of the *Majles* would, in any case, not last longer than three months".[20]

News of the bombardment of the *Majles* was not immediately made public in Tabriz. This was due to the decision of Mirza Khan Tarbiyat, a well-known Tabrizi Constitutionalist who was in charge of the telegraph office at the time. Instead, he informed the Council during a closed meeting, thus enabling the Council to take swift independent action and impose its authority on parts of the city.[21] The Council, having taken control of the arsenal, eventually proceeded to arm the volunteers it had already begun training in special courses months beforehand.[22] The Tabrizis had clearly been expecting the arrival of such troubled days and were not unprepared to act in defense of their political ideals.

The thirteen months from June 1908 to July 1909 which followed Mohammad Mirza's *coup d'état* were a decisive stage in the constitutional movement in Iran. Despite the fact that, for the time being at least, the Shah's coup successfully hindered the functioning of a constitutional government, the overall long-term effect of his violent intervention was to galvanize the movement. The propertied classes, who rather easily abandoned the barricades in the early days of the movement and, in some cases, even pretended that social harmony prevailed among the people, were now shocked into new consciousness. It was glaringly clear that the constitutional movement had the capacity to bring about serious changes to the old, established socio-political structures. On the other hand, ordinary people were coming to realize that a constitutional government did not result in everyone "eating a kebab as long as the span of a hand". The latter quotation refers to a statement made by one of the proponents of the revolution, Sheykh Salim. During the early days of the movement in Tabriz, he had assured the people that when the constitution came such would be the benefits which they would enjoy.[23]

Generally speaking, the part which Azerbaijan, and especially the Tabrizi Constitutionalists, played during the course of these thirteen months of war and famine was so impressive that, from that time on, Azerbaijan was seen by many Iranians as the centre from which any future progressive political change would originate. Kasravi, who was an eyewitness of the events of Tabriz's "revolution", compares Tabriz to Paris in the following words:

> In Tabriz during the Constitutional Revolution as in Paris during the French Revolution, the *sans-culottes* and the propertyless poor reared their heads. The driving force of these men was towards anarchy. First to overthrow the despotic power of the Court, then to turn against the rich and propertied classes. It was with the backing of such men that

Danton and Robespierre rose to power. In Tabriz no Danton and Robespierre appeared but if they had, we would have had own "reign of terror". Instead we lived through a period of chaos, instability and fear.[24]

As mentioned above, the Tabrizi Constitutionalists reacted swiftly to the news from Tehran and managed to gain control of part of the city. Meanwhile, the rival conservative, royalist group, *Eslamiyeh*, brought other parts of the city under their banner. They warned the people of Tabriz to dissociate themselves from the "Constitutionalist Babis and infidels by hanging a white banner outside their residences".[25] Tabriz was a city divided into two camps. The "Père Lachaise" of Tabriz was Amir Khiz, which, along with the neighbourhoods Maralan and Khiyaban, formed the barricade of the Constitutionalists. Except for Amir Khiz, the Royalists had control of the north of the city, i.e. the Davachi, Sorkhab and Shishkelan districts. This division of the city remained in force for several months.[26]

In these circumstances, the Tabriz Council was replaced by a loose military organization, commanded by Sattar Khan, a Sheykhi horse dealer from Amir Khiz who, together with the mason Baqer Khan, also a Sheykhi and from Maralan, gathered all the volunteers, armed them and founded a paramilitary group whose members were known as *Mojahedin*. These *Mojahedin* of Tabriz, whose numbers have been estimated as high as 10,000,[27] carried on a "cat and mouse" war, skirmishing off and on with the royalists. During these months, the *Mojahedin*, to voice their demands, often sent telegrams to Tehran, such as:

The unfortunate Azerbaijani, despite the lies of slanderers with ulterior motives, is not a wicked insurgent, nor a rebel, nor does he lay claims to sovereignty; he is not seeking after independence or separation, nor does he wish to cause a bloody uprising or to take revenge. On every occasion, he has declared to his opponents and to all the world that his sacred goal and lost beloved is Iran's Constitution of eternal dominion, and his cherished Ka'ba is the National Assembly of Tehran. As for his equitable judge and arbitrator of all differences, it is none other than that "Holy Book", the Constitutional Code.[28]

The royalist camp was led by 'Ayn od-Dowleh whom the Shah had recently appointed as governor when the former governor, Mokhber os-Saltaneh, appeared to be hesitating to confront the Constitutionalists head on.[29] 'Ayn od-Dowleh, besides having the support of important clerics such as Imam Jom'eh and Mirza Sadeq,[30] derived his chief local support from different tribal groups, in particular the Shahsevans.

The *Mojahedin*, on the other hand, enjoyed the moral support of all revolutionaries and reformists outside Azerbaijan. In Istanbul, the *Sa'adat* Society, which was founded by Iranians in exile, promoted the ideals of the Tabrizi Constitutionalists on the international level.[31] Armenian and Georgian Social Democrats, at the request of their Azerbaijani counterparts, crossed the border to give their support to the "communards" of Tabriz. Kasravi estimates that there may have been as many as a hundred of them – mostly experts in making bombs.[32]

The history of social democracy in Tabriz goes back to the end of the nineteenth century. "Since 1898 there had been a series of closed meetings in Tabriz, during which the participants had spoken about the political affairs of the country ... In 1904, they published a declaration in which they called themselves *Ejtema'iyun 'Amiyun* (a term equivalent to Social Democrats)."[33] Since they were a centrally organized clandestine party, the *Ejtema'iyun 'Amiyun* of Tabriz soon became known as the "*Markaz-e Gheybi*" (the Secret Society).[34] Besides taking part in the street battles during the civil war, the Tabrizi Social Democrats attempted to organize the workers of the city into trade unions. Strikes were planned and, generally, efforts were made to explain in popular terms the meaning of the "Iranian Revolution".[35]

As the civil war dragged on, the court was faced with a series of problems which culminated in financial exhaustion. The government, having run out of money, was at a loss how to pay its troops and banks refused to make available any further credit. The court was barely maintaining its authority in the capital but such power as the Shah had retained was not to last much longer. Strikes centring around the bazaar took place and resulted in discreding the Shah with his two allies, the British and Russians, who, in 1907, had concluded an alliance known as the Anglo-Russian Agreement according to which the two old rivals intended to divide Iran into separate spheres of interest.[36]

After thirteen months of bloody civil war, the co-ordinated efforts of the Constitutionalists succeeded in deposing the Shah. The

Constitutionalist armed forces were closing in on the capital from north and south, and had formulated a series of demands which included "the obligation on the government's part to consult with the local *Anjoman* concerning the appointment of governors".[37]

By now it was even too late for the Shah to redeem the situation by accepting the demands of the Constitutionalists. The Shah was obliged to abdicate and he took refuge in the Russian consulate. Consequently, his twelve-year-old son, Ahmad, was nominated as the new Shah. The other important political results of this struggle were that the electoral law concerning representation in the *Majles* by class and occupation was repealed and the provinces were allowed a greater number of deputies. On the basis of these changes, the Second *Majles* was convoked.

By the summer of 1909, the political scene in Iran had significantly changed from what it had been four years earlier. The recent dramatic events of the civil war served to accelerate the rise of political awareness and the consciousness of class identity. This tendency was particularly visible once the Second National Assembly began to function. Iran was entering a new political phase which may perhaps best be described as "the crisis of liberty".

The Second *Majles* and the Formation of Political Parties

The First *Majles* had not been a parliament of parties. Political parties only appear on the Iranian political horizon during the proceedings of the Second *Majles*.[38] As one might expect from the brief remarks above, the pioneers in forming and organizing parties as a political institution in Iran were the Social Democrats.

One of the earliest attempts to create a Social Democrat party in Iran was by Heydar Khan 'Amoghlu, who was later to be the First Secretary of the Iranian Communist Party. He spent fifteen months (1903–4) in Mashhad employed as an electrical engineer and there tried, unsuccessfully, to organize a political group. In his memoirs he recalls:

> During the whole period that I was living in Khorasan, however hard I tried to set up a political group, I never succeeded in doing so. The reason was that the people were not yet ready for this.[39]

Faced with this failure in Khorasan, Heydar Khan 'Amoghlu went to Tehran, where he established the Tehran branch of the Social Democrats.[40]

Simultaneously in 1904, the Tabrizi Social Democrats, as mentioned above, published their first political manifesto, in which they called themselves the *"Ejtema'iyun 'Amiyun"*. It was another three years before the Khorasan branch of the Social Democrats was founded – with the publication of their own manifesto entitled *Maram-nameh va Nezam-nameh-e Sho'beh-e Irani-ye Jam'iyat-e Mojahedin Moteshakkeleh dar Mashhad* (The Program and Regulation of the Iranian branch of the *Mojahedin* of Mashhad). The Social Democrats chose the 15th of Sha'ban (September 1905), the birthday of the Twelfth Imam, to announce the birth of the new party's local branch.[41]

These parties, as well as other like-minded groups, were, in one way or another, in contact with the *Hezb-e Sosiyal Demokrat-e Iran (Ejtema'iyun 'Amiyun)* (the Social Democrat Party of Iran), which had been founded in Baku in 1905.[42] This party was itself an offshoot of another party called *Hemmat*, which had been created one year earlier in Baku with the avowed task of organizing the Muslim labourers of Transcaucasia.[43]

Soon after the formation of the Second *Majles* (15 November 1909), the radical deputies began to organize their own parliamentary political group. Pilosiyan, an Armenian Social Democrat, wrote from Tabriz to Taqizadeh, the radical Azerbaijani deputy to the *Majles*, urging him and his companions to intensify their efforts to form a political party.[44] Shortly thereafter, *Ferqeh-e Demokrat-e Iran* (the Democrat Party of Iran) was founded, with a central committee made up of eight members.[45] At first the name chosen for the party caused some concern among certain Social Democrats. In a letter to Taqizadeh, Pilosiyan asks him whether "he knows a Persian or Arabic word which could be employed as an equivalent of 'Democrat'... since the Iranians show hostility to foreign names".[46] But it would seem the deputies in Tehran were too excited by matters in the parliament to pay attention to philological problems.

The parliamentary group of Democrats consisted of some twenty-seven members, twelve of whom were Azerbaijanis.[47] The group included: "Eight civil servants, five journalists, five religious leaders, one landowner and one doctor. Of the five religious leaders, there were three Sheykhis and one was a clandestine Azali."[48]

In their first published manifesto called *"Maram-nameh-e Ferqeh-e Siyasi-ye Demokrat-e Iran – 'Amiyun"* (The Program of the Democrat Party of Iran – 'Amiyun), the Democrats pleaded for a "strong, legitimate and centralized government" which, "by implementing various necessary reforms, would enable the Iranians as a *nation* to safeguard their freedom and independence".[49] A little later, the concepts of political centralization, ethnic integration and national unification were elaborated in an editorial article entitled "We are One Nation" which appeared in the leading Democrat newspaper, *Iran-e Now* (The New Iran). The following excerpt is representative of the spirit prevailing in these Democrat circles:

> Tyranny, with its different titles and numerous names, has driven us apart and made us enemies of one another. Tyranny has presented the single, united Iranian *mellat* (nation) as divided in form and identity, has alienated us from one another ... Consequently, the single Iranian group, all of whom have grown up in one land and breathed the poisoned air of tyranny to the same extent, seem to imagine that their enemy is their own brother, either because he speaks another language or because he praises God in a different way ... Every tyrannical state and all absolute rulers have always acted like this and all the famous tyrants of the world imposed this kind of system. In order to extend the power of their oppressive government over everyone, all the tyrants of the earth have always had recourse to a policy of dividing a united group and turning them against one another. And our tyrants in Iran are not to be outdone by anyone in this respect. They have successfully adopted the principles of *Jesuitism* (sow discord in order to rule) nor do they ever forget these principles.

Having in this manner diagnosed the evil policy that tyranny exercised everywhere in the world, the editorial went on to describe the constitutional movement as the only viable remedy available to the diverse peoples of Iran:

> In the same way that tyranny has divided us and sown the seeds of mutual hatred in our hearts, so liberty and the present

constitutional movement – which are the result of a bloody
protest against the principles of the previous regime – must
provide the basis for affection and unity among ourselves. In a
government which exercises power in the shadow of the
mortal struggles (*mojahedat*) of this homeland's self-
sacrificing children – and those *mojahedin* strove to attain
freedom and equality without differences of *mellat* or religion
– there must no longer be talk of national conflict and
religious dispute ... Today our homeland, this dear mother
who has experienced so much grief, calls out to all her
children with her sad voice, calls all Iranians to unite together,
whether that Iranian is a Muslim or a Jew or an Armenian,
whether he is a Zoroastrian or a Turk or a Persian. Iranians are
one nation, albeit a nation which has spoken different
languages and worships God in various ways.[50]

Of the ten newspapers and journals run by the Democrats, five were
published in Tehran and one in Tabriz.[51] The most influential of them
was *Iran-e Now*, a daily whose "real and actual editor, as well as the
principal writer, was, however, Mohammad Amin Rasulzadeh".[52]

Rasulzadeh (1884–1955) was a Social Democrat from Baku who began
his political career by joining the Hemmat Party in Baku. For a short time
he was editor of *Takamol*, the Hemmat Party's official newspaper. In 1908,
after *Takamol* had been banned by the Tsarist authorities, the Social
Democrat Party of Caucasia sent Rasulzadeh to Rasht, the capital of Gilan,
to assist the Iranian Social Democrats and the Constitutionalists in their
struggle against the Shah. Following the Constitutionalist march on Tehran,
he joined the Social Democrats in Tehran to form the Democrat Party.[53]

In addition to his numerous articles which appeared in *Iran-e Now*, he
was a pioneer figure in the development of political polemics,
especially in his arguments with *Ferqeh-e E'tedaliyun* (the Moderate
Party). In one of his articles criticizing the Moderate Party's program,
after first reviewing the programs of various Russian and British political
parties, he adds: "Our beloved homeland, Iran, cannot be an exception in
the evolutionary process which every human society has gone through."
And he therefore concluded that: "Clashes between the propertied
classes and the *nation* are inevitable."[54]

Soon enough the spirit of these "inevitable clashes" had spread across
the whole country. The enthusiastic parliamentary debates were not

contained within the walls of the *Majles*. The streets of Tehran turned into a battlefield of bloody clashes between the Democrats and the Moderates. The Democrats were responsible for the death of Amin ol-Molk, an influential figure in the Moderate Party, as well as Seyyed 'Abdollah Behbahani, the prominent *mojtahed* (high-ranking clergyman) and advocate of the Constitution. Eventually this campaign of violence backfired on the Democrats and they themselves fell victim to severe attacks. In the end, important Democrat leaders, such as Heydar Khan 'Amoghlu, Taqizadeh and Nowbari, were forced to leave the country.

By adopting terrorist tactics, the Democrats not only lost their credibility as advocates of legality and pluralism, but unfortunately contributed substantially to bringing about the interlude in modern Iranian history which Abrahamian has aptly called "the period of disintegration".[55]

The other major factor, however, in bringing about political disintegration was pressure from foreign powers. In October 1910, Britain, known as "the Southern Neighbour" in Iranian political parlance, delivered an ultimatum to Iran concerning the security of southern Iran. By doing so, Britain set an example for the Russians to follow. Russian troops had already occupied the northern provinces. In November 1911, the Tsarist government presented Iran with its own ultimatum, which amounted to nothing less than an attempt to reduce the north of the country to the status of a semi-dependent colony.[56] However, while the *Majles*, which enjoyed the support of the "crowds" in the street, resisted the Russian ultimatum, the weak Iranian government decided to accept the ultimatum and dissolve the parliament. This seemed to be the only effective measure available to the deputies in face of the crisis which had arisen.[57]

The Grand National Assembly which we saw referred to above as the "beloved Mecca" of the Revolutionaries, was, in the end, dissolved by the very "lovers" themselves.

World War I: Departure of the Old Order, Arrival of the New Ideas

The outbreak of World War I did not stop the process of political disintegration in Iran. In fact, increased foreign pressure caused the long-standing rift in Iranian politics to widen. Meanwhile, the occupation of the north and south of Iran by Russian and British troops was to provoke the Ottoman forces to invade western and northwestern Iran early on in the war. If we add to this list of disasters the activities of the "German Lawrence", especially among the southern tribes, we begin to get an idea of how powerless the Iranian government was during this period.

The central government was so divided and ridden by factions that the different cabinets which were formed never lasted more than a few months. And yet the government itself was not the sole source of power in the country. As Blucher, a contemporary observer put it, "there were *two sources* for exercising *political power* in the country, the *official* one which included the government and its connections, and the *unofficial* source", which he explains consisted of "the national forces".[58]

The Iranian government's early reaction to the outbreak of the war was to declare Iran's strict neutrality in the *farman* of 1 November 1914. On the other hand, what sense was there in the government's announcing its neutrality when a sizeable part of Iran's territory was occupied by the Entente's forces? When Mostowfi ol-Mamalek, the prime minister of Iran, approached the Russian authorities and asked that they withdraw their troops from Azerbaijan because their presence gave the Turks a pretext for invading Iran: "The Russian minister appreciated the Iranian viewpoint but inquired what guarantees could be given that after the withdrawal of Russian forces, the Turks would not bring in theirs."[59]

It seems clear that had Iran's government been strong and firmly established, it might well have been able to pursue a policy of neutrality. The fact is, however, that both the Shah, who was crowned in July 1914, and the cabinet of Mostowfi ol-Mamalek, were utterly impotent. This impotence on the government's part can only be explained by the absence of a centralized state in Iran.

As a result of their inability to remain neutral, some Iranians chose what they considered to be the safest path in seeking an alliance. Germany, because of its geographical distance, appeared to be a preferable ally. In contrast to the British, whose interests in India automatically made them pursue a policy of intervention in Iran, Germany at first sight seemed to present no direct threat. In its relations with Iran, Germany could even claim this advantage over the Russians and the Ottomans when they offered themselves as allies. It was true that the Germans "made persistent efforts to acquire a place in the sun", but they were always particularly careful not to antagonize the Russians.[60]

Anti-Russian and anti-British sentiments consequently made the Democrats see the Germans as suitable allies. When the Third *Majles* was convened in December 1914, thirty out of the one hundred and thirty-six deputies were members of the Democrat Party.[61] The pro-German activities of the Democrats were viewed with mistrust and dismay by the British and Russians who decided to increase the number of their occupying forces in Iran. The situation became so acute that the Russian troops stationed in Qazvin, a hundred miles north-west of Tehran, marched on Tehran, threatening to occupy the capital. The thirty Democrat deputies, accompanied by some journalists and influential politicians, set out on their "long march", first stopping in Qom where they formed the "*Komiteh-e Defa'-e Melli*" (the National Defence Committee), then falling back to Kashan, and finally establishing themselves in Kermanshah, where they called themselves the "*Hokumat-e Melli*" (the National Government). The *Hokumat-e Melli* which had the official recognition as the central power and as such was the sole legitimate government of Iran, could not persist in face of the increased pressures brought to bear by the British. In 1916, Kermanshah fell to the British forces and the *Hokumat-e Melli* came to an end.

Meanwhile, inspired by pan-Turkish and pan-Turanian sentiment (envisaging a greater united homeland for all Turkic people), the Ottomans opened a new front against the Entente forces in Azerbaijan. The immediate result was that Azerbaijan became one of the major battlefields in the World War I. As part of their military strategy, the Russians, British and Ottomans all pursued policies which aimed at stirring up or aggravating the existing animosities between the different ethnic and religious groupings in the province. Promises were made with regard to setting up a sovereign state for Kurds, Assyrians, Armenians and Azerbaijani Muslims. Such demagogic manipulations led to the most bloody and barbaric confrontations among these ethnic and religious groups. During the struggles of the constitutional movement, although Azerbaijan was split between reform-seeking Constitutionalists and the conservative Royalists, it had none the less been possible for Muslim Azerbaijanis to make common cause with the Christian Georgians and Armenian volunteers. Now, thanks to foreign manipulation, Azerbaijan became "a divided land", where the heads of various tribes and communities were engaged in unifying the *Ümmet-i Islam* under the banner of *Ittihad-i Islam* (Unity of Islam).[62]

The Russian Revolution of February 1917 appeared to have a more immediate impact in Gilan than in Azerbaijan. Along with the general consternation among the Russian troops, what could be observed in Azerbaijan was a shift in attitude on the part of some units in the Russian army towards the local people. In Tabriz Russian *saldats* began to address Tabrizis as "friend" or "comrade", but in the early days there was no real initiative from the Russians to spread the idea of radical change.[63] Furthermore, seven years of war and continuous military occupation made the Azerbaijanis loth to react enthusiastically to the Iranian Social Democrats' call to join in the revolutionary surge descending from the north.

By 1917, the Iranian Social Democrats in Baku, who had been engaged in clandestine political activities since the beginning of the war, announced the formation of their own independent political party, *Ferqeh-e 'Edalat* (the Justice Party). The party's first newspaper *Beyraq-e 'Edalat* (The Banner of Justice) did not last very long. It was replaced by *Hürriyat* (Liberty) and *Yoldash* (The Comrade) which were bilingual Azerbaijani-Persian publications. The chief editor and one of the major contributors to these newspapers was Mir Ja'far Javadzadeh (Pishevari).

In 1918, the Justice Party sent a group of eighteen party members to Gilan, under the leadership of Asadollah Ghafarzadeh, first secretary of the party. Although the first attempt by the party to establish contact with Kuchak Khan, the leader of the *Jangali* rebel movement in Gilan was a failure, the party soon sent a second group of twenty members to Gilan. In June 1920, the Justice Party held its first congress in Anzali, Gilan's major port on the Caspian.[64] At this congress, consisting of fifty-one voting members, seventeen of whom were Azerbaijanis, the Justice Party was renamed the Communist Party of Iran and a Minimum Programme was formally approved and adopted.[65] Article Four of the Programme called for the establishment of a "People's Republic of Iran, an independent and indivisible sovereign Republic".[66] One year later, in July 1921, the Khorasan provincial committee of the Communist Party of Iran (Justice Party) published its program. In this document the national unity of Iran is emphasized:

> Our aim is to establish a government in Iran which originates
> with the toiling Iranian people.[67]

During these early days of the Iranian Communist Party, it is clear that
the party did not conceive of Iran as a land made up of separate nations
and there was no mention of the Leninist concept of "the right of a
nation to self-determination, the right to secede from others and to form an
independent national state".[68] Only seven years later would such a view
emerge, namely in the new program ratified at the end of the Second
Congress of the Communist Party of Iran which was held at Rostov.[69]
Here, for the first time, Iran was officially described as a land where "many
nations" live. The task of the Iranian Communist Party now became that of
"fighting for the total freedom of these nations, even to the extent of their
seceding from the central government".[70]

* * *

While the spirit of Communism was spreading its wings over Caucasia,
in neighbouring Anatolia pan-Turkism, having replaced the rival schools
pan-Ottomanism and pan-Islamism, was flourishing.

The origins of pan-Turkism go back to the beginning of the century,
when both pan-Ottomanism and pan-Islamism failed to cope with the
ever growing problems of the Ottoman Empire. "Ottomanism had
proven a failure. Islamic loyalty still dominated the sentiments of the
great mass of Turks, as it had done for centuries past, but its modern
political avatar, pan-Islamism, had won only limited successes, and
held, moreover, a diminishing appeal for the western-educated,
westwardlooking younger intellectuals."[71]

Indeed, it was the Ottoman-Turk *münevver ul-fikirler* (intellectuals)
who first began to shed the aura of contempt associated with the name
Türk. Mehmet Amin, for instance, expresses the new sense of national
pride in his poetry:

> I am a Turk, my faith and my race are mighty ...
> We are Turks, with this blood and with this name we live.[72]

What began as a lack of resentment at being called a *Türk*, soon evolved into a positive sentiment of pride and came to embrace the concept of a Turkish nation. Surprisingly enough, the one who baptized pan-Turkism was not himself a subject of the Ottoman Empire. In 1904, Akçuroğlu Yusuf (later known as Yusuf Akçura), a Tatar from the Russian Empire, published a pamphlet called *Üç Terz-i Siyaset* (Three kinds of Policies), which soon came to be known as the manifesto of the pan-Turkists. In this famous declaration, which was originally printed in Cairo by Turks in exile, Akçuroğlu Yusuf discusses the inherent historical obstacles blocking the advance of pan-Ottomanism and panIslamism and advocates *Ittihad-i Etrak* (the Unity of Turks, i.e. pan-Turkism) as the sole concept which is able to sustain the *Türk milleti* (Turkish nation). He admits that he "does not know if the idea still has adherents outside the Ottoman Empire", especially in *Qefqaziyeh ve Şumali Iran* (Caucasia and northern Iran), but he hopes that in the near future his views on Turkish identity will attract the support of many Turks wherever they live.[73]

Ittihad-i Etrak, or as it was later named by Akçuroğlu Yusuf, *Türkçülük* (Turkism),[74] was soon adopted as a policy by political parties and "cultural organizations" in the Ottoman Empire. In 1908, *Türk Derneği* (the Turkish Society) was founded in Istanbul to study the "past and present activities and circumstances of all the people called *Türk*".[75] *Türk Derneği* was followed by another "society" called *Türk Ocağı* (the Turkish Hearth). In its manifesto, written in 1912, this later society proclaimed as its chief aim "to advance the national education and raise the scientific, social and economic level of the Turks who are the foremost of the people of Islam, and to strive for the betterment of the Turkish race and language".[76]

The issues which these "societies" still had to address were: who is a Turk and where is his homeland? Zia Gökalp (1876–1924), the most influential nationalist and one of the founders of the *Türk Ocağı*, in a poem published in 1911 and entitled *Turan*, describes the Turkish homeland in the following terms:

> The country of the Turk is not Turkey, nor Turkistan. Their country is a vast eternal land: *Turan!*[77]

Later, in his much publicized book *Türkçülük Esasları* (The Principles of Turkism), Zia Gökalp reiterates the old beliefs and adopts a more "realistic" approach in defining Turk and the Turkish homeland. By "Turk", he now means "a nation which possesses a culture peculiar to itself; therefore a Turk can have only one language, only a single culture".[78] Realizing the obstacles confronting his former utopian notion of assembling all Turks in the land of *Turan*, he now excludes the Tatars, Kirghiz and Uzbeks from sharing in the ideal unity and only focuses on the Oghuz Turks:

> Today, the Turks for whom cultural unification would be easy are the Oghuz Turks, that is the Turkmens; for the Turkmens of Azerbaijan, Iran and Khwarizm, like the Turks of Turkey, belong to the Oghuz, or Turkmen unity.

He then describes the kind of unity he proposes:

> A political unity? For the present, no! We cannot pass judgment today on what will happen in the future, but for the present our goal is only cultural unity of the Oghuz peoples.[79]

The outbreak of World War I, with the Ottomans fighting Russia, paved the way for the flourishing of pan-Turkism. For the pan-Turkists the Russians were not only *kafirs* (infidels), but also invaders who had occupied areas south of the Caucasus which were considered as part of the Islamic Turkic homeland. Therefore, the war against Russia could be promoted with all the sanctions of *jihad*.

The Russian Revolution of 1917 and the collapse of the Russian Empire made many pan-Turkists believe that the time for liberating the fatherland and unifying the Turkish nation had come. Although this optimism did not last for very long and the Bolsheviks soon showed that they would not tolerate any change in the territory of the empire, none the less for some years the veteran partisans of pan-Turkism were still busy employing any possible means for realizing their old dream.

Contrary to their expectations, the achievements of pan-Turkists in Azerbaijan during and immediately after World War I were not very impressive. Although the province for years remained under quasi-occupation by the Ottoman troops, their attempts to create a solid base of support among Azerbaijanis ended in failure. Pan-Turkish newspapers, such as *Azarabadegan*, which was published in the Azerbaijani language, did not succeed in facilitating Azerbaijani-Ottoman relations. Furthermore, the Ottomans never enjoyed the support of local political parties. Their relations with the Democrats were particularly strained. With the prolonged presence of Ottoman troops in Iran, relations with the Democrats steadily deteriorated. On one occasion, the Ottomans even went as far as to arrest the Democrats' popular leaders Khiyabani and Nowbari and sent them into exile.[80] Although later they tried to justify their action by accusing Khiyabani of "collaborating with the Armenians against the forces of Islam",[81] nevertheless, what they did resulted in whipping up serious anti-Ottoman sentiment among the Democrats, who, at the time, were preparing to take control of the province.

The Revolt of Khiyabani

During the days of the constitutional struggle, when Tabriz was offering resistance to Mohammad 'Ali Mirza's royalist *coup d'état*, there appeared on the political scene a young radical preacher who had been elected as a member of an important local provincial council and was destined to play a prominent role in local events.[82] The preacher, Sheykh Mohammad Khiyabani, was born in 1880 in Khameneh, a village in the vicinity of Tabriz. His father was a merchant who maintained an office in Petrovsk (later renamed Makhachkala in the Russian Soviet Federal Socialist Republic). Having finished primary school in his home village, Khiyabani went to Russia and worked for a while in his father's office. When he returned to Tabriz, he then attended a seminary school and became a qualified preacher.[83]

At the beginning of the Constitutionalist movement, Khiyabani was holding the post of imam in two mosques in Tabriz, as well as being a mathematics teacher at the Talebiyeh school, where his lectures were attended by Ahmad Kasravi, who was to become a distinguished historian and an opponent of Khiyabani.[84] In the conflict between the *Anjoman-e Tabriz* and the *Eslamiyeh*, Khiyabani aligned himself with the Constitutionalists, and it is from that point in time that his career really began. In the election for the Second *Majles*, he successfully stood as a candidate for Azerbaijan and then took up his seat in the *Majles* in Tehran along with the other eleven elected deputies.

During the early days of the Second *Majles*, when deputies felt obliged to declare their affiliation with one of the political parties, although Khiyabani denied being a member of any particular party, he acknowledged that he attended the meetings of the parliamentary fractions of the Democrats.[85] In a rather lengthy speech delivered in Parliament, he is on record as having dissociated himself from both the *Ejtema'iyun 'Amiyun* (Social Democrats) and those Democrats who sympathized with republicanism. And in the same speech, he declared before parliament that as far as he was concerned, he would never consider joining any particular political party.[86]

As it turned out, Khiyabani was unable to maintain this independent stance indefinitely. Seven years later, in March 1918, in conjunction with Nowbari and Chaychi, he announced publicly the re-establishment of the Democrat Party, and subsequently he began to publish the newspaper *Tajaddod* as the party's organ.[87] Thanks to the firm stand which Khiyabani had taken against the Russian ultimatum of November 1911, and the controversial speeches he had made on the subject at that time in the *Majles*, the re-established Democrat Party soon began to enjoy widespread popular support, both inside and outside Azerbaijan.

When famine broke out in Azerbaijan during the winter of 1918, the measures taken by the Democrats, which included distributing grain among the people, naturally increased the Party's reputation and popularity, both in the home province and throughout Iran generally. In a region where there was a deep-rooted tradition of heroic banditry, such actions on the part of the Democrats were bound to make Khiyabani appear as the new Robin Hood of that day and age. By this time, the Democrats had established control over Tabriz and a few other important cities in Azerbaijan.[88]

However, by the summer of 1919, when the Ottoman troops returned to Azerbaijan, the honeymoon for the Democrats was over. Yusuf Zia, a civilian political adviser to the Ottoman army, saw to it that the rank and file of the Democrats was broken and dispersed. Once again the old tattered banner of *Ittihad-i Islam* was hoisted aloft. With the support of Khiyabani's opponents, Yusuf Zia intensified his activities, in particular by initiating a new campaign of pan-Turkism. An important instrument for the propagation of pan-Turkish ideals throughout the province of Azerbaijan was the newspaper *Azarabadegan* which was founded at this time.

Shortly after the arrival of the Ottomans, Khiyabani, Nowbari and

Badamchi were arrested and sent into exile. Not only did the Iranian government officials in Tabriz not raise objections to the decision of the Ottoman authorities, but the rumour quickly spread through Tabriz that the Ottomans were in fact acting at the request of the Iranian government. In particular, the Heir Apparent, Mohammad Hasan Mirza, was considered to have played a major role in these political machinations.[89]

Khiyabani and his fellow Democrats were deeply perturbed by what they perceived as the local government's willingness to collaborate with the enemy. Throughout the preceding year, although the Democrats presented themselves as a political alternative, they had consciously tried to stay on good terms with the government and to avoid unnecessary head-on confrontations. Now, however, they felt that the government had betrayed them. When, after the Ottoman withdrawal from Azerbaijan, Khiyabani returned from exile, he went on to become the most prominent leader among the Democrats. But he had learned a bitter lesson which he would never forget. From now on he was committed to a policy of radical change in Iran, and more specifically, he was convinced of the necessity of greater local autonomy for Azerbaijan.

Khiyabani's revolt really begins with his election campaign for the Fourth *Majles*. The election itself was held during August/September 1919. Of the nine deputies elected to represent Tabriz and the city's suburbs, six were candidates put up by the Democrat Party, the most famous among them being Khiyabani himself.[90]

The central government was anything but pleased by the results of the election. The prime minister, Vosuq od-Dowleh, alarmed by the increasing activities of the Democrats, decided to dispatch a group of forty-three policemen headed by two Swedish chief officers to assert the central government's authority and to "reorganize" the police departments throughout Azerbaijan.[91] According to the British consular report: "The Swedish officers from the start seem to have played their cards very badly and to have let it be generally understood that they intended to suppress the Democrat Party."[92]

Relations between the police department and the Democrats went on steadily deteriorating. Major Burling, the Swedish chief officer, had the task of imposing the central government's authority in a region which was on the brink of political collapse. Being a Christian, his mission had very little chance of success. The Democrats took every opportunity to exploit his Achilles' heel and profited greatly by whipping up popular religious sentiment against him. On one occasion, when the police arrested a Democrat sympathizer, the Democrats demanded his release and called on their members and supporters to arm themselves and gather before the premises of the party's newspaper. Subsequently, the crowd marched to the police station and forced the release of the jailed individual. Not long after this, the Democrats formed a *Hey'at-e Ejtema'i* (Public Commission) and published a declaration calling for "public peace and order" and "the restoration of the Constitution in Iran".[93] Khiyabani's uprising was now well under way.

It did not take Khiyabani and his fellow Democrats long to establish their control over local affairs. On 24 June 1920, less than two months after the above mentioned events, Khiyabani announced the formation of a local government which he called the *Milli Hükumat* (the National Government). This announcement took place with pomp and ceremony in the 'Ali Qapi – the central government's provincial headquarters – while the crowd sang the *Marseillaise* which they had adopted as their anthem.

By *Milli Hükumat*, Khiyabani had in mind a popular government rather than a national one. On many occasions in his speeches and writings, Khiyabani had used the expression "free and independent *mellat* of Iran", when addressing the nation of Iran as a whole. These earlier usages of the term *mellat* clearly indicate that he had not been specifically referring to a particular ethnic group on those occasions. Apparently, his use of *milli (melli)* or *millat* was not rigorously consistent. In any case, *Melli Hükumat*, as employed to describe the newly set up local government of Azerbaijan, was never intended to convey the meaning of an independent Azerbaijani nation-state.

In an interview with the British consul in Tabriz, when Khiyabani was asked "whether he objected to Tehran's authority", he "categorically denied the accusation made against him" and "in the most positive terms... assured" the consul that: "There was nothing of a separatist nature in their [the Democrats'] movement". Moreover, "he considered Azerbaijan as an integral part of Persia".[94]

One of the key issues for Khiyabani and his fellow Democrats was how to dissociate themselves as fully as possible from the foreign powers. Their relations with the Ottomans, in view of the latter's early stance against Khiyabani, remained cold and distant. And the British, too, were not likely candidates for an alliance, considering their long-standing anti-Democrat attitudes and policies. The only foreign power which might conceivably act as a sponsor on behalf of the Democrats was the newly born state whose revolutionaries had recently toppled the Imperial Government of Tsarist Russia.

Originally, the Azerbaijani Democrats welcomed the 1917 Russian Revolution and instructed their party's provincial committee to establish friendly reciprocal relations with "those groups in Russia which are not only struggling for democracy in their homeland but also respect the fundamental sovereignty of other nations".[95] It was not long, however, before the policies implemented by the revolutionaries on the other side of the Araxes River made the Democrats of Azerbaijan adopt a more cautious, protective attitude towards their giant neighbour.

On 27 May 1918, when the new Republic of Azerbaijan was founded in the territory lying north of the Araxes River and to the south-east of Transcaucasia, the adoption of the name Azerbaijan caused consternation in Iran and especially among Azerbaijani intellectuals. Khiyabani and his fellow Democrats, in order to dissociate themselves from the Transcaucasians, decided to change the name of the province to *Azadistan* (Land of Freedom).[96] By way of justifying this decision, they referred to the important "heroic role" Azerbaijan had played in the struggle to establish the Constitution in Iran which, in their view, warranted adopting the new name *Azadistan*.[97]

All along Khiyabani maintained that "he had no desire or intention of severing Azerbaijan from Iran"[98], and he repeatedly declared this stance publicly. None the less, many observers, especially the British, were convinced that he was in fact a separatist.[99] In face of any such accusations from his political opponents, Khiyabani made no concessions. He never abandoned his early aim of winning more autonomy for Azerbaijan within the framework of Iran. However, it was this goal in particular which he set himself that caused many politicians, including Kasravi, to turn their back on the *Milli Hükumat*. Opponents like Kasravi were firmly committed to the idea of a strong, centralized government, whose power base would be located in the capital city of Tehran, rather than in the provinces. They believed that the capital was the only suitable and legitimate base from which to introduce radical changes into the provinces of Iran. Consequently, when, at a later date, Moshir od-Dowleh's popular cabinet replaced the despised government of Vosuq od-Dowleh, Khiyabani's opponents in the Democrat Party did not hesitate to align themselves with the new government against Khiyabani's *Milli Hükumat*.

Khiyabani's uncompromising policy not only made it impossible for him to negotiate with the central government but he was unable to co-ordinate his efforts with other contemporary regional movements in Iran. He was adamant in his opposition to any form of foreign interference, whether direct or indirect, in Iran's political affairs, and consequently was against co-operating with Kuchak Khan, the leader of rebellion in Gilan. For instance, when Kuchak Khan called for the formation of a popular front with the purpose of restoring the Constitution in Iran, Khiyabani went so far as to compare him to Vosuq od-Dowleh:

> What is the difference between you and Vosuq od-Dowleh? He wants to rule Iran with the assistance of the British forces and you would do the same with the backing of the Russians.[100]

By the time Moshir od-Dowleh appointed Mokhber os-Saltaneh Hedayat as governor of Azerbaijan in August 1920, Khiyabani's days were numbered. Mokhber os-Saltaneh reached Tabriz in September and within one week of his arrival, on 12 September, the Cossack Brigade[101] was deployed to take control of all the strategic points throughout the city. In a short time, the Cossacks had achieved their objectives and fifty Democrats had been killed, including Khiyabani. The central government's authority was unambiguously re-established over the whole region.[102]

Although Khiyabani's power was short-lived, he exercised an important influence on political thought and attitudes in Iran, especially with regard to reformist trends. His initiative to set up his government as an alternative to the central government's authority in Azerbaijan caused a major split in the reformist camp. While the modern tendency within the *Nahzat-e Melli* (Popular Movement) was towards playing down the central government's functions and granting more autonomy to the provinces, the traditional current in reformist politics was still wholly committed to establishing a strong, centralized (not necessarily despotic) government in Iran. The successful suppression of Khiyabani's revolt can be taken as a sign of the widespread vigour and legitimacy which this traditional current of thinking still enjoyed.

3

The Reign of Reza Shah:
One Country, One Nation

Today you Deputies of the Majles wish to make Sardar-e Sepah, Reza Khan, a King. The honourable gentleman is now not only Prime Minister, but Minister of War and Commander-in-Chief of the armed forces as well. Today our country, after twenty years of widespread bloodshed, is about to enter a phase of retrogression. One and the same person as King, as Prime Minister, as Minister of War, as Commander-in-Chief? Even in Zanzibar no such state of affairs exists!

From a speech by Mosaddeq during a session of the Parliament, concerning the change of dynasty, 31 October 1925.

Building a Modern Nation-State

The tragic conclusion of Khiyabani's revolt marked the beginning of a historical period during which Azerbaijan, as well as the rest of Iran, underwent far-reaching changes in all sectors of life. After Khiyabani's death, apart from two consecutive incidents, there was almost no trace of open incitement to revolt expressed in Azerbaijan for the next twenty years.

The first of these incidents, which took place immediately after the fall of Khiyabani, was the insurrection led by Qiyami, one of

53

Khiyabani's associates. Qiyami called those taking part in his insurrection the "*Qiyamiyun Enteqamiyun*" (Revenge Insurgents), but he was unsuccessful in his efforts to maintain the momentum of Khiyabani's revolt. He was particularly active in Kalaybar in the district of Ahar, north Tabriz.[1]

The second of these episodes was the uprising of Major Lahuti, the commander of the Tabriz gendarmerie. On 1 February 1922, Lahuti challenged the central government's authority by seizing the governmental offices in Tabriz and setting up the *Komiteh-e Melli* (the National Committee). The uprising didn't last more than one week. By the end of February, Lahuti was obliged to flee from Tabriz. He sought refuge "in the land of the Soviets", where he began his career as a revolutionary poet.[2]

Though not involved in the suppression of Khiyabani, Reza Khan, as head of the Cossack Brigade, personally conducted the military operation directed against Lahuti's insurrection in Tabriz. Just one year earlier, on 21 February 1921, Reza Khan, together with the journalist Seyyed Zia Tabataba'i, had successfully launched a *coup d'état* in Tehran. It was to be another four years before Reza Khan would have himself crowned Shah of Iran. Having thus founded the Pahlavi dynasty, Reza Shah went on to rule for another twenty years before abdicating and going into exile in 1941, under pressure from the Allies.

The Policy of Centralization

Reza Shah's policy of centralizing government power and implementing modernization in Iran was precisely what the vast majority of Iran's urban population, in particular the middle classes and the intelligentsia, hoped for and expected. As early as 1914, many popular politicians were taking a stance in relation to the question of the country's modernization. In the program of his second cabinet, which was rejected by the *Majles* in 1914, Mostowfi ol-Mamalek proposed the following: the abolition of the old pensions system, the speedy completion of the new Code, the founding of a secular law school to train personnel for the Ministry of Justice, the establishment of several schools for girls, and new laws concerning telegraphic communications.[3]

That same year, Moshir od-Dowleh presented his cabinet before the Third *Majles* with a program which proposed "formulating commercial codes, enacting bankruptcy laws, the establishment of a teachers' college for women, the adoption by all schools of a uniform curriculum and uniform textbooks, the gradual transformation of *maktab-khanehs* (religious schools) into secular elementary schools, and the formation of a Chamber of Commerce".[4]

The process of centralization, which included such harsh and disruptive measures as transferring tens of thousands of nomads and forcing them to settle on the land, generally enjoyed the support of many members of the intelligentsia, especially those with liberal and left-wing leanings. It was the common belief in such circles that only a centralized, powerful (though not necessarily despotic) government would be capable of solving the country's growing problems of underdevelopment, while at the same time safeguarding the *nation's unity* and *sovereignty*.

The magazines *Iranshahr* (Land of Iran) and *Ayandeh* (The Future) were pioneers in publicizing these views. *Iranshahr* was first published in Berlin, in June 1922. The editor, Hoseyn Kazemzadeh, maintained close contact with intellectuals in Europe who were involved with Iranian studies and his magazine was soon exercising a powerful influence in political and intellectual circles in Iran. During the five years of *Iranshahr*'s existence, forty-eight issues appeared and special attention was often paid to Azerbaijan. Indeed, there were nine long articles which were exclusively devoted to the subject.

When, in 1923, the Turkish magazine *Yeni Mecmu'a* (The New Journal) reported on a conference concerning Azerbaijan held by *Türk Ocağı* (the Turkish Hearth) in Istanbul, *Iranshahr* was quick to react. During the conference, Roshani Beg, a well-known pan-Turkist, had condemned the Iranian government for its atrocious, oppressive and tyrannical policies towards the Azerbaijanis living in Iran. He called on all Azerbaijanis in Iran to unite with the new-born Republic of Turkey.[5] In reply, *Iranshahr* published an article by J. Marquart, the eminent German Iranist of the early twentieth century, which dealt with the historical bonds existing between Azerbaijan and the rest of Iran. At the end of the article, there appeared a poem by 'Aref, the Iranian radical Constitutionalist poet, denouncing the Turkish language by saying:

The Turkish tongue should be torn out by the roots.

The legs it stands on should be cut off in this land.
Sweep across the Araxes bearing the Persian tongue!
Oh, breeze of dawn, arise! Tell the people of Tabriz:
The pleasant land of Zoroaster is no place for Genghiz![6]

While such issues of *Iranshahr* attempted to provide historical background,
the magazine *Ayandeh* took on the task of propounding the necessary
conditions for the "unification" and "Persianization" of all Iranians as a
nation. The first issue of *Ayandeh* contains an introductory article written by
the editor, Mahmud Afshar, and entitled *Gozashteh – Emruz – Ayandeh*
(Past – Present – Future). After expressing his concern for Iranian unity,
Afshar emphasizes the importance of accepting Persian as the national
language of Iran. He believes this is the only effective means for bringing
about cultural and political unification:

> What I mean by the national unity of Iran is a political,
> cultural and social unity of the people who live within the
> present day boundaries of Iran. This unity includes two other
> concepts, namely, the maintenance of political independence
> and the geographical integrity of Iran. However, achieving
> national unity means that the Persian language must be
> established throughout the whole country, that regional
> differences in clothing, customs and such like must
> disappear, and that *moluk ot-tavayef* (the local chieftains)
> must be eliminated. Kurds, Lors, Qashqa'is, Arabs, Turks,
> Turkmens, etc., shall not differ from one another by wearing
> different clothes or speaking a different language. In my
> opinion, until national unity is achieved in Iran, with regard
> to customs, clothing, and so forth, the possibility of our
> political independence and geographical integrity being
> endangered will always remain.[7]

And Mahmud Afshar went further by propounding the practical steps
which he thought were necessary to take in order to achieve national
unity:

> The Persian language must become established in all parts of
> Iran and gradually replace the foreign languages. This task
> can only be accomplished if elementary schools are founded

everywhere, and if laws are passed which make education compulsory and gratis, and these laws see to it that the necessary means for this are provided.

And by way of eliminating ethnic divisions and fostering national unity, he adds:

Thousands of low-priced attractive books and treatises in the Persian language must be distributed throughout the country, especially in Azerbaijan and Khuzistan. Little by little the means of publishing small, inexpensive newspapers locally in the national language in the most remote parts of the country must be provided. All this requires assistance from the state and should be carried out according to an orderly plan. Certain Persian speaking tribes could be sent to the regions where a foreign language is spoken, and settled there, while the tribes of that region which speak a foreign language could be transferred and settled in Persian speaking areas. Geographical names in foreign languages or any souvenirs of the marauding and raids of Genghiz Khan and Tamurlane should be replaced by Persian names. The country should be divided from an administrative point of view if the goal of national unity is to be achieved.[8]

In another article, entitled "*Mas'aleh-e Melliyat va Vahdat-e Melli-ye Iran*" (the Question of Nationality and National Unity in Iran), Mahmud Afshar describes "the Iranian nation" as:

A group of people united on the basis of common race, religion, social life, and history, who have lived together for centuries on common land.[9]

In the same article, Mahmud Afshar declares quite explicitly: "Iranian national unity will always remain fragile and fragmentary as long as there continues to be a difference between the languages spoken in Iran." It is doubtful, he points out, whether the common religion will be able to function for very long as a basis for Iranian national unity.[10]

The measures here proposed for accomplishing a complete unity of Iranians are worked out in more detailed form and at greater length, but they are basically the same as those he recommended in his earlier articles. The only new consideration which he introduces to the problem has to do with the type of government which would best be able to carry out this important undertaking. He is convinced that only "a strong government with effective powers (*moqtader*)" would be up to the task, and at this point he adds by way of parenthesis that such an advanced, empowered government "is not to be confused with a despotic regime".[11]

Generally speaking, Reza Shah, apart from the above mentioned provision about despotism, met all the demands voiced by such intellectuals as Hoseyn Kazemzadeh and Mahmud Afshar. As a result of the Shah's educational reforms, the traditional religious *maktab-khaneh* was replaced by the modern primary school. These schools increased in number from 440 in 1922 to 2,401 in 1942. During that same period, the number of pupils attending these schools rose from 43,025 to 244,315.[12] Moreover, in 1922, there were only 46 secondary schools with an enrolment of 9,308 students. By the end of Reza Shah's reign, the number of functioning secondary schools had risen to 320 with 26,812 students.[13] The new school books were all in Persian and published in Tehran. They replaced the old Koranic and classic texts previously in use. Meanwhile, the teaching of other languages spoken in Iran was strictly forbidden. By 1930, even Arabic had been eliminated from the primary school curriculum and was only taught in secondary schools.

Not only was Persian now the national language of Iran, but all the other ethnic languages in the country were banned. It was not permitted to publish books and newspapers in any language other than Persian. In June 1935, the prime minister, Forughi, presented his cabinet to the Tenth *Majles* and took the opportunity to announce the formation of a new institution called the *Farhangestan*, a kind of Academy or Cultural Institute. Its task was to be "the purification of the Persian language by introducing new Persian words to replace the Arabic and foreign ones".[14] The press was under the strict surveillance of a special branch in the police department which exercised censorship not only over the contents of what was published, but was also concerned with the purity of the language.[15]

To achieve greater national uniformity, Reza Shah, in January 1938, ordered the setting up of a government office called the *Sazeman-e Parvaresh-e Afkar* (the Department for Fostering Thought). The head of this new department was the minister of justice, who was now charged with the task of guiding and directing the younger generation towards service to the homeland.[16]

Reza Shah's policy of the forced transfer and settlement of nomads officially began in 1932. Under very harsh conditions, tens of thousands of Kurds were resettled in Mazandaran (northern region of Iran), as well as in Khorasan (the north-east) and Isfahan and Yazd (central Iran). Azerbaijanis were driven into Kurdistan, while the Bakhtiyaris and Lors were forced to settle in the central and southern parts of Iran.[17]

Traditionally, Iran had been geographically divided into four large *Iyalat* (provinces) and numerous *velayat* (districts). Azerbaijan was originally one of these *Iyalat* with its own *vali* (governor). Between the end of 1937 and the beginning of 1938, two special laws were passed which abolished the old administrative system. Iran was divided into *ostans* – *ostan* being a pure Persian word introduced by the *Farhangestan*, and equivalent to *Iyalat* which is of Arabic origin. The *ostans* were divided into *shahrestans* (counties), the latter being subdivided into *bakhshs* (municipalities) and *dehestans* (rural districts). Each *ostan* had its own *ostandar* (governor general) and every *shahrestan* its own *farmandar* (governor), both of these administrators being directly appointed by the Shah. The Ministry of the Interior was responsible for appointing mayors and other municipal officials.

According to this new administrative division of the country, Azerbaijan was divided into two *ostans*: Eastern Azerbaijan with Tabriz as its capital, and Western Azerbaijan, its chief city being Reza'iyeh (formerly Urumiyeh, but renamed in honour of Reza Shah). As a result of this reshuffling, Eastern Azerbaijan not only contained regions inhabited by Azerbaijanis, but also took in parts of Kurdistan, including the cities of Mahabad and Sardasht.

* * *

During Reza Shah's reign, Azerbaijan gradually lost its former commercial pre-eminence. Having once been known as the gateway to Iran's trade with the western world, Azerbaijan was now reduced to the sole function of being Iran's granary. Reza Shah's policy of centralizing commerce in Tehran, along with the problems Azerbaijani merchants faced in their trade relations with the new-born Soviet regime across the northern border, are the major factors which led to the region's commercial decline. The Russian Revolution of 1917, which was followed by civil war, disrupted Russo-Iranian trade for some years, but by 1927 the Soviet Union had once again become Iran's biggest single trading partner. With specific reference to the north of Iran during this period, Banani sums up the state of affairs with regard to trade as follows:

> The rich agricultural provinces of northern Iran depended upon the Russian market for the sale of their surplus grain, rice, tobacco, cotton, wool, hides and fruit. These provinces, however, had relatively free access to the Russian market, so long as Russia did not choose to apply the terms of her state foreign trade monopoly to Iran. Afterwards, this privilege was partially withdrawn in 1928 and completely denied in 1930.[18]

Reza Shah's policy of industrialization singled out Mazandaran, the province on the southern shores of the Caspian where Reza Shah was born, and the central provinces of Iran for preferential treatment. As a result of this policy, Isfahan (known eventually as the "Manchester of Iran") and Mazandaran grew to be the core of Iran's wool industry, while Tehran became the heart of Iran's high technology production. As an index of the Shah's priorities, it is noteworthy that, during the period 1931–41, of the twenty new factories set up in four Azerbaijani cities (Tabriz, Reza'iyeh, Miyandoab and Maragheh), only two of them were directly sponsored by the government.[19] During this same period, the Iranian government invested in twenty of the one hundred and thirty-two factories which were set up in the central and northern provinces of the country.[20]

The centralized, strong government with effective powers which was personified by Reza Shah, while implementing the demands of many of the Iranian liberal intelligentsia, was however unable to tolerate the very existence of such an intelligentsia. In the long run, many of these intellectuals, who had in one way or another prepared the ground ideologically for Reza Shah's coming to power, were to suffer dearly as a result of the Shah's success. Several intellectuals were killed, imprisoned or fled into exile during these years. Even a conservative observer such as the American financial adviser, Millspaugh, who lived in Iran for several years, remarked that although "the Constitution, laws, Parliament and Cabinet survived" during the reign of Reza Shah, none the less:

> In actual practice [Reza Shah] acted completely contrary to
> the spirit of the Constitution and violated many of its
> provisions, notably the bill of rights. Elections took place,
> but the Shah controlled them. The puppet parliament, cowed
> and corrupted, passed laws in due form, but strictly in
> accordance with the King's order. The Prime Minister and
> ministers took their appointment and instruction from Reza
> Shah and resigned at his bidding. He destroyed such freedom
> of the press as had previously existed, as well as speech and
> assembly.[21]

4

The Rebirth of the Autonomous Movement in Azerbaijan

With the creation of relative freedom in Shahrivar *1320 (August 1941), the social currents which had remained stagnant behind the dictatorial barrages broke forth like a roaring torrent ... A new generation of intellectuals arose to undertake the task of changing and transforming prevalent conditions. But they had no particular ideology. Many young men filled with passion did not know whether they were Fascists or Communists. All they knew with absolute certainty was that everything must be changed and a new world in accordance with everyone's hopes and desires must come into being.*

K. Maleki, *Khaterat-e Siyasi*, p. 330.

The New-Born Democracy in Turmoil

In September 1939, when the army of the Third Reich invaded Poland, few would have foreseen that in less than two years the whole world would be drawn into the conflagration of war. Failing to achieve air superiority on the Western fronts, Germany turned its energies eastward. It invaded Yugoslavia and Greece, and attacked the Soviet Union along a 2,000-mile front on the 22 June 1941.

63

From the very outbreak of the war, Iran adopted an official policy of neutrality and for two years Iran's neutrality was respected on the part of both the British and the Soviets. However, when the Germans began fighting on an Eastern front, both these major powers changed their policy toward Iran. The change in their policy was primarily an attempt to bolster up the Soviet Union's defence efforts which were on the verge of collapse. In comparison with other routes available for shipping supplies to the Soviet Union (from San Francisco to Murmansk or Arkhangelsk), the Persian Gulf–Caucasus route was by far the most practical and convenient. The question then arose of how to set up and assure the smooth running of this vital corridor.

The option of convincing the Iranian government to abandon its policy of neutrality and to co-operate with the Allies was simply impractical and fraught with uncertainties. Although the Iranian government was eager to avoid antagonizing the Allies, its pro-German policies, particularly in the form of ever-growing economic ties, were already considerable. By 1941, Germany's share of Iranian foreign trade had risen to between 45.5 per cent and 48 per cent.[1] In the same year, the official number of German subjects holding employment in Iran through the Iranian prime minister was 690,[2] though British sources put the estimate at 2,000.[3] Whatever the exact figures may have been, the Allies used the presence of these German residents as a justification for invading Iran on 25 August 1941. But in fact the major reason (which was consistently omitted in pertinent British documents) was the British government's desire to secure control over Abadan and the southern oil fields.

The Iranian army which was never formally institutionalized and, for the last twenty years, had depended directly on the person of Reza Shah, was not able to consolidate itself and resist the military invasion of the Allies. There were only a few minor incidents of resistance by some units of the Iranian armed forces, otherwise the immediate result of the Allied invasion was extensive chaos and disarray, not only within the rank and file of the army but throughout the civil administration of the country as well.

Two days after the invasion had begun, the prime minister, Mansur, presented the resignation of his cabinet to the Twelfth *Majles*, and the following day, 28 August, Forughi, who was an elderly, well-educated, upper-class politician, formally introduced his caretaker cabinet before the same *Majles*.

Forughi saw as the cabinet's primary task the maintenance of law and order in a country which was on the brink of utter turmoil. In pursuing this goal, he was quick to realize that the stick had lost its clout and, consequently, it was time to hold out the carrot. He soon proved successful in managing the transfer of the imperial crown from Reza Shah to the latter's son, Mohammad Reza Shah. On 16 September 1941, the old despot Reza Shah abdicated in favour of his son and went into exile, eventually to die abroad in 1944. On 17 September, Mohammad Reza, now the second Pahlavi, took the ceremonial oath of accession in the *Majles* and pledged before the Iranian people that, as a constitutional monarch, along with revering the Constitutional Code, he would take every precaution to avoid making the mistakes his father had made. Indeed, he would do his best to rectify any such mistakes.

To appease the public's sense of grievance, Forughi launched a campaign to prosecute the old guards of Reza Shah's regime, especially the secret police. Moreover, he was successful in getting the *Majles* to ratify a bill which obliged the government to free all political prisoners. Likewise, in order to weaken any possible opposition from the ex-Shah's supporters, as well as to comply with the growing demands of the intelligentsia, he lifted the severe censorship affecting newspapers and periodicals, and made it easier to form political parties.

When the Allies invaded Iran, there were only twelve newspapers and periodicals in the country. Between 1941 and 1947, that number rose to five hundred and eighty, of which forty were daily newspapers.[4] In the same period the number of political parties in existence went from zero to twenty-one.[5]

In introducing the above mentioned measures, Forughi enjoyed the support of both the British and the Soviets. In view of the Persians' long-standing "xenophobia", as noted by the British ambassador at the time,[6] the Allies tried to align themselves with the opponents of the old regime and to justify the occupation of Iran by disseminating anti-Axis propaganda which did have antidespotic and liberal aspects to it.

The early policy which the Soviets adopted in Iran was to distance themselves from direct involvement in the day-to-day politics of the country and, at all costs, to avoid doing anything which would jeopardize their relations with the British:

> The most notable demonstrations of friendship by the Russians toward us were after the entry of Anglo-Russian forces into Persia in August 1941.[7]

One of the most striking examples of this friendship which clearly underlined the co-ordinated war policies of the Allies in Iran, was the publication of the newspaper called *Mardom-e Zedd-e Fashist* (The People Against Fascism). Its first issue came out on 1 February 1942. The editorial board included members representing a wide spectrum of political views. Besides the known pro-Soviet Communists, Iraj Eskandari and Bozorg Alavi, were to be found pro-British figures such as Mostafa Fateh, who was a high-ranking employee in the Anglo-Iranian Oil Company. Anvar Khameh'i, an ex-Marxist who was a member of the editorial board of *Mardom*, in his recently published memoirs comments on the Anglo-Soviet joint effort in founding the newspaper that:

> The Soviets agreed to provide the paper and the printing facilities, while the British were willing to meet any other needs.[8]

But perhaps the most significant event in Iranian political life during the post-invasion period was the formation of the *Tudeh* Party.[9] On 29 September 1941, about twenty political activists met in Tehran in the house of the veteran Democrat, Soleyman Mirza, to form a political party. Several of these political figures possessed a certain notoriety and had colourful careers. Among them were members of the outlawed Communist Party, as well as veteran Democrats and Nationalists. But the organizing core of the assembly consisted of the young, educated Communists who had become known as members of "The Fifty-Three" (*Panjah-o Seh Nafar*).[10]

The group known as "The Fifty-Three" was a Communist circle formed around the periodical *Donya* (The World), which was founded in 1934 and went on publishing for three years.[11] When, in 1937, Reza Shah's secret police informed him that *Donya*, far from being a theoretical scientific journal, was a front for the Communist Party of Iran, he did not hesitate to suppress it immediately and arrest all its associates. Some of the latter received prison sentences of up to ten years. The famous leader of the group, Dr Taqi Arani, an Azerbaijani physicist, was killed in prison, not long after being sentenced to ten years in solitary confinement.

In its first proclamation, the Tudeh Party presented itself as a "legal Constitutionalist Party" which was committed to "the independence and sovereignty of Iran". The party stated that its endeavours were aimed not only at achieving those "liberties which were embodied in the Constitutional Code for the *mellat-e Iran* (the Iranian nation)", but also that it advocated a "series of *eslahat* (reforms) with regard to landholding, health, taxation and education". By educational reform the party meant: "Free and compulsory education for everyone".[12]

One of the major reasons for the growing popularity of the Tudeh Party, especially among the urban working and middle classes, was the extreme economic crisis which the country was experiencing. Similarly, it was the grave economic crisis which finally caused Prime Minister Forughi to withdraw and give up his seat to Soheyli.

From its first days of coming to power, Forughi's cabinet was faced with rapidly mounting food shortages, particularly with regard to wheat, which was becoming scarce everywhere throughout the country. Several factors combined to aggravate the situation. An atmosphere of uncertainty prevailed among the farmers since the Allied invasion. Food distribution was hampered by lack of transportation and the bad state of the roads connecting urban centres with the villages. And, generally speaking, there was a shortage of manufactured materials. Finally, the Tripartite Treaty of Alliance,[13] signed on 29 January 1942, obliged the Iranian government to meet the needs of Allied troops passing through or stationed in Iran. The economic crisis which resulted not only forced Prime Minister Forughi to resign, but also made it impossible for his successor, Soheyli, to survive.

Forughi's cabinet (on the demand of the British) took the decision to devalue the Iranian currency from 68 to 140 rials to the pound sterling, and increased the amount of money in circulation in Iran (a demand of both the British and the Soviets). Neither measure led to any economic improvement but rather deepened the crisis. In 1941, the amount of money in circulation did not exceed 1,850 million rials. Two years later, this sum had risen to 6,320 million rials.[14] The effect which these monetary policies had upon the rapid rise in the cost of living was staggering. By the end of 1942, the cost of living index indicated a rise of 439 per cent since the beginning of that year.[15]

As a final measure by way of implementing its policy of maintaining order, Forughi's cabinet convened the Thirteenth *Majles*, which, for the most part, had been constituted during the last days of Reza Shah's rule. Despite widespread protest because the deputies had been appointed and not elected, Forughi officially opened the Thirteenth *Majles* on 4 December

1941, and in so doing he enjoyed the support of both the British and the court. However, this decision of the government had important immediate consequences for political life in Iran. The arena of political action now shifted from parliament to the streets of the big cities. Those political groups which felt deprived of a voice in parliament turned their energies to mobilizing crowds as a means of exerting pressure on the government.

Nor were the streets the only political battlefield. Hundreds of newspapers began to be published. These new organs of political expression represented the views of scores of political parties and trade unions which sprang up immediately after the Allied invasion. Most of these new parties and newspapers had ties of one kind or another with one of the two occupying foreign powers. The Soviets exerted influence on the northern parts of Iran, including Azerbaijan, part of Kurdistan, Gilan, Mazandaran and Khorasan, while the British zone consisted of the southern regions of the country. Meanwhile, in the capital, Tehran, the two foreign powers undertook a joint military occupation and martial law was declared.

Dreyfus, the American Minister in Iran at the time, in a letter to the US Secretary of State, assessed the situation in the following terms:

> Politically, the present confused and unsatisfactory situation derives from violent change from dictatorial to democratic government for which the country was ill-prepared, and from popular reaction to virtual occupation of the country by two powers regarded as hostile.[16]

Faced with an economic crisis of unmanageable proportions and an acute food shortage, Foroughi presented his resignation to the *Majles* and the young Shah, and cast his vote in favour of Soheyli, a loyal monarchist bureaucrat, in a session held behind closed doors on 4 March 1942.

Soheyli's appointment makes manifest the gravity of the political crisis which Iran was then experiencing. There were, undoubtedly, numerous other trustworthy and more capable politicians who could have tackled the tasks confronting the nation more effectively than Soheyli. The main obstacle which hindered such politicians from accepting the premiership was the very existence of the Thirteenth *Majles*. For many popular politicians, such as Mosaddeq, the Thirteenth

Majles was no more than an assembly of Reza Shah's hand-picked deputies.[17]

By 30 July 1942, after one hundred and forty-four days as prime minister, Soheyli felt obliged to step down from office. The cabinet which had been formed around him had taken as its two top priorities solving the problem of food shortages and guaranteeing public order. In both these aims they had failed.

When Soheyli announced his resignation, which everyone had been expecting for some time, efforts were made to find a suitable replacement for him. However, the same political state of affairs which had permitted the appointment of a mediocrity like Soheyli still prevailed, namely, the unwillingness of competent statesmen with politically "clean hands" to co-operate with the *Majles*. In reply to the US Secretary of State's question as to whether any Iranian politicians existed who were competent to deal with the ever-mounting problems confronting Iran, Dreyfus wrote:

> There are in Iran few persons of integrity and proven reliability, but the few either are not available or refuse a cabinet position.[18]

The man who was thought by many to be qualified to deal with the national crisis, and who was finally nominated to the premiership after prolonged negotiations, was Ahmad Qavam (Qavam os-Saltaneh). He was a wealthy member of the landowning aristocracy with a background of long-standing service in government administration. It was almost twenty years since Qavam had last appeared on the political scene, having at that time also held the post of prime minister.[19] During the reign of Reza Shah, however, he had first fled into exile and then lived in forced retirement on his extensive tea plantations in the north of Iran.[20]

The fact that Qavam's estates were located in the area occupied by the Soviets led to a widespread rumour that he was on very good terms with the Russians. As fanciful and exaggerated as such hearsay may have been, it was generally true that Qavam enjoyed the support of the Allies.[21] What made his premiership particularly difficult, however, were his strained relations with the court.

Upon ascending the Peacock Throne, the young Shah, as a constitutional monarch, had taken a solemn oath to remain aloof from the parliamentary workings of government. In fact, the legal restraints which, in view of his father's abuse of power, had been placed on the Shah's powers had reduced him to being no more than a national figure-head. But by now it was clear that Mohammad Reza Shah was seeking an illegitimate degree of personal power. This was nowhere more obvious than in the area of military affairs. According to the Constitution, the armed forces were under the direct control of the Ministry of War.

Being only too aware of the Shah's appetite for power, Qavam purposely left the post of minister of war empty when he presented his Cabinet before the *Majles* on the 13 August 1942. The conflict between the court and Qavam began from his first day in office.

In the event, it did not prove difficult for the court to turn the prevailing economic crisis, in particular the food shortage, to its own advantage, and, as with his two predecessors, to bring about Qavam's downfall. Indeed, Qavam himself was, from the beginning, fully aware of the capital importance of coming to grips with the economic problems swiftly and effectively. When, on the eve of his assuming the premiership, Qavam was asked in a press interview what his program would consist of, he picked up a piece of bread from his desk and replied: "This is my program. If I can put bread of good quality in the hands of all Iranians, other problems will be easy to solve."[22] During the six months that he remained in office, all his attention was devoted to tackling the problem of food shortages.

On 8 December, four months after Qavam had become prime minister, when it was clear that he was still unable to solve the problem of food shortages, rioting broke out in the streets of Tehran. The violence was of a scale hitherto unknown in the city and went on for two full days.[23] According to one eyewitness account, the riots were spontaneous,[24] but the American ambassador to Iran felt that political motives played a decisive role in causing the incident:

> Political intriguers used food shortage as a sentimental issue
> to gain their own ends ... It seems to me probable that the
> Shah is responsible for the demonstration with the ultimate
> object of setting up a military government including his
> group of officers.[25]

Qavam was obliged to call out the army to restore law and order in the streets and, as an additional measure to reduce the political tension, he banned the press for forty days. In so doing, he wished to appear decisive and capable of coping with the extreme situation but it was clear by then that his days in politics were numbered. Qavam was losing in his power struggle with the Shah, partly because he had underestimated the latter's competence. Finally, on 13 February 1943, the *Majles* put an end to Qavam's six-month battle against the crown by calling into question his competence which led to his resignation. Meanwhile, the Shah went on consolidating his forces in anticipation of round two.

The Fourteenth *Majles*: Its Formation and the Question of National Representation

Soheyli's second term of office began four days after Qavam's departure. The same reasons which had led to his first term of tenure had once again been in operation to bring about his present appointment. Furthermore, his election was perceived by many observers to be a friendly gesture to the Soviets on the part of the *Majles*. After Qavam, Soheyli was thought to be the politician who most enjoyed the Soviets' confidence.[26] In face of what was now viewed as the Soviets' slow but steady advance in the war, especially after their remarkable victory at Stalingrad in January 1943, the *Majles* had every political reason for taking this step.

The main task confronting Soheyli during his second term as prime minister was to see that elections were held for the Fourteenth *Majles*. This was not at first sight an easy task to carry out properly. The country was still subjected to occupation by the two Allied powers. In particular, the Soviets, now that they were emerging as victorious in the war, were altering their stance towards Iran. The earlier policy of minimal interference in Iran's domestic affairs and avoidance of antagonizing any of their Allies was shifting to a policy of challenge and confrontation. Previously, Iran was regarded as a "corridor" through which vital supplies reached the Russian front, and efforts had been made not to "interrupt the flow of these supplies".[27] But a new wind was now blowing, and the Soviet Union was not acting with timid caution as it had during its early days of occupying Iranian territory.

The elections for the Fourteenth *Majles* were the first parliamentary elections in twenty years in which independent political parties could take part. As Abrahamian points out, prolonged, the most competitive and hence the most meaningful of all elections in modern Iran ... the results were determined not only by the state, but by the relative strengths, on the one hand, of competing social forces, and, on the other hand, of organized groups, especially political parties, parliamentary fractions and their foreign protectors, within the government bureaucracy".[28]

Of the more than one dozen political parties campaigning for the parliamentary elections, there were two in particular which stood out as distinctive from all the rest and representing opposite poles of the political spectrum. On the extreme right, was the *Eradeh-e Melli* (the National Will), headed by Seyyed Zia Tabataba'i. He had engineered Reza Shah's *coup d'état* of February 1921, only to be eventually forced by the latter to go into exile. Not long after Reza Shah's abdication, he had returned to Iran with the approval of the British. To the left of the spectrum was the Tudeh Party which "after the Battle of Stalingrad, January 1943, became the increasingly one-sided pro-Russian Party".[29]

Although admittedly a "pro-Russian" party, the Tudeh Party still regarded itself, according to the party's official newspaper, *Rahbar* (The Leader), as a non-Communist Constitutionalist party which even sought to win over capitalist support:

> Labelling the Tudeh Party of Iran as Communist is the result of the efforts of Seyyed Zia's group. By this means they are trying to make Iranian capitalists and merchants afraid of us. But the label is erroneous and far from the truth. The Tudeh Party of Iran is a Constitutionalist party in favour of the Constitutional Code. It is our conviction that the ideas of Communism and Socialism were born out of social conditions which do not exist in Iran, and if one day there comes to be a Communist Party in Iran, that party will most definitely not be the Tudeh Party.[30]

An important ally of the Tudeh Party in the election campaign was the *Jebheh-e Azadi* (the Freedom Front), which had been founded during the summer of 1943 at a political convention which brought together fourteen different newspapers and journals. The proclamation which the Freedom Front issued as a summary of their political views called for:

– An intense struggle against any form of deviation from the principles of the Constitutional Code and a national government.
– Curtailing the power of agents of tyranny and reaction throughout society.
– Striving to eradicate the principles and institutions of the dictatorial period, and the implementation of a true constitutional government.
– Striving to concentrate the forces of the nation and to create unity among the partisans of freedom.[31]

Among the signatories of the proclamation was Ja'far Pishevari, who had started publishing the tri-weekly newspaper *Azhir* (Alarm) in Tehran in May 1943.[32]

Thanks to the Freedom Front's support, not only in Tehran but in the provinces as well, the Tudeh Party succeeded in forming a caucus of twelve deputies in the *Majles*. However, their rival, the pro-British caucus *Fraksiyon-e Mihan* (the Patriot Caucus), enjoyed a stronger position in the Parliament since they could count on the allegiance of twenty-one deputies, including Seyyed Zia himself.[33]

The Fourteenth *Majles* was convened on 26 February 1944, though its formal term started three weeks later, on 16 March. Although the parliament was destined to acquire a particularly colourful image in the annals of parliamentary proceedings in Iran, "producing as many as 7 premiers, 9 cabinets and 110 cabinet members"[34], during the two-year period of its existence, in the view of many deputies the political problems of the past remained unsolved, namely the question of the nation's sovereignty and geographical integrity.

The first undertaking of the new *Majles* was to examine the credentials of the elected deputies. Out of a total of one hundred and thirty-six deputies holding seats in parliament, two were rejected. These two were the first and second elected deputies for Tabriz, Kho'i and Pishevari. Indeed, there was a third deputy whose credentials were rejected, but the deputy in question was able to secure his seat when a second round of elections was held.[35]

The number of deputies for Tabriz in the Fourteenth *Majles* was originally nine: Kho'i, Pishevari, Eskandari, Sadeqi, Seqat ol-Eslam, Ipakchiyan, Panahi, Mojtahedi and Sartippur. Kho'i and Pishevari were highest in popularity on the electoral list having received 15,883 and 15,780 votes respectively, out of a total of 47,780 votes cast.[36]

In an unusually stormy session of the *Majles*, forty-eight of the ninety-nine deputies who were present, voted for Kho'i and another forty-eight voted against him, three deputies abstaining from the vote.[37] Ten days later, on 13 July, another session of the *Majles* took place during which the credentials of the second deputy from Tabriz were subjected to scrutiny. After a long debate concerning voting procedures, the *Majles* decided that the vote would be secret. The outcome was quite dramatic for the left and the liberal wing of the *Majles*. Of one hundred votes cast, forty-seven approved of Pishevari's credentials and fifty rejected them.[38] The discussion which followed concerning the validity of the vote was surrounded by the usual general clamour which prevailed in the *Majles*.[39]

The following day, an editorial printed in block letters appeared in *Azhir*. It attests to the reaction on the part of Tudeh Party sympathizers to the rejection of the Tabriz deputy. The tone of its declarations is harsh and threatening:

> We are proud that the representatives of violence, money, hypocrisy and deceit have not recognized us as one of their number, but have cast their vote against us. We see this treacherous action as one of numerous manifestations in reaction to the social struggle. Our judgement of our opponents is nonpartisan, whereas the nation's judgement of them will be severe, merciless and deadly. From this day, a new page in the history of our social struggle is beginning, a page filled with pride.

The editorial went on to emphasize the undemocratic mechanism which allowed a few individuals to nullify the legitimate political will of the mass of voters:

> With 50 scheming votes, they have nullified 16,000 votes of the sincere and honest people of Tabriz. This is the biggest step which the reactionaries, in their ignorance, have taken against themselves and to our profit. This seeming defeat, which is in reality a victory, will not hold us back from the *jihad-e moqaddas* [holy war] we have begun against the reactionary forces. Hopelessness and despair are for impotent people. Through the powerful force of unity of the nation's freedom-

loving elements and the steadfast, patriotic press, we will destroy
the palace of cruelty, violence and tyranny, betrayal and
duplicity, and in its place we will raise the banner of true
constitutionalism and Iran's real national freedom. We are not
like a willow tree that trembles in such winds as these. We have
proved ourselves. Our purpose and goal is the uprooting of
tyranny and injustice. Final victory will only ever be achieved
through battle, self-sacrifice, and struggle. The future belongs to
us. Let us continue the combat.[40]

The justification proffered by the parliamentary opponents of the Tudeh
Party for their rejection of Kho'i and Pishevari was the accusation
(quite common and well-known those days) that they had only been
elected thanks to the interference of foreign powers. And, indeed, the
Soviets and the British did interfere wherever they could during the
elections for the Fourteenth *Majles*, though not always with success:

In some places in the Northern Zone, right-wing Persians
were elected in the teeth of opposition from Russian supported candidates. The Tudeh Party had definitely hoped for
Russian support of all their candidates in the Northern Zone
and the fact that it was given in but a few cases is another
indication that it is not their present policy to give hundred
percent support to any one party. It can very well be said the
British, too, interfered in the elections. British support ... was
largely confined to such methods as talking to the most
influential people in a particular district and to give advice.[41]

Nor were the elections in Azerbaijan by any means an exception in this
respect. The Tudeh Party, believing that "the Fourteenth *Majles* will
decide the destiny of Iran", initially presented a list of six candidates
for Tabriz. The candidates chosen were 'Ali Amir Khizi, Ja'far
Pishevari, Rahim Hamdad, Aqazadeh Shahin, Ahmad Esfahani, and
'Abolqasem Musavi.[42] In the rival political camp, there were "self-
seeking" industrialists such as Jurabchi, Calcuttachi and Kho'i, who
were "prepared to spend large sums of money to gain *Majles* immunity
for the furtherance of their interests".[43] Commenting on the social
atmosphere in which the two political groups were confronting one
another, the British consul in Tabriz concludes his remarks as follows:

> The countryside is still definitely conservative: the class
> consciousness of the town proletariat is not yet developed
> and, with few exceptions, the merchant class wishes to go
> its own way untrammelled by social legislation and
> taxation such as the advanced elements demand.[44]

The Iranian government was seriously concerned about the outcome of
the elections in Tabriz. By postponing the election date, it hoped its
acting governor-general would have time to reach a compromise with
the Soviets, who had their own list of candidates.[45] The Soviet-
supported candidates were Ipakchiyan, Mashinchi and Pishevari. Of
them, only Pishevari was also on the electoral list of the Tudeh Party.

The Tabriz elections finally began on the 2 March and lasted for
eighteen days. The only polling station in the whole city was located in
the governor-general's headquarters and that was closed "at the same
time as the factories".[46] This and other such measures taken by the
governor-general led the Tudeh Party to raise objections as to how the
elections were being conducted.[47] On the other hand, the anti-Tudeh
candidates, by way of discrediting their opponents, repeatedly referred
to Pishevari as "an ex-political prisoner who had committed crimes
against the state and nation". They emphatically urged the prime
minister and the *Majles* "not to accept his credentials [as legitimate]".[48]

In the event, the Fourteenth *Majles* did not hesitate to use its powers
against the Tudeh Party's Azerbaijani candidates. However, the *Majles*'s
decision to reject two out of the nine deputies for Tabriz appears to have
been biased. Indeed, all the denunciations concerning the deputies were
based on the general circumstances in which the elections took place,
rather than any concrete charges intended to disqualify the individual
candidates themselves. As Mosaddeq later remarked: "Nothing could
justify the act of the *Majles*, since the polling process was the same for
all the deputies."[49]

The Fourteenth *Majles*: Its Survival and the Question of the Country's Welfare

The new *Majles* was officially convened on 26 February 1944. Within
less than three weeks of that date, Soheyli handed in his resignation and

the vacated post of prime minister was occupied by Sa'ed, a sixty-nine-year-old Azerbaijani diplomat. Having studied in Russia and then having served as Iranian Ambassador to Moscow, Sa'ed was to all appearances particularly suited to deal with the Soviets' foreign policy. However, after eight months of constant struggle to find a satisfactory form of relationship between Iran and the Soviet Union, he admitted defeat and abandoned the task. During his eight-month period as prime minister, his primary concern and that of the four different cabinets formed under him had been to cope with the new demands of the Northern Neighbour.

Even while Soheyli was preparing to hand in his resignation, reports began to circulate concerning the visit to Tehran of delegates of the British company, Shell, and the two American companies, Standard Vacuum and Sinclair Oil. The purpose of the visit, as emerged at a later date, was to study the possibility of oil exploration and extraction outside the southern region of Iran, which region was already being exploited exclusively by the Anglo-Persian Oil Company.[50] The initial reaction of Sa'ed's government was by no means reluctant or overly cautious. By employing two American advisers to examine the proposals of the companies, the government demonstrated a willingness to co-operate in the venture.[51] However, the stormy session which dealt with the issue in the *Majles* made it clear that the government was not going to have an easy time of it.

Following a comment made by a deputy with regard to the government's secrecy in the matter, Radmanesh, a leading member of the Tudeh Party's eight-deputy caucus in the *Majles*, rose to his feet and made clear his party's policy concerning oil concessions by declaring:

> I and my comrades are completely opposed to giving concessions to foreign countries. In the same way that Iran is capable of building its own railroad, I am certain that, with the help of our own people and capital, we are able to extract all this country's resources of wealth ourselves.[52]

At this early date, the Tudeh Party's position with regard to the issue could not be clearer. However, when one month later the Soviet delegation approached the Iranian government with the same demands for themselves, the Tudeh Party's leadership, as well as Prime Minister Sa'ed, were faced with making a decision which would be crucial for their political careers. For the Tudeh Party in particular, this moment was a turning point in the course of its history.

On 15 September 1944, Sergei Kavtaradze came to Tehran for a lengthy visit as head of the Soviet oil delegation.[53] In a press interview, Kavtaradze frankly stated his government's views with regard to demanding an oil concession in Iran's northern regions. The geographical zone intended for exploitation included Azerbaijan, Gilan, Mazandaran, and part of Khorasan.[54] The first steps the Soviets undertook to win the desired concessions consisted of direct negotiations with Sa'ed's Cabinet. For his part, however, Sa'ed hesitated to commit himself to any firm position, but, while alluding to the difficulties within the *Majles*, simply adopted a "wait and see" policy.

Meanwhile, the Soviets turned their attentions to putting pressure on the Iranian government. One measure they took was to request the Tudeh Party to change its old stance concerning oil concessions and to support a proSoviet policy. In a series of editorial articles published in the party's official newspaper, the party's earlier intransigent position was modified into a more nuanced, ambiguous attitude which concerned itself with examining "the content of each concession" and "the circumstances in which it was accepted".[55]

But the catastrophic step (in terms of its public image) which the Tudeh Party took was to acquiesce to the Soviet request that the party demonstrate in favour of oil concessions to the Soviet Union.[56] The demonstration went ahead in the streets of Tehran on 27 October 1944, under the protection of Soviet troops. The presence of the latter spelled disaster for the political future of the Tudeh Party and the Iranian Communist movement in general. Only two months previously, at the end of its first congress, the Tudeh Party had declared its absolute rejection of foreign concessions with the words:

> our party is against all economic concessions which
> weaken the country's independence and impose economic
> slavery on the nation.[57]

At the time, all such declarations on the part of the Tudeh Party greatly increased its popularity, particularly among the intelligentsia. By abandoning this earlier position, the party immediately lost the support of a large segment of that same intelligentsia.[58] Although the party leadership for a long time tried to justify the change in their stance,[59] it is only recently that the veteran leaders of the Tudeh Party have published their memoirs in which they admit the "catastrophic result" of their action.[60]

Two days after the Tudeh Party's demonstration, Mosaddeq, in a long speech delivered to the *Majles*, rejected the Tudeh Party's argument that since the British enjoyed an oil concession in the south of Iran, a similar concession should be given to the Soviets in the north in order to maintain a balance between the two powers. By way of denouncing any type of concessions, he promoted the notion of *"Movazeneh-e Manfi"* (Negative Balance), i.e. keeping balance by denying everyone any concessions, as an alternative to *"Movazeneh-e Mosbat"* (Positive Balance). With regard to the latter, he declared:

> The nation of Iran wishes for political balance, that is, balance which is to the country's advantage. The nation of Iran will never agree to positive balance, and from the first day I entered this *Majles* I have been opposed to financial agreements and all undertakings which the [foreign] states, after August 1941, have concluded with a view to positive balance.[61]

Being dissatisfied with Sa'ed's non-committal policy with regard to their aims, the Soviets thought they had a better chance of realizing their goals under a new government which they hoped to influence by escalating the pressure they were capable of bringing to bear. Sa'ed's government proved to be too fragile when pitted against Soviet influence. On 11 November 1944, despite enjoying majority support in the *Majles*,[62] Sa'ed stepped down from the premiership.

The British reaction to Sa'ed's resignation was not unpredictable. The Foreign Office assumed that:

> if the Persian government are forced to give all the oil in the north to Russia, the natural tendency will surely be to give a concession in the south to an American company, so as to enlist the interest of the United States government.[63]

Such a situation had the potential of "endangering H.M. Government's interests in the region". Consequently, the Foreign Office instructed Sir Reader Bullard, the British ambassador in Tehran, to make it known that the British government "wants the appointment of a new Persian prime minister, who will follow the same policy as Sa'ed over the granting of concessions".[64]

Beyond any shadow of a doubt, the Soviets had welcomed Sa'ed's resignation. It was evident that achieving this objective had been at the heart of their new policy of offensive action. But, as subsequent developments were to show, the Soviets had been overly optimistic with regard to what they hoped to gain by removing Sa'ed. The latter's resignation was not in fact the end but rather the beginning of an unstable period of political struggle and intrigue.

On 25 November 1944, Bayat became the new prime minister. He was from an upper-class family and had been a deputy in the *Majles* for quite some time. It was during the first days of Bayat's short-lived term in office, while the *Majles* was still studying the latter's proposed cabinet program, that Mosaddeq managed to have his famous bill passed which prohibited any future Iranian government from granting oil concessions to foreigners. One week later, on 8 December, Kavtaradze, the head of the Soviet oil delegation, denounced this act of the *Majles* as ill-advised, and then returned to the Soviet Union after his lengthy sojourn in Iran.

The early campaign which the Tudeh Party launched against Mosaddeq (they went as far as accusing him of serving British interests)[65] did not continue for long. Realizing how much discontent their stance on oil concessions was generating among their own rank and file, the party organs and its allied newspapers eventually began to direct their concern to "the country's welfare and unity under the Constitutional Code". The central demand put forward during this campaign was for the implementation of the neglected Articles 90–93 of the Supplementary Code concerning *Anjoman-ha-ye Iyalati va Velayati* (the provincial and district councils).

The pioneer newspaper throughout the campaign was *Azhir*, understandably so, since its editor-in-chief was Pishevari who had been rejected by the *Majles* as a legitimate deputy for Azerbaijan. By calling for the implementation of the above mentioned Articles and championing the right of the provinces and districts to have their own local councils, the newspaper demonstrated its commitment to the Constitutional Code and, at the same time, attempted to promote the councils as an alternative to the *Majles* itself. In a long editorial entitled *Anjoman-ha-ye Iyalati va Velayati Borandehtarin Selah-e Mobarezeh ba*

Afkar-e Tajziyeh-Talabi (the Provincial and District Councils, An Effective Weapon Against Separatism), Karim Keshavarz, one of the newspaper's editors, accused Seyyed Zia Tabataba'i's party of fomenting separatist sentiment among the southern tribes, whereas he declared that:

> Implementing the Constitutional Code means implementing justice and equity, applying laws to promote the dissemination of culture and knowledge, granting good material conditions to people and having them participate in the running and supervision of their local affairs. These are measures which if applied are not only capable of preventing the spread of separatism but, by their regular and sustained application and enforcement, are capable of building a truly *independent and indivisible*, free, powerful, and democratic Iran.[66]

The Tudeh Party's caucus in the *Majles*, as well, now began to take every opportunity to draw attention to the issue of "Iranian national unity" which they believed could "only be preserved by the Constitutional Code being applied" by "the sole sovereignty of the Central Government".[67] But by the time this vigorous and outspoken commitment to the principles of Iranian Constitutionalism had become one of the Tudeh Party's hallmarks, the office of prime minister had passed into the hands of Sadr ol-Ashraf.

Many observers have judged Bayat's five-month premiership to be the golden months of "political democracy" in Iran. Although parts of the country were still under foreign occupation and martial law, political parties and trade unions enjoyed an unprecedented degree of freedom. They were free to organize mass rallies and even strikes,[68] and the press was able to write on almost any topic without fear of strict censorship. Like everyone else, the Tudeh Party profited from the open political atmosphere, though, according to the recently published memoirs of a former party leader, the party did not seem to appreciate the prevailing climate of relative tolerance:

> The period of Bayat's government was the freest and most favourable period for the Tudeh Party throughout the years of the wartime governments. The Party's newspapers and press enjoyed an unprecedented freedom and

wrote exposés with regard to nearly all the authorities, including the Army and the Court ... Alas, the Party did not take sufficient advantage of the freedom, and instead of striving to preserve Bayat's Cabinet, to a certain extent they even contributed to his downfall.[69]

Bayat's relatively strong commitment to Constitutionalism and the drastic measures which he was prepared to undertake during his five-month premiership mobilized many "sources of power" against him.[70] Formerly old rivals, the court and the right-wing parties headed by Seyyed Zia Tabataba'i, were now prepared to sink their differences and unite against Bayat. On 17 April 1945, his premiership was terminated, not, as in the case of previous ministers, by his resigning, but as a result of his failure to receive a vote of confidence from the *Majles*. Of ninety deputies present, only forty-four voted in his favour, which was below the required majority. As Khameh'i notes, the vote of no confidence from the *Majles*, rather than voluntary resignation, which terminated Bayat's premiership, was perceived as very exceptional:

Among all the Prime Ministers during the fifty-three year period of Pahlavi rule, the record of Bayat's government, with the exception of Mosaddeq's government, was the most positive. He entered the political arena with bravery, accomplished several outstanding achievements, ran the government in accordance with the Constitutional Code, defended himself heroically, and fell. He was the first Prime Minister, after the month of *Shahrivar* [referring to Reza Shah's abdication on 16 September 1941], who would not accept to resign but fell through a vote of no confidence from the *Majles*.[71]

The very day that Bayat was deposed, proceedings were instigated to find a suitable successor. It took the *Majles* two weeks to produce a nominee, but, in the event, the new prime minister lasted only four weeks in office. On 3 June 1945, Ebrahim Hakimi, who had been raised in Azerbaijan and had long-term experience in government administration, left the parliamentary chamber without having had the opportunity to exercise his powers as an elected prime minister. Hakimi was no more than an interim figurehead who was meant to ease the transition from Bayat's relatively pro-Constitutionalist government to the "strong man" regime which the conservatives had in mind for the immediate future.

The right-wing coalition, consisting of the Shah and Tabataba'i's supporters, wanted to nominate a "strong" figure as prime minister who would preside over the coming elections for the Fifteenth *Majles* and conduct the elections in a way which served their interests. As it turned out, the candidate they chose was the widely detested figure, Mohsen Sadr (Sadr ol-Ashraf), a seventy-four-year-old religious, conservative politician who had served as a judge in the Justice Department during the thirteen-month period known as *Estebdad-e Saghir* (the Short-Term Despotism: June 1908–July 1909) when many Constitutionalists had been condemned to death during the prosecutions carried out by the Justice Department at the orders of Mohammad 'Ali Mirza.

Sadr ol-Ashraf persistently denied the accusation of having taken part in these prosecutions,[72] but in attempting to discredit him his opponents, in particular the Tudeh Party, never passed up the opportunity of calling attention to his former employment in the Justice Department and dubbed him *"Jallad-e Bagh-e Shah"* (the Executioner of Bagh-e Shah).[73]

From the moment he took office, Sadr was confronted by a solid opposition. A clique of fifty-four deputies led by Mosaddeq was determined to obstruct the parliamentary session and make it impossible for the *Majles* to have the quorum which Sadr desperately needed in order to introduce his cabinet. The obstruction lasted thirty-five days and only ended when the Prime Minister promised he would hand in his resignation once his cabinet had been introduced to the *Majles*.[74] This promise, however, he failed to keep.

In continuing its campaign of opposition, the Tudeh Party characterized Sadr's government as a bulwark of "despotism and anti-Constitutionalism", while presenting itself as the true guardian of Iranian Constitutionalism and an uncompromising advocate of Constitutionalist principles. The fortieth anniversary of the Constitutional Revolution provided the leaders of the Tudeh Party with an occasion to display their loyalty publicly. On 5 August 1945, by way of celebrating the Constitutional Revolution, the Tudeh Party organized mass rallies and street demonstrations in those cities where it had sufficient support to do so. In Tehran, the party was able to call onto the streets tens of thousands of sympathizers, most of whom simply wished to protest against the failure of successive cabinets to introduce necessary reforms.

At the end of the rally, Iraj Eskandari read out a resolution in which, among other things, the Tudeh Party demanded the formation of provincial and district councils, in the belief that such bodies were "an inseparable part of the achievements of the Constitutional Revolution".[75]

The Sadr government, which had been voted in by conservatives primarily in the hope that it would be able to meet the challenge of the Tudeh Party, now found itself confronted with ever-increasing effective opposition from that quarter. Indeed, the Tudeh Party's rally of 5 August was only one more instance of the offensive political campaign that the party had begun since the beginning of 1945. When Germany surrendered on 7 May 1945, the Tudeh Party, which was founded as an anti-Fascist party and throughout its five years of political life had eagerly looked forward to the defeat of the Axis, had every reason to believe that "the future was promising" and that the party was entering a flourishing phase of political activity. Likewise, when in July 1945 the Labour Party came to power in Britain, the Tudeh Party reacted with enthusiasm and felt it was cause for celebration at party headquarters. In a letter to the new British prime minister, Clement Attlee, the Tudeh Party expressed its hope "of enjoying the new Labour government's support in establishing democracy in Iran".[76]

However, these happy days in the annals of the Tudeh Party were not destined to continue indefinitely. The government now decided to take every possible measure to limit the party's activities and to assure that there would be no chance of such a "troubled black ship" appearing on the country's political horizon in the future. After refusing to honour his promise to step down from office, Sadr ol-Ashraf put a motion before the *Majles* proposing that, as long as foreign troops were stationed on Iranian soil, there should be a postponement of the parliamentary elections. Traditionally, the right-wing parties profited from the government's interference in parliamentary elections. In the present circumstances, with the Soviet presence in the north of Iran, it was obvious that Sadr ol-Ashraf's motion was specifically aimed at denying the Tudeh and its allied parties any advantages from eventual Soviet interference.[77]

On 23 August, the government's attack against the Tudeh Party entered a new phase of intensity. On that date, the party's newspaper, *Rahbar*, was banned by order of the military commandant of Tehran. Four days later, the headquarters of the Tudeh Party in Tehran were occupied by government military forces, which was quite astonishing in view of the fact that Tudeh Party deputies still held their seats in parliament.

While these and other such clashes were occurring between the government and its opponents in the centre and southern parts of Iran, disturbing news was reaching the capital to the effect that the north of Iran, especially Azerbaijan, was on the verge of political turmoil.

Azerbaijan Poised to Leap

Other than the minor resistance which the Iranian army offered at Qushchi, a village near Urumiyeh, Soviet forces encountered no serious obstacle to their invasion of Azerbaijan in August 1941.[78] In less than one month, the Soviets had stationed a total of 40,000 men on Iranian soil, spreading them over an area which extended westwards from the Araxes river to Sharifabad, a village near Qazvin.[79] The Soviet occupation of Azerbaijan lasted for almost five years. It was not until May 1946 that the last Soviet soldier departed for home and withdrew across the border. During those five years, Azerbaijan lived through the most crucial period of its modern history.

As in most other parts of Iran, the economy in Azerbaijan suffered great setbacks during the years of World War II. There was soon a general shortage of essential commodities which at times resulted in famine and the spread of epidemics. As early as January 1942, a catastrophic shortage of bread occurred in the city of Tabriz, which then counted a population of 220,000 inhabitants.[80] The bakers were forced to sell potatoes instead of bread, though bread was considered the staple diet locally.[81] On 17 March angry crowds took to the streets and marched on the governor's headquarters, chanting: "We are hungry, we want bread!"[82]

Whereas in the country as a whole the cost of living for 1943 rose 400 per cent compared with 1941,[83] economic conditions in Azerbaijan were deteriorating to a far greater extent. An early report describing Azerbaijan's economic situation states that:

> Business generally is very restricted and, in view of the
> difficulties of obtaining fresh supplies, prices of all

commodities have gone up by 200 to 250 percent over
last year's prices.[84]

Some years later, R.W. Urquhart, the British consul at Tabriz, undertook an impressive survey which clearly demonstrates how drastically
prices increased for basic commodities like bread, rice and sugar,
particularly over the last two years the survey covers. In the same
survey, one finds to one's astonishment that a workman's average wage
at that time was 10 rials per day. At the end of his bi-monthly report,
the British consul ironically remarks on the atmosphere of frustration:

> Indeed, a bitter jest is increasing among the crowds that
> anti-Fascism is some new kind of bread.[85]

The unjust distribution of food supplies throughout the country made
many Azerbaijanis believe that in the eyes of the central government
Iran meant only the capital, Tehran. In an official telegram to the
government, the Tabrizis complained:

> Since the invasion, the textile ration has only been 1.5
> metres and 1/3rd of the city's inhabitants have not even
> received that. Furthermore, Tabrizis have not received
> their sugar rations for the last six months of 1943.[86]

In face of what was perceived to be blatant discrimination and mismanagement on the government's part, questions of the following type were
frequently hurled at the Tehran-based authorities:

> While the sugar ration in the capital is 1.5 kilos per
> month, why is the ration for Azerbaijanis no more than
> 400 grams, and that is not per month but rather, per
> season?![87]

The government had no adequate answer to this type of question, and
did not seem seriously interested in Azerbaijan's problems. As the
British consul remarked, most of the government "officials from the
south find Tabriz and Reza'iyeh (Urumiyeh) nothing more than dull
villages", where they can "make money and get back to Tehran, or
anywhere down south".[88]

TABLE 1
Prices of some commodities in Tabriz*
(1938–43)[89]

Commodities (per kilo)	June 1938	June 1941	June 1942	Feb. 1943
Wheat	0.59	1.65	1.11	13.00
Bread	0.69	1.50	1.10	12.00
Rice	3.00	3.30	6.00	32.00
Sugar-moist	4.00	5.95	7.50	100.00
Sugar-loaf	4.30	7.00	8.50	113.00
Mutton	2.60	5.20	6.00	116.00
Kerosene	1.35	1.65	2.65	4.00
Firewood	0.21	0.36	0.30	0.55
Charcoal	0.50	0.80	1.20	2.80
Milk	0.85	1.25	1.60	3.20
Potatoes	–	1.00	1.60	3.60
Fowl (each)	4.00	10.00	1.60	40.00
Eggs (each)	0.10	0.17	0.30	1.10
Ghee	10.80	16.00	36.00	68.00
Tea	44.00	70.00	120.00	180.00

* Prices in Rials

During the early days of the Soviet occupation, after the central government's authority in Azerbaijan had been abrogated, a number of rebellions occurred in the region, the most notable of which was the peasant uprising under Sumali Qasem. According to Chashm Azar, a leading member of the *Azerbaijan Demokrat Ferqehsi* (ADF), not long after the Soviets were installed in Azerbaijan, Qasem escaped from prison and returned to Suma, the village where he was born (in the district of Biagush, near Sarab). There he gathered together the landless peasants and incited them to attack the local landlords and notables. Having confiscated the estates of the rich landowners and distributed land among the poor peasants, Qasem was able to hold

power in the region for a time. In his memoirs, Gholam Yahya
Daneshiyan, a prominent leader of the ADF, gives accounts of similar
events in the district of Sarab.[90] The Tudeh Party also acknowledged
the occurrence of these rebellions. In the 24 May 1945 issue of *Rahbar*,
the party's official newspaper, the following remarks appeared:

> After the month of Shahrivar [Reza Shah's abdication and
> the beginning of the foreign occupation], as a reaction to
> twenty years of repression, wherever the peasants saw that
> the chains of reaction and dictatorship had loosened, they
> organized themselves and fought. They stepped to the fore
> and perhaps in some places the peasants were even the cause
> of tumult and disorder.[91]

One reason why these uprisings failed was indirect pressure from the
Soviet authorities. As mentioned previously, the Soviets' early policy
in Iran was primarily concerned with maintaining peace and order so
that "the Persian corridor for supplies and aid" would keep functioning
smoothly. A corollary of this policy was to avoid any form of confrontation with the Iranian government. In this connection, the remarks of
the British consul, who had recently arrived in Tabriz, are worth citing:

> I had left Tabriz in 1937. The intervening years have
> brought no great changes to the outward appearance of this
> province or of its inhabitants, but they have given reality to
> that nightmare of all politically minded Persians: the Rus-
> sians are here. I had heard so much before leaving London,
> at various points on the way, and at Tehran, of the Russians'
> intransigence, of their machinations and unscrupulous
> methods, that I approached my consular district warily,
> ready for trouble at the first post. I met with none. If anyone
> wishes to learn from my two months' experience in Russian-
> occupied Azerbaijan, let him register that the Russians,
> certainly no angels, are equally certainly no ogres.[92]

A very striking change which followed the termination of Reza Shah's
twenty years of autocratic rule was the emergence of a new kind of
political pluralism. Such freedom had not existed for many years and
was a virtually unknown phenomenon as far as younger generations in

Iran were concerned. As early as October 1941, the first political circle in Azerbaijan was formed. It was known as *Azerbaijan Jam'iyati* (the Azerbaijan Society). According to Chashm Azar, whose memoirs have recently been published in Baku, among the primary demands voiced by the society was "the formation of provincial and district councils which are guaranteed by the Constitutional Code".[93] The same source describes the following men as the chief architects of the society: Akhgari, Helal Naseri, Rahimi, Rezian, Chavoshi, Shabestari and Shams.[94] On 1 November 1941, the Azerbaijan Society published its first issue of the newspaper, *Azerbaijan*, which was written in the Azerbaijani language.[95] It was almost twenty years since a newspaper in the Azerbaijani language had appeared. The event attracted much attention from observers concerned with political developments in the region.[96]

Shortly after the founding of the Azerbaijan Society, other political circles and societies were formed. In January 1942, a group of eight formally educated men and women, some of whom had previous political experience, met in Tabriz to set up *Azerbaijan Zahmatkeshlar Tashkilati* (the Azerbaijan Toilers Association).[97] On the central committee of the Association were: Padegan, Vela'i, Qadiri, 'Elm Dust, Mizani, Nunkrani, Hambarsonian and Hajizadeh. In the Association's published manifesto, they, too, called for the creation of provincial and district councils in Azerbaijan.[98]

In February 1942, the "anti-Fascist" newspaper *Mardom* was founded in Tehran. Immediately thereafter, a network of anti-Fascist committees were formed in the Azerbaijani cities of Ardabil, Maragheh, Urumiyeh, Sarab, Ahar and Tabriz, their primary task being to "spread anti-Axis propaganda and give aid to the Allied Forces". In addition to providing plays, films and exhibitions, and installing loudspeakers in the city to transmit the broadcasts of "News of the Allies", the Tabriz committee also published a highly propagandistic newspaper in Azerbaijani entitled *Yumuruq* (The Fist).[99] By then, Azerbaijan had three Azerbaijani-language newspapers, the third one being *Vatan Yolunda* (Towards the Homeland), which was published by the Soviet Department of Propaganda.[100] All together, a total of twenty-one newspapers was published in Azerbaijan between October 1941 and September 1945. Fourteen of the twenty-one were in Persian, three in Azerbaijani, another three were bilingual, and one was in Armenian. Out of this total, right-wing parties controlled six newspapers, all of which were published in Persian. The others were run by leftist or liberal organizations.[101]

After the early days of relative freedom, the central government gradually began to reassert its administrative authority over the region. By mid-April 1942, Soheyli's government, fearing it was losing control over the province, launched its first offensive campaign in Azerbaijan. All local newspapers were banned, and the existing associations and societies were forbidden.[102] The reaction on the part of the Soviets was consistent with the general policy they had adopted at this point. They considered the governmental crackdown as a matter of Iranian internal affairs, and did not respond to local calls for intervention.[103]

However, the central government was too weak to sustain its repressive measures throughout the province for any great length of time. Due to the fluctuations of party alliances in Tehran, the outlawed societies gradually began to reappear on the political scene and the banned newspapers were once again being distributed in the cities. Moreover, new political groups were now emerging to give their support to the old ones, groups such as *Markaz-e Tarafdaran-e Demokrasi* (the Centre of the Sympathizers of Democracy), which was founded in Tabriz during the summer of 1943.[104] But no sketch of political life in Azerbaijan during the Soviet occupation would be complete without considering the activities of the Tudeh Party and the labour movement in that province.

On 7 April 1942, seven months after the Tudeh Party's formation in Tehran, the local branch of the party was officially founded in Tabriz under the name of *Komiteh-e Iyalati-ye Azerbaijan-e Hezb-e Tudeh-e Iran* (the Azerbaijan Provincial Committee of the Tudeh Party of Iran).[105] The active nucleus of the Tabriz branch consisted of: Mirza 'Ali Birang, who died shortly thereafter, Aqazadeh Shahin, the editor of the newspaper, *Shahin*,[106] as well as Padegan, Vela'i, Asadi, Eskandari, Kaviyan, Shabestari and Kalantari.[107] Shortly thereafter, the Tudeh Party set up branches in other cities of Azerbaijan, e.g. Zanjan, Urumiyeh, Ardabil, Astara, Maragheh and Miyaneh. Some of the founding members of these branches were later to become well-known figures in local politics. Examples of such men are Gholam Yahya Daneshiyan, Chashm Azar and Shandermani, who were Tudeh Party leaders in Urumiyeh, Sarab and Miyaneh respectively.

The first Tudeh Party conference in Azerbaijan was known as the Tabriz Conference and was held in the provincial capital towards the end of 1942. The procedural structure of the conference was very similar to that of the party's Tehran Conference which took place in October of the same year. Among other issues discussed at the Tabriz Conference was the urgent need to convoke a provincial congress. None the less, it took almost two more years before the Party was able to organize such a congress.

The Tudeh Party's first provincial congress was held in Tabriz on 11 January 1945. One hundred and forty-five delegates[108] took part in the congress.[109] What emerged most clearly during the four-day congress was the fervent commitment on the part of the delegates to the Iranian Constitutional Code. However, there were also delegates on hand who vigorously advocated support for the Azerbaijani language and wished to see Azerbaijani recognized as the second official language in the province after Persian.

Growing concern for the language question was illustrated by an incident which took place at the party's Second Tehran Conference held in August 1945. On that occasion, Ahmad Hoseyni, an Azerbaijani guest delegate, refused to address the audience in Persian. The chairman of the conference was obliged to employ a party member, 'Ali Shamideh, to act as interpreter during Hoseyni's address. Conflicts over the Azerbaijani language seemed to be symptomatic of an even larger dispute which was threatening to divide members of the Tudeh Party in Azerbaijan.

Reports were reaching Party headquarters in Tehran that party members in Azerbaijan were dividing into two separate camps which eventually came to be known as *Yerli* (Local) and *Muhajir* (Immigrant). The latter label was applied to those Azerbaijanis who had lived for long periods, in some cases for generations, in Russian (later Soviet) territory. By 1937, as a result of Stalin's policy of repatriation, a great number of such Azerbaijanis had crossed the border to settle once again in Iran. These *Muhajirs* having previously assimilated Russian culture and language, were, from the outset of the Soviet occupation of Azerbaijan, prone to align themselves with the Soviet authorities.

In view of the growing factional strife between these two camps in the Tudeh Party's Azerbaijani branch, the party's central committee appointed Khalil Maleki, a prominent party leader and himself an Azerbaijani, as the central committee's inspector in Azerbaijan. Maleki's mission was to find a practical solution to the divisiveness which threatened to upset the Tudeh Party's stability and hamper its future progress in the province. To facilitate his task, Maleki was given "the full power to expel all unsuitable elements from the party".[110]

Qiyami and Malek were assigned by the party to assist Maleki, but his task was not easy. He was confronted by a strong, entrenched pro-Baqirov tendency throughout the party's local organization.[111] The ideological tactic Maleki adopted was to emphasize Azerbaijan's Iranian identity, and to elaborate on the concept of national unity as the mainstay in preserving the country's sovereignty. His attitude to such topics as nation, national cohesion, national sovereignty, and language is well illustrated in an address he gave before party members in Tabriz:

> The general characteristics which constitute a nation are said to be unity of language, unity of governmental jurisdiction, unity with regard to economic policy or mutual economic interests, and finally, a cultural unity, i.e. literature and such like. However, on closer inspection, the history of nations both past and present shows that there never was even one nation which possessed all the above mentioned forms of unity. Likewise, there have been many nations which had some of the mentioned factors of unity and others which have not, without any harm resulting to the national unity of those nations.

And by way of dealing with the language question, Maleki comments:

> And here I will refer only to unity of language. Surveying the various kinds of nations, it is obvious that a difference of language does not cause a lack of national unity, nor does it follow that if two nations speak the same language that this leads to their national unity ... Moreover, the fact that Turkic is the language of Azerbaijan is in no way the cause for a lack of national unity, nor is there any necessity to eliminate Azerbaijan's mother tongue. Condemning the mother tongue of Azerbaijan will not have the slightest effect on strengthening national unity, and without this measure an Azerbaijani will feel himself to be more Iranian than any other Iranian. The only guarantee of our national unity is the Iranian national will to preserve the independence and integrity of Iran's soil, despite any propagandistic tales from the north or the south.

All political parties and groups which enjoy some social

standing, despite their differences in program or ideology, have no difference of opinion whatsoever with regard to preserving the integrity of Iran's soil ... The fact that Azerbaijan's language is different from the language of other parts of Iran is not a cause of weakening national unity. The nation is made up of different social classes, and each class which manifests itself through its own special party, uses its representatives to fight against other parties or cooperate with them, and thus, through consultation and intellectual struggle, a balance and order is effected in the relations between the different classes of society. And it is this which prevents the dissolution of national unity.[112]

Maleki attempted to impose the Tehran party line by reshuffling the posts of some party officials, expelling others as undesirable elements,[113] and introducing a more nationalist tone to party life in Azerbaijan.[114] It was soon evident that to put party affairs in proper order far-going change and drastic reform were necessary.[115]

Maleki's mission was not limited to promoting unity within the Tudeh Party in Azerbaijan and bolstering its activities. He was also charged with the task of reshaping the structure of the province's labour union which had been maintaining close contacts with the Tudeh Party.

During the period of Soviet occupation, the city of Tabriz with its 35,000 "industrial" workers[116] was the natural focal point of the labour movement in Azerbaijan. The pioneers in forming the first labour circles at this time were the workers in the city's textile mills and matchmaking factories.[117] The city's first formal labour organization, however, was founded by a labour activist from Tehran. In September 1942, Khalil Enqelab Azar, a leader of the Tehran-based *Ettehadiyeh-e Kargaran-e Iran* (the Union of the Workers of Iran) set up a local branch of that union in Tabriz.[118] In a situation where inflation was mounting, conditions were especially favourable for launching a labour movement,[119] and Enqelab Azar met with enthusiastic support on the part of the majority of the city's workforce.

The Tudeh Party in Azerbaijan was by no means pleased with Enqelab Azar's initiatives and the success of his efforts. The party had, in fact, formed its own labour union in Tehran six months earlier, but was reluctant to support a similar labour movement in the territories under Allied occupation. Since most large factories in Tabriz were producing for the Red Army, any union activities which might jeopardize industrial output were understandably problematic in the party's judgement.

However, now that the Tudeh Party found itself confronted with a rival labour union operating in Tabriz, it seemed expedient to found a local branch of *Showra-ye Markazi-ye Ettehadiyeh-ha-ye Kargaran-e Iran* (the Central Councils of the Union of the Workers of Iran) which was directly attached to the party. In the very first proclamation given out by the newly formed union, Enqelab Azar was condemned in no uncertain terms as being a traitor, and an appeal was launched for "all workers in the local factories to remain at their jobs producing goods for the Red Army".[120]

Because of "the undesirable activities" of Enqelab Azar and his union with regard to organizing industrial disputes, the Soviets eventually demanded his expulsion from the city. Likewise, the newspaper *Trud*, which was the official organ of the Soviets' labour councils, launched an all-out offensive against this rival labour organization and labelled one of the early architects of the union, Yusef Eftekhari, as "rogue and a provocateur".[121]

In the end, however, the two rival labour unions joined ranks and formed a new organization which bore the lengthy name of *Showra-ye Mottahedeh-e Iyalati-ye Ettehadiyeh-ha-ye Kargaran va Zahmatkeshan-e Azerbaijan* (the Provincial Council of the Federated Unions of Workers and Toilers of Azerbaijan).[122] The fusion took place on 2 August 1944. The newly founded labour union was managed by a twenty-seven-man central committee which proceeded to elect the Tabriz lampoonist, Biriya, as the union's vice-president.[123] The "amalgamation" of the two unions, which some observers believed was brought about under pressure from the Soviet Union,[124] brought to a close the short-lived history of Azerbaijan's independent labour movement. To begin with, the Tudeh Party was enthusiastic in its reception of the newly founded union. But it was soon clear to party leaders that Biriya, by imposing his absolute authority and controlling the union's affairs with an iron fist, was alienating many supporters of the Tudeh Party.[125]

When World War II came to an end and the Red Army ceased to give out commissions to the factories of Azerbaijan, the economic life of the province went into a grave decline. According to the British consul at Tabriz:

all the city factories are now believed to be losing money or
at best barely covering running expenses.[126]

But it was not only the region's factories that were affected by the
changed situation. Employers in numerous other sectors of the local
economy depended on market demands generated by the war. According to an American consular report, the post-war economic crisis in
Azerbaijan was beginning to make some people believe that granting an
oil concession to the Soviet Union would bring economic prosperity to
the region.[127] By the summer of 1945, unemployment began to hit
those working in the consumer goods production sector. The Tabriz
tobacco factory laid off more than 300 of its workers.[128] The labour
union proposed a series of measures to the central government aimed
at bringing down unemployment. These measures consisted, in the
main, of job-creating projects which never had a real chance of getting
off the ground in view of the chaos reigning in Tehran's noisy
parliamentary chambers. Now more than ever, the populace believed
that the solution to the economic problems afflicting Azerbaijan lay in
the creation of provincial councils.

From the beginning of 1944, it was the common demand of almost
every political gathering in the region that the Constitutional Code be
applied, especially Articles 90–93, which were concerned with the right
of the provinces to have local assemblies. For the period between 1944
and 1945, there are reports describing fifteen political meetings or
demonstrations which took place in the cities of Tabriz, Ardabil,
Meshginshahr, Marand, Sarab and Urumiyeh, and at each of these
meetings the demand was made for provincial councils.[129]

While the autonomous movement was gathering momentum in
Azerbaijan, the Tudeh Party leadership was at pains to make it clear
that it was in favour of autonomy, not separatism. The party wished to
discourage anyone from interpreting its policy as a desire for
Azerbaijan to secede from Iran. In reaction to a Radio Ankara news
broadcast which alleged that the provincial council of Azerbaijan had
demanded that Azerbaijan secede from Iran and join the Soviet Union,
the party newspaper, *Rahbar*, promptly declared:

> Firstly, Azerbaijan doesn't have a provincial council, and
> secondly, if such a Council did exist, how and when would it
> ever make a statement like that?! Furthermore, where is there

an Azerbaijani who would make such a demand to the detriment
of the territorial integrity of his beloved homeland, Iran?[130]

While the Tudeh Party and the labour union endeavoured to win wide
public support for the creation of provincial councils in Azerbaijan, the
various right-wing parties in the province emphatically dissociated
themselves from the policy. Parties such as *Vatan* (Homeland) and
Esteqlal (Independence) in Tabriz, or *Anjoman-e Kheyriyeh* (the Charity
Society) in Miyaneh, constantly accused the Tudeh Party of causing
"social change" and unrest, and calling for secession from Iran. As
S.G. Ebling, the American consul at Tabriz, remarked:

> The reactionary sympathies of the landed proprietors are
> shared by the local "aristocrats" or representatives of the old
> families, government employees, the police and the
> Mohammedan religious leaders such as the mullahs and
> mojtahids ... [who] are opposed to any change in the present
> economic and political organization.[131]

As regards the question of seceding from Iran, the local branch of the
Tudeh Party did everything within its power to convince the right-wing
parties of the region that its commitment to preserving Iranian territorial
integrity was above suspicion. Avoiding the issue of the Soviet Union's
policy of annexing adjacent territories, one party spokesman attempted
to strengthen the image of the local Tudeh Party's loyalty to Iran by
criticizing the expansionist aspirations of neighbouring Turkey:

> For some time now Turkish government authorities have
> fostered the claim to leadership of the east ... and unfurling the
> worn out map of pan-Turkism, they pore over it with regret and
> desire in their eyes ... They should be told that there is no
> Azerbaijani who will lift a finger to the detriment of the
> territorial integrity of his dear homeland ... An Azerbaijani
> loves his homeland, Iran, more than any other Iranian, and in
> all circumstances he is ready and willing to make sacrifices to
> defend its freedom, independence and territorial integrity.[132]

Despite all such assurances, the Tudeh Party did not succeed in its
efforts to allay the fears of its opponents. The atmosphere of relative

calm which prevailed between the opposing camps did not last for long. By mid-1945, reports indicate that clashes between rival political groups in the region were beginning to reach alarming proportions. Tudeh Party members and party offices were the main targets of right-wing attacks. The *khans* (tribal leaders) of such tribes as the Zolfeqari and the Shahsevan are alleged to have been the organizers of this offensive campaign.[133]

As examples of the wide-ranging disorders of the day, the following cases of paramilitary activity and growing violence in Azerbaijan were reported by the Tudeh Party's official newspaper, *Rahbar*. In Zanjan, the armed Zolfeqaris led the anti-Tudeh attack and had established almost total control in their area.[134] In Ardabil, Yurtchi, the well-known Shahsevan khan, enjoyed the full support of the local mullahs. He now saw to it that *jihad* (holy war) was declared against the Tudeh Party in his region. Likewise, Esfandiyari and Mozaffar Solati, two wealthy landowners, were arming mobs in Maragheh,[135] while the Charity Society was organizing its own military groups in Miyaneh.[136] In Sarab, the well-known Tudeh Party activist, Gholam Yahya Daneshiyan, was stabbed by members of a mob controlled by the municipal authorities.[137] And finally, in Urumiyeh, after the acting governor, Colonel Zanganeh, banned all Tudeh Party activities, several houses of Tudeh supporters were set on fire.[138]

Perhaps the most extreme of these clashes occurred on 10 August when a group of Tudeh supporters, by way of celebrating the anniversary of the Constitutional Revolution, decided to march to the village of Liqvan which is not far from Tabriz. Hajj Ehtesham Liqvani, the chief landowner of the region, put a stop to the festivities by attacking the demonstrators. The Tudeh supporters took the case to court in Tabriz and having received legal sanction for their procession, set out once more to march to Liqvan, this time accompanied by the court magistrate. In the armed clash which took place outside the village, eight people were killed, including Hajj Ehtesham Liqvani himself.[139]

The Liqvan incident was the first occasion when the left-wing parties in Azerbaijan decided to arm themselves in face of their opponents. In a telegram sent to the government in Tehran, the party's Azerbaijani branch declares:

> Liqvan was the first entrenchment where the slogan "one fist against another and blood for blood" was put into practice.

> And from now on, this slogan will remain the code of
> practice for the combatants of Azerbaijan.[140]

Moreover, *Rahbar* reported that at the end of a deliberative conference
held in Tabriz, one hundred and fifteen delegates from thirty-three local
branches of the Tudeh Party in Azerbaijan unconditionally declared:

> Elections for provincial and district councils must be carried
> out by whatever means possible. It is thirtyseven years now
> that these councils have been suspended. The people (*ahali*)
> of Azerbaijan will not allow the Constitutional Code to
> remain ineffective.[141]

The Prime Minister Sadr clearly demonstrated his indifference to any
such declarations. He stated in a session of the parliament that he would
not be the least concerned even if a hundred such telegrams were sent
to Tehran.[142] Meanwhile, rumours were pouring into the capital from
Tabriz indicating that "Azerbaijan was boiling over and ready to rise in
revolt".[143] Had the central government earlier on showed signs of
concern for Azerbaijan's wellbeing, the present state of tension would
not have reached such a high level. Many Azerbaijanis felt that the
central government had not only failed to respond to their call for
reform and change but also, from the time of Soheyli's premiership,
had adopted a policy of outright repression in the province. Finally,
under the premiership of Sadr, government repression reached its peak,
and it was too late to effect a political compromise which would avoid
a final confrontation.

5

The Democrat Party of Azerbaijan

In Iran social classes are not very distant from one another, especially the lower classes such as workers, peasants, small businessmen and artisans. In most cases they have common interests. For this reason, there is no basis in Iran for the formation of a political party which is class oriented in the true sense of the word. Presently in this country, any party or parties which aimed at safeguarding the interests of those classes with the above mentioned common interests would be most likely to succeed.

J. Pishevari, "Is There a Genuine Party in Iran?",
Azhir, no. 156.

The Party's Formation

From ancient times, Iranian history has been characterized by periodic alternation between a centralized and decentralized form of government. During periods when there is an absence of central government with strong and effective powers, centrifugal forces are obviously least hampered in their tendency to foster separate, heterogeneous political developments in the different regions of Iran. This has often resulted in uneven political development and, in particular, in a lack of unified political thinking at the national level. At such times, it is difficult for the central government to sustain a coherent national policy throughout the country. The political opposition finds it equally difficult to adopt a coherent political platform. Both the government and the opposition are faced with the problem of how to mobilize optimal support for a "national" party with a viable "national" program. Ever since the existence of political parties in Iran, this has been a dominant concern of party policy makers, and especially political strategists in the opposition camp.

Immediately after World War I, the early Democrats were faced with the problem of formulating policies with nation-wide application. Likewise, during World War II, the Tudeh Party had to cope with the difficulty of shaping a coherent national policy. The Tudeh Party, which was created on the model of the late Comintern "United Front" rather than the old single class, proletariat style party,[1] chose to adopt a national policy based on a class-oriented movement. It did not take long, however, for the Tudeh Party leadership to realize that it was impossible for the party's endorsed policy to find supporters at the national level. Though it was possible for the party to display proudly its banner outside party headquarters in Tehran, circumstances were such in Isfahan, for instance, that it was not safe for Tudeh Party members to acknowledge their political views openly. Whereas party members and sympathizers in the south were obliged to adopt *taqiyyeh* (dissimulation) in order to live in security, throughout the north Tudeh Party branches enjoyed the privilege of living in the so-called "liberated land".

In the prevailing atmosphere, there were some veteran Communists, such as Pishevari, who rejected the Tudeh Party's program and advocated a *melli* (national) rather than a *tabaqati* (class) policy. At this stage in his career, Pishevari was obviously using the term *mellat* to refer to the whole nation of Iran, including Azerbaijan. The main arguments of this old guard may be summed up as follows:

a) Class differentiation and consequently class consciousness in Iranian society have not yet developed to the point where it was meaningful to speak of *class interests* and a *class struggle*.

b) It was the foreign imperialist powers rather than the class of native property owners who presented the real barrier to Iran's further economic and political development.

In a series of articles which were published in *Azhir*, Pishevari frankly discarded the concept of a class-based political party in Iran, pointing out that:

> In underdeveloped countries, defining the social standing of individuals, or even that of groups and classes, is very difficult. For example, in our own Iran social classes have scarcely appeared at all in the classic form which is to be seen in the advanced world. Between the large-scale landowner and the peasant there is a numerous group of small landowners who, by varying degrees, fill the space between the two classes, in fact to a certain extent, they have even linked and joined them together. The majority of city workers still practise a craft and work in their own hut together with apprentices. The majority of our industrial capitalists still have their hand in trading, or even in large-scale landownership.[2]

Moreover, Pishevari elaborates his views on the nature of political parties in Iran by adding:

> In countries like Iran which are not advanced ... it is impossible for a political party based on class, in the full sense of the concept, to come into being. Even if such an organization did exist, it would definitely be very weak. And it is on this basis (i.e. class solidarity) that most political parties in the advanced countries have managed to become a national and mass movement.[3]

One year later, in September 1945, at a time when the newly born *Azerbaijan Demokrat Ferqehsi* (the Democrat Party of Azerbaijan - ADF) was no more than a few days old, Pishevari, in an article entitled *"Ferqehmiz Tarikhi Ishi"* (Our Party's Historical Task), assessed the Tudeh Party in the following terms:

> In practice, the Tudeh Party arose in the form of a class-based party. No one but workers, peasants, and some intellectuals from the lower classes were allowed to enter this party. The duties and the slogans of the party were designated by the interests of these classes and groups alone. For this reason, people called the Tudeh Party a party of the left and

the members of this party used leftist slogans. We, however, by way of safeguarding national freedom, extend a helping hand to everyone, to the landowners and the peasants, to the workers and the capitalists. We will all strive together on the road to Azerbaijan's prosperity and happiness.[4]

Indeed, those who signed the early declaration of the ADF, men such as Pishevari, Shabestari and Padegan, consciously avoided making any reference whatsoever to class distinctions in their statements, and saw to it that the wording of the declaration would be representative of the broadest social spectrum. On 3 September 1945, the declaration was published in Tabriz in a bilingual form (Persian and Azerbaijani). Besides the three persons already mentioned, there were twenty-eight other signatories to the declaration, including even landowners, merchants and other notables.[5] According to ADF documents, Pishevari undertook a long and detailed consultation with Shabestari in *Shahrivarin avvallerinde* (late August 1945). He then handed over the newspaper *Azhir* to one of his colleagues in Tehran and departed for Tabriz, where, along with Shabestari, he deliberated with Padegan, who was then chairman of the Tudeh Party Committee of Azerbaijan, and attempted to convince him of the necessity of establishing a new political party for Azerbaijan.[6]

Among those who believe that the ADF "project" was chiefly invented and directed by the Soviets is Anvar Khameh'i. According to Khameh'i, Pishevari left Tehran some time between the end of July and the beginning of August *(nimeh-e avval-e Mordad)*, i.e. not at the end of August, and while in Tabriz he used his influence to have Ovanessian and his group deported, the latter being opposed to the pro-Baqirov tendency. Moreover, Pishevari succeeded in replacing Amir Khizi with Padegan, as chairman of the Tudeh Party's Azerbaijan Committee.[7]

The ADF's early declaration consisted of twelve articles. After referring to its firm commitment to maintaining *esteqlal va tammamiyat-e Iran* (Iran's independence and territorial integrity), the *Ferqeh* demanded *azadi-ye dakheli* (internal freedom) and *mokhtariyat-e madani* (cultural autonomy) for the *mardom* (people) of Azerbaijan. In this connection, it was stated that the Azerbaijani language should be the sole language used for teaching during the first three years of primary school, after which time Persian was to be introduced as the "state language". Both languages were then to be employed throughout higher education. Likewise, the ADF called for early elections for the provincial and district councils. As regards Azerbaijan's economy, the party declared its willingness to find new "transit channels" for the export of local products and pledged itself to a policy of establishing new industries as well as maintaining old ones. It added that the taxes collected in Azerbaijan would be spent locally with the welfare of the province in mind. As for landownership, the ADF would limit itself to confiscating those lands which had been abandoned by landowners who fled Azerbaijan. The property would then be distributed, without any restrictive conditions, among the farmers who worked the land. Land taxation would continue according to the old system, except that "those illegal taxes which were invented by the landowners" would be abolished. Finally, on the issue of representation, Article Nine of the declaration, after objecting to the present way that Azerbaijan was represented in the *Majles*, stated that: "Since four million Azerbaijanis live in Iran, therefore Azerbaijan, instead of having only twenty seats in the *Majles*, should occupy some one-third of the parliament's seats."

After justifying its actions by saying "it is only natural that anyone who wishes law and order to be established throughout the country should begin by first putting everything in order in his own home", the Declaration of the ADF closes by praising a democratic Azerbaijan and a free, independent Iran, and in particular by praising the *Ferqeh-e Demokrat-e Azerbaijan* as the true guide to liberty in Azerbaijan as well as in Iran as a whole.[8]

Although the ADF, during the following year, elaborated upon these early demands (as will be examined in Chapter 6), implementing what had been called for in the September Declaration (*Shahrivarin Muraji'at-namehsi*) was to remain the party's primary challenge. The crucial demand, so it appeared to many Iranian outsiders, was the decision to adopt Azerbaijani as the official (albeit not the "state") language of the province. In the eyes of many Iranians, even those who made up the liberal wing of the political spectrum, the adoption of any language other than Persian as the official language amounted to nothing less than the first step on the road towards secession.

For many Iranian intellectuals who had grown up in the post-Constitutionalist era when Iran was passing through a phase of disintegration and when the central government of Reza Shah seemed to be the only means of forcing the pieces of the vast jig-saw puzzle together, the Persian language appeared to be the primary bond which guaranteed the nation's territorial integrity. Liberal newspapers such as *Azadegan* (The Free Minded), *Aras* (The Araxes), *Darya* (The Sea), and *Iran-e Ma* (Our Iran), while promptly expressing their sympathy for the early demands of the ADF, none the less took exception with the party's position on the language question.[9]

In an editorial entitled *"Zaban-e Melli-ye Hammihanan-e Azerbaijani-ye Ma Parsi Ast"* (the National Language of Our Azerbaijani Fellow Countrymen is Persian), the newspaper *Iran-e Ma* reconfirmed its support for the ADF, and urged the central government and the *Majles* to respond favourably to the party's "just demands". However, the editorial went on to voice its dissatisfaction with the Azerbaijani Democrats' use of certain specific terms:

> We do not here wish to haggle over words but, in our view, it would be far more appropriate if the Democrat Party's authors would say and write *"mardom-e Azerbaijan"* (the people of Azerbaijan), instead of *"mellat-e Azerbaijan"* (the nation of Azerbaijan).[10]

And with regard to the language issue:

> In the view of our writers, it is perfectly obvious that the local language of Azerbaijan deserves respect. However, in our opinion the local language of Azerbaijan can definitely not be the national language of our Azerbaijani fellow countrymen because we do not consider the people of Azerbaijan to be a nation separate from ourselves and our other fellow countrymen.[11]

On the other hand, the bilingual newspaper *Azerbaijan* which began publishing on 5 September as the ADF's official organ made clear in its first issue the ADF's uncompromising commitment to adopting Azerbaijani as the official language of the province:

> Over the years, many traitors and foreigners have striven to destroy our language or to hinder its development. This effort became especially widespread during the period of Reza Shah's regime which was inimical to freedom. But we have indicated that we have not renounced our language.[12]

A comparison of the stand taken by the old Azerbaijani Democrats on the language issue with that expressed in the ADF's declaration clearly demonstrates how the Azerbaijani language had evolved from being a means of communication to being a means of identity. Neither Khiyabani and his companions, nor even Pishevari during his pre-ADF political career, were particularly keen to promote the use of the Azerbaijani language. It is undeniable that the drastic measures promulgated by Reza Shah to suppress languages other than Persian elicited a negative reaction from members of the non-Persian intelligentsia. However, the resentment which the Shah's language policy aroused had never resulted in so far-reaching a program as the ADF put forward in its Declaration. Language, along with any other emblems of ethnic and national identity, has an inherent potential for mobilizing popular support and can be used to bring the "crowds into history". This was precisely what Pishevari was doing in September 1945.

The Pishevari of September 1945 was not the same as the Pishevari of a few years earlier, or even of a few months earlier. Up until then, he had been living in Tehran, working as editor of *Azhir*, a Persian-language newspaper. Meanwhile, he had become aware that in order to mobilize the Azerbaijanis in a mass ethno-political movement he would need to find some unifying element which he could stress, some element which transcended class divisions and distinguished the Azerbaijanis from their fellow Iranians. Championing the Azerbaijani language proved to be the most effective rallying point around which to unite the population of the province. Some have speculated that Pishevari's sudden concern for the language question was due to influence emanating from Soviet Azerbaijan, influence from men such as Baqirov and Mirza Ibrahimov, a Soviet Azerbaijan essayist, who was also an advocate of Greater Azerbaijan.[13]

The chief barrier to organizing a new party based on an Azerbaijani identity was the existence of the Tudeh Party. The Tudeh Party was the only party on the left which enjoyed wide support in the province, having already recruited those people who were potentially politically minded. Consequently, at first sight it appeared almost impossible for the ADF to compete successfully with an old national broad-left party which most importantly had been enjoying the support of the Soviet Union. Furthermore, since the Tudeh Party's constitution did not allow its members to join other political parties, the only course of action open to the founders of the ADF was to attempt to liquidate the

Azerbaijan provincial committee of the Tudeh Party and urge the committee members to join the ADF. It is interesting to note that there were individuals among the provincial committee's leadership who believed that, in the long run, such developments would serve the interests of the Tudeh Party. The party would be dissociated from involvement in the controversial conflicts with the central government and thus be able to maintain its legal status in the capital.

After the early consultation between Pishevari, Padegan and Shabestari, Badegan, who was chairman of the Tudeh Party's provincial committee, was put in charge of dissolving this committee. Padegan's brief visit to Tehran was in reality simply to inform the Tudeh Party's central committee of the decision which had already been taken. According to Fereydun Keshavarz, then a member of the central committee and the party's deputy in the *Majles*:

> The day before announcing the formation of the Democrat Party of Azerbaijan, the Central Committee of the Tudeh Party held a meeting in my house because I enjoyed parliamentary immunity and the party headquarters were occupied by soldiers ... I was in the meeting when I was summoned because Padegan, the Secretary of the provincial organization of the party in Azerbaijan, had arrived from Tabriz and had urgent business ... I took him into the meeting ... He said before the meeting: "I have just arrived from Tabriz and must return immediately. I have come to inform you that tomorrow our whole party organization in Azerbaijan will separate from the Tudeh Party of Iran and, with the agreement of our Soviet comrades, will join the Democrat Party of Azerbaijan, the formation of which is to be announced tomorrow." The Central Committee appointed Iraj Eskandari to write a letter of protest to the Communist Party of the Soviet Union which he did, but a reply to this letter was never received.[14]

In his memoirs Iraj Eskandari, who at that time was the First Secretary of the Tudeh Party, confirms the allegation made by Keshavarz with regard to the "inconsiderate act" undertaken by the founders of the ADF. He writes:

The Tudeh Party was wholly unaware of the formation of the *Ferqeh*. For that reason it came as a great surprise ... We found ourselves confronted with a *fait accompli*, and we were against it.[15]

On 7 September, four days after the foundation of the ADF, the provincial committee of the Tudeh Party convoked a conference. The only item on the agenda was to administer the last rites to the provincial committee and call upon the committee's members to join the ADF.[16]

The emergency conference of the provincial committee opened at Tabriz with an attendance consisting of one hundred and ten party activists "representing" 65,700 party members in Azerbaijan.[17] After a "lengthy debate on the necessity of founding the ADF", the conference passed a motion calling for fusion with the ADF, on the condition that five of the representatives on the ADF's provisional founding committee be drawn from the Tudeh Party's provincial committee. Subsequently, Qiyami, Badegan, Sheykh Hasan Borhani, Vaqef and Yadollah Kalantari were elected to the new positions. Likewise, Pishevari, Shabestari, Rafi'i and Biriya were nominated as the non-Tudeh Party members to the provisional committee.[18] The fusion, however painful to some of the old party members, was now accomplished, and the ADF's membership jumped from 50 to 65,750.[19]

The reaction throughout Azerbaijan to the formation of the ADF and its "fusion" with the Tudeh Party's provincial committee was not entirely sympathetic. In Reza'iyeh (Urumiyeh), a group of six trusted notables of the city gave their support to the ADF on the condition of certain small alterations in the party's declaration,[20] while in Zanjan, the party branch expressed its hesitation to join the ADF in no uncertain terms.[21] These instances of reluctance, however, were the least of the ADF leadership's worries. In an editorial entitled "*Güj Birikdedir*" (Strength Lies in Unity) which was published in *Azerbaijan*, after "welcoming the provincial committee's decision on fusion with the ADF", the author admonishes those who still believe in the Tudeh Party's "principles", that:

Joining the Tudeh Party's provincial committee to the *Ferqeh* does not mean imposing the party's principles on the ADF. On the contrary, it means accepting the program of the ADF. Our chosen path is clear. We are not aiming at class struggle.

> Our *Ferqeh* is a national one. Except for traitors and those
> who oppose the Constitutional Code, every Azerbaijani may
> join the *Ferqeh*.[22]

The British consul in Tabriz also confirmed the latest shift in political
developments. When comparing the Tudeh Party to the ADF, he
commented on the open-door policy of the ADF in the following terms:

> While not all can belong to the Tudeh, everyone can be a
> Democrat.[23]

The first conference the ADF held (13 September 1945) elected a
provisional organizational body consisting of eleven members presided
over by Pishevari, and proposed that the Party's first congress be held
in twenty days' time.[24] The ADF's first congress took place in Tabriz
on 2 October and included a total of two hundred and forty-seven
delegates representing thirty-eight district, municipal and county
committees.[25] The varied composition of the delegates is quite interesting. According to an opposition source, those taking part in the
congress included such diverse social types as the *hajji*, *mullah*,
bazargan (merchant), *ra'is-e il* (tribal head), *rowshanfekr* (intellectual),
and *Komonist-e vajih ol-melleh* (popular Communist).[26]

The ADF's three-day congress came to a close on 5 October, when
it published its constitution containing fifty-one articles. After a lengthy
introduction which stressed the necessity of the ADF's formation, the
constitution went on to deal with a wide range of subjects such as:
general politics, economics, agriculture, education, art, justice, the
military, and the question of nationality. The main points made in the
constitution, which were not all that different from what had already
been put forward in the early declaration, were as follows:

– The ADF commits itself to safeguarding the independence and
territorial integrity of Iran, while endeavouring to establish *milli va yerli*
(national and local) autonomy for Azerbaijan which is defined in civic,
economic and cultural terms.
– The ADF shall endeavour to establish democracy throughout the
country and to that end supports the formation of a central democratic
government based on parliamentary elections.
– The ADF is in favour of altering the existing electoral law in order

to establish universal suffrage: i.e. extending the vote to everyone (including women for the first time) over the age of twenty. Anyone between the age of twenty-seven and eighty may stand for office.

– The ADF supports the introduction of a labour code which will limit work to eight hours a day, forbid child labour, acknowledge trade unions and establish the right to social benefits.

– The lands of those landowners who have already left Azerbaijan will be confiscated by the provincial government and all illegal forms of land taxes will be abolished.

– There will be universal and compulsory free education which will recognize the right of minorities living in Azerbaijan (e.g., Armenians, Assyrians and Kurds) to study in their own language.

– Some democratic measures will be introduced into the existing structure of the military.

– Any other distinct *millet*, like the Azerbaijanis, will have the right to use its own language and exercise national and local autonomy through its provincial and district councils.[27]

As mentioned above, the ratified constitution of the ADF was not radically different from the party's early declaration. In addition to noting some new points in the constitution such as the introduction of universal suffrage and the concern for carrying out some reforms in the army, one may draw attention to their usage of the term *millet*. In the early declaration, the Azerbaijanis were referred to as a *khalq* (people), whereas in the constitution, the Azerbaijanis are described as a particular *millet* (nation) like other nations living in Iran. The introduction of this new term was by no means fortuitous. A few days before the publication of the ADF's constitution, the question of *milliyat* (nationality) and *taba'iyat* (citizenship – *staatsangehörigkeit*) was discussed in detail for the first time in an editorial published in the newspaper *Azerbaijan*. In reaction to a recent article by Mahmud Afshar, in which the latter had once more stressed Iranian unity and Iranian national identity,[28] the columnist of *Azerbaijan* made it clear that the ADF was perfectly aware of the terminology it used:

> *Milliyat* and *taba'iyat* are two different concepts. Although we consider ourselves to be *taba'eh-e* Iran, we preserve our *milliyat* as Azerbaijanis.[29]

In addition to the constitution, the ADF's first congress drew up the *Ferqeh*'s regulations. The organizational structure of the ADF, as formulated by the Congress, was not very different from the hierarchical structure of the Tudeh Party. The lowest level of organization was the *howzeh* (cell) consisting of five to seven members. This was followed by the District Committee with fifteen to twenty-one members, the County Committee with twenty-one to twenty-seven members, and finally the Central Committee with thirty-one to forty-five members. The Executive Committee of the ADF, consisting of seven to eleven members, who were elected directly by the Central Committee, was in charge of the *Ferqeh*'s current affairs.[30]

During the last session of the Congress, the deputies elected a Central Committee of forty-one members, headed by Pishevari, as well as a twelve-member Disciplinary Committee.[31] Although the Central Committee was soon to vote for an eleven-member Executive Committee, in practice the body which ran the affairs of the *Ferqeh*, was a core of five persons: Pishevari, Shabestari, Biriya, Javid and Padegan,[32] only two of whom, Biriya and Padegan, had previously been active in the Tudeh Party.

The month which followed after the Congress was a brief interim period during which the ADF stood poised for the attack. Having spread its organization over all of Azerbaijan, now the party leadership's main concern was how it could go one step further and take over complete control of the province. On 8 November the *Ferqeh*'s Central Committee convoked its first plenum. *Azerbaijan*, the ADF's official organ, in an article entitled "*Ikinji Dowranin Sho'arlari*" (the Tasks of the Second Period), described the proceedings of the plenum and commented on what it felt would be its "very important" consequences. It summed up the activities of the plenum in the following terms:

– The first phase in the history of the ADF, when the *Ferqeh* was chiefly engaged in deploying its organization throughout the whole province, had now reached completion.
– All previous measures of the ADF constituted the necessary practical steps before entering upon phase two which will be to set up the governmental structure of autonomy.
– The next step of the ADF will be the formation of provincial and district councils in Azerbaijan.

1. Political activists attending the founding conference of the Democrat Party of Azerbaijan. Tabriz, September 1945

2. A memorial meeting for the Azerbaijani Constitutionalists. Tabriz, March 1946

3. Gholam Yahya Daneshiyan, Commander in Chief of the Armed forces of the Autonomous Government of Azerbaijan together with a group of Feda'iyan. Zanjan, April 1946

4. Members of the Tabriz Plenum Committee of the Democrat Party of Azerbaijan.

Top row: Mohammad Biriya, Sadeq Badegan, Mir Ja 'far Pishevari, Mirza 'Ali Shabestari, Mir Rahim Vela'i

Second row: Mir Mehdi Chavoshi, Mir Qasem Chashm Azar, Javad Mahtash, Zaynalabedin Badkoubehchi, Khalil Azarbadegan, Jar 'far Kaviyan, Veram Mirakiyan, Kazem Hashemnia

Third row: Adel Adeliyan, Soqra Qaderi, Rasam Moze 'zadeh, 'Ali 'Askar Diba'iyan

Fourth row: Hoseyn Jeddi, Najaf Beshavard, Reza Rasuli

Fifth row: Taqi Karimi, Qahreman Qahremanzadeh, Borhaneddin Sobhi

– After the formation of the provincial and district councils, it will be time to elect Azerbaijan's deputies to the Fifteenth *Majles* which is soon to be constituted.[33]

As was to be expected, the editorial in *Azerbaijan* also referred to "the practical military measures" adopted by the plenum. According to Chashm Azar, who at the time was a member of the Central Committee: "After busying itself with political decrees, the task which then confronted the plenum was how to realize them in practical terms."[34]

It appears that no one in the plenum was against undertaking military action. However, the question was whether to attempt a simultaneous armed insurrection in Tabriz and a few other big cities, or to adopt a strategy of small-scale guerrilla fighting for short periods, with the ultimate aim of disarming the Central Government's army barracks throughout the province. In view of the unexpected reaction of the Central Government, the plenum voted for the second option.[35]

Shortly after the plenum was held, the ADF began to organize militia-like armed groups called the *Feda'iyan*. Some months later, a more regular type of army known as *Qizilbash* was also established, but the role of the *Feda'iyan* as the military backbone of the ADF was to remain crucial throughout the ensuing events. The *Feda'iyan* were recruited primarily from rural areas and they were presented as an alternative to the country's gendarmerie.

To begin with, most of the officers in charge of training the *Feda'iyan*'s new recruits were deserters from the army of the Central Government. They came from different parts of Iran but there was a significant core of them who were rebel officers who had fled to the Soviet Union after an abortive attempt to launch a guerrilla war in the north-east of Iran a few months earlier.[36] Out of a total of twenty-eight officers residing in Shaholan, a first group of seven crossed the border into Iranian Azerbaijan and reached Tabriz by mid-November. The group consisted of two colonels, three captains and two lieutenants. These officers were soon joined by a second group of ten lieutenants who arrived via the same route. By the beginning of December 1945, almost all of these officers were active in different parts of Azerbaijan. It is interesting to note that most of these officers came from non-Azerbaijani speaking parts of Iran and, consequently, were not as directly affected as their local companions by the much debated language question.[37] Although to begin with it made no difference that most of these officers were not of Azerbaijani origin, by the end of the autonomous government's term of existence the ethnic origins of the officers came to have a vital significance for a particular group in the ADF, a group which included a few members of the leadership itself.

By the end of November, armed groups of *Feda'iyan* had begun their offensive in the west and north-west of the province. Among the first cities to be taken by the *Feda'iyan* were Maragheh, Marand, Miyaneh, Sarab and Ardabil. On 25 November, the guerrilla forces had advanced to positions close to Zanjan, a city less than two hundred miles west of the capital, Tehran. Zanjan, though not administratively part of the Province of Azerbaijan, is culturally speaking considered the western frontier of Azerbaijan, due to its dominantly Azerbaijani population.

The *Feda'iyan*'s success in taking control of these cities was due, at least in part, to the passive support they received from the Soviet army which still maintained a hold over the province. Among the measures which the Soviet army took to support the ADF early on may be mentioned the handing over to the *Feda'iyan* of guns which had mostly been seized from the Iranian army during the August 1941 invasion, as well as hampering the central army's transportation of supplies in Azeraijan.[38] Soviet support moved on to a new, more active level when Iranian government troops *en route* to Azerbaijan to reinforce local garrisons were stopped at the Soviet check-point just outside Tehran.

On 17 November, the Iranian Foreign Office sent an official memorandum of protest to the Soviet authorities, reminding them that the Soviet Union had signed the Tripartite Treaty of Alliance on 29 January 1942, and thereby pledged itself not to interfere in Iran's internal affairs. The same memorandum informed the Soviet Union that the Central Government intended to send "two battalions and a company of the gendarmerie to Azerbaijan in order to strengthen local government forces and restore law and order in the province".[39] However, a few days later, when the above-mentioned troops set out from Tehran for Azerbaijan, they were unexpectedly intercepted by the Red Army at Sharifabad. Though to many observers the situation appeared "fraught with danger",[40] it was clear that the ADF's star was in the ascendant.

In the ten days from 10 to 20 November the ADF made a supreme effort to mobilize maximum crowd support. During those ten days, a series of well-planned, synchronized rallies was organized in almost all the major cities of Azerbaijan. The focal point of all these gatherings was the demand for the immediate formation of the provincial and district councils.[41] At the end most rallies, the crowds instigated an "election" to choose members of a delegation which would represent them in an assembly scheduled to be convened shortly in Tabriz.

On 20 November 1945, seven hundred and twenty-four "delegates" representing some 150,000 Azerbaijanis came to Tabriz to attend a gathering which was initially called the National Congress of Azerbaijan. However, by the end of its second day of proceedings, the delegates adopted the more decisive and authoritative sounding name of the Constitutional Assembly of Azerbaijan.[42] Despite the controversial nature of the legitimacy of the Assembly's authority,[43] in the statement addressed by the Assembly to "His Imperial Majesty the Shahanshah, His Honour the head of the *Majles*, and His Honour the Prime Minister", the following explanation for recent events was presented:

> The people (*khalq*) of Azerbaijan, as a result of innumerable historical causes and great events which it is impossible to enter into here, possess their own nationality (*melliyat*), language, manners and customs, as well as other special characteristics of their own. These peculiar qualities give them the right, while respecting the independence and territorial integrity of Iran, to be free and empowered to determine their own destiny, in accordance with the Atlantic Treaty, like all the other nations of the world. The people of Azerbaijan have political, economic and cultural ties with the other provinces and districts of Iran and in view of the sacrifices which this people have made with regard to establishing the government of Iran (the present government of Iran was in reality founded by Azerbaijanis), they seek their *mokhtariyat-e melli* (national autonomy). Nor do they in any way wish that the fulfilment of this desire should result in territorial losses to Iran, or Iran's partition. The people of Azerbaijan are fully committed partisans of the principles of democracy which in Iran has taken the form of the Constitution. Azerbaijan, like all the provinces and cities of Iran, will send representatives to the *Majles-e Showra-ye Melli* (the National Parliament) and will participate in paying just taxes.[44]

The statement then goes on to describe in more concrete terms the

functional structure of Azerbaijan's autonomous government as follows:
The National Congress of Azerbaijan ... will elect a
thirty-nine man National Commission for the running of
Azerbaijan's internal affairs. This Commission will have the
power to take whatever measures are necessary for putting
into practice the nation's wishes and to enter into discussion
with the competent authorities [of the Central Government].
At the same time, the Commission will see that elections are
held for the *Azerbaijan Milli Majlisi* (the National Assembly
of Azerbaijan), as well as for the National Parliament.[45]

At the end of its proceedings, the National Congress (later to be called
the Constitutional Assembly), headed by Shabestari, did elect thirty-nine
delegates to sit on the *Hey'at-e Milli* (the National Commission). The
Commission's chief task was "to prepare the ground and take the
necessary steps" in order to hold elections for a new provincial
assembly, i.e. the *Milli Majlis* (the National Assembly).[46] According
to the minutes of the proceedings of the Congress, while some deputies
wanted to retain the old name for the future assembly, i.e. the
Anjoman-e Iyalati (the provincial council), certain "radicals" who were
on hand succeeded in getting the new name adopted: *Milli Majlis* (the
National Assembly).

On 27 November, the voting, which was to continue for five days,
began, these being the first elections in Iranian Parliamentary history in
which women were to take part.[47] In ADF documents there is no
reference to the number of votes cast in the elections for *Milli Majlis*
(the National Assembly). The only precise figure recorded is the
number of votes cast in the city of Tabriz for the twelve nominated
deputies: Pishevari, Biriya, Qiyami, Padegan, Javid, Rafi'i, Shabestari,
Elhami, Nikju, Ipakchiyan, Mashinchi and 'Azima. A total of 23,951
votes were cast.[48]

At this point the ADF, which was claiming a membership of
200,000[49], and a regional Parliament consisting of 100 deputies,[50]
was ready to assume the governing of the whole province. In a
communiqué issued by Pishevari, the new era in the ADF's history was
proclaimed in the following terms:

When the help of Allah and victory arrive, then you will see
the people joining the religion, rank upon rank of them. (Koran)

Azerbaijan has entered a new era of history. The great success
in the elections held for the National Assembly clearly demonstrates that the time is now right for seizing power.[51]

Eighteen months earlier, when Pishevari's legitimacy had been
contested by the *Majles* in Tehran and he published his well-known
harsh and threatening declaration of 16 June 1944, it is doubtful
whether he could have foreseen that, in less than two years, he would
be occupying the post of *Bash Vazir* (Prime Minister) at the head of his
own cabinet in Azerbaijan. Pishevari was successful in presenting an
image of being a moderate politician. He was conscious of the existence
of Islamic values in contemporary society in Azerbaijan and was able
to exploit them when the time called for it.[52] Likewise, he was aware
that he needed to form a political organization with a wide popular
appeal, wider even than that of a broad-left political party like the
Tudeh. The structure and policies of the ADF reflected the changed
attitudes of the older Pishevari, in contrast to the young Pishevari who
as a Communist had conceived of political organization as primarily
based on a dedicated core of professional revolutionaries.

A Profile of the Party Leadership

One of the striking features of the Iranian Constitutional era was the
emergence of an intelligentsia whose mode of understanding society was
based on socio-political ideas of west-European origin. Despite the
diversity of their political views, what singled out the so-called
mostafrang (westernized) members of the Iranian intelligentsia from the
home-grown variety of educated or learned individual was the model of
society which they took for granted. The West European model of
society presupposed a coherent, class-layered society, which by
definition was organized around the distinctive concepts of *nation* and
state. From the extreme conservative right to the radical left, Iranian
politically minded intellectuals were united in their acceptance of the
idea that political activity consisted in correlating the relationship
between these two "given" entities.

Seyyed Hasan Taqizadeh, a conservative Constitutionalist, Mahmud

Afshar, an intellectual of a more liberal cast of mind, and Taqi Arani, an eminent Marxist of the mid-1930s, all belonged to different political camps, and yet they all viewed society from the perspective of class, rather than that of ethnicity. Taqizadeh took refuge in Britain, Afshar received his higher education in France, and Arani first became acquainted with Marxism in Germany during the Weimar Republic. Although their political destinies were to prove so dissimilar, their west-European experience endowed them with the same set of socio-political assumptions. These might have been very different indeed if they had originally embarked for Tsarist Russia, or later the revolutionary Soviet Union.

As mentioned earlier, Khiyabani was the first political figure from the reformist Democratic camp who strove to concentrate political change on the provincial level. In so doing, he was distancing himself from his former companions, men such as Bahar, or Soleyman Mirza Eskandari. At a later date, those leaders in the Communist Party of Iran who advocated the right of Iranian "nations" to self-determination, notwithstanding their differences in political outlook from Khiyabani, were perpetuating Khiyabani's conception of the nature of regional movements and the Central Government. It is noteworthy that Khiyabani and many of the later Communist Party leaders were well acquainted with the social milieu in Tsarist Russia and had spent a great part of their lives in the Caucasus which was then under Russian colonial administration.

The leaders of the Tudeh Party, on the other hand, had grown up in the era of Reza Shah and were well acquainted with West European schools of political thought. Despite being Marxists, during the early days of the party's life they continued the *mostafrang* tradition of the Iranian intelligentsia, rather than following in the footsteps of their predecessors in the Communist Party. It is worth mentioning that out of the fifteen prominent figures involved in founding the Tudeh Party, six had received their higher education in Western Europe and two in Tehran. Only two had studied in the Soviet Union.[53] Abrahamian underlines this significant point when he describes the leaders of the Tudeh Party as "Persian intellectuals who had come to Communism through the Marxism of Western Europe", rather than the "Leninism of the Bolshevik Party".[54]

By contrast, no one in the ADF leadership came from a background specifically shaped by direct west-European experience. All seven top leaders of the ADF – Pishevari, Shabestari, Padegan, Javid, Kaviyan, Daneshiyan and Biriya – either studied or spent considerable lengths of time as political activists in Tsarist Russia or, later, the Soviet Union.

Mir Ja'far Pishevari (formerly Javadzadeh Khalkhali) was born in 1892 in Khalkhal, a city of eastern Azerbaijan located near the Caspian Sea.[55] In 1905, he left Iran and went to Baku with his father who was seeking employment in the Caucasian oilfields. Pishevari's career as a journalist began in 1917 when he contributed an article to *Achiq Söz* (The Divulged Word), an Azerbaijani language newspaper which was published in Baku.[56] Later, he continued his journalist career by writing articles in *Azerbaijan Joz'-e la-Yanfak-e Iran* (Azerbaijan, an Inseparable Part of Iran), the official party organ of the Baku Committee of the *Ferqeh-e Demokrat-e Iran* (the Democrat Party of Iran).[57]

In mid-1919, after joining the *Ferqeh-e 'Edalat* (the Justice Party), Pishevari was appointed chief editor of the party's bilingual newspaper *Hürriyat* (The Liberty) and the associated newspaper *Yoldash* (The Comrade). His editorials usually open with criticism of various policies of the Iranian government and point out the need for social change, apparently along the lines of a "proletarian revolution". And while adopting a patriotic tone, he would often emphasize that Iran was a "*nation* with a distinguished history and identity". In an article entitled "*Iranda Inqilabi Fikri Lazimdir*" (A Revolution in Thinking is Necessary in Iran), after praising "Iranian customs and traditions", he adds:

> It is a known fact that Iranians are a historical nation which, despite having suffering numerous ups and downs in the past and adopted many religions and beliefs, has nevertheless been able to preserve its six-thousand-year-old culture and tradition.[58]

The conclusion which he goes on to draw is not unpredictable:

> Only a proletarian revolution is capable of achieving continuity in Iranian history.[59]

The upheaval caused by the *Jangali* revolt in the northern province of Gilan interrupted Pishevari's career as a revolutionary journalist. By late May 1920, he was sent to Gilan as a member of the *Ferqeh-e 'Edalat*'s Second Mission "to establish relations"[60] with Kuchak Khan, and carrying on guerrilla warfare, was undermining the central government authority in the region.

The high point in the history of the *Jangali* movement was, indeed, in June 1920 when the *Jangalis* in collaboration with the Communist Party founded a republic in Gilan, known as "the Soviet Socialist Republic of Iran". In the first Cabinet of this short-lived government, Kuchak Khan held the office of Commissar-in-chief of the republic. However, the honeymoon of the Communists and *Jangalis* did not last long. Following a *coup d'état* orchestrated by the Communist Party, Kuchak Khan was deposed and a second cabinet was formed, in which Pishevari directed the Commissariat of Internal Affairs of the republic.[61] Furthermore, by way of continuing his career as a journalist, Pishevari became editor of a Communist Party newspaper called *Komonist-e Iran* (The Communist of Iran) which was published in Rasht, the capital of Gilan, but only survived a few months.[62]

In September 1920 the famous Congress of the Toilers of the East was held in Baku.[63] Although Pishevari's (Javadzadeh's) name is not mentioned on the list of the Iranian delegates who attended the congress,[64] according to an account of one of the participants, Pishevari was among the group designated by the Communist Party to attend the Congress.[65]

On his return to Iran, Pishevari was confronted with the deep crisis of the *Jangali* movement and one more departed for the Soviet Union, this time as the deputy of the Tabriz Committee of the Communist Party of Iran to the Third Congress of the Communist International which was held in Moscow during the period June–July 1921.[66]

From 1922, after his second return to Iran, Pishevari resided in Tehran, where he became actively involved in the country's newly born trade union movement and founded the newspaper *Haqiqat* (Truth) which was associated with the movement and soon acquired some measure of influence.[67] The government closure of the newspaper marked the beginning of a new phase in Pishevari's life. During the next eight years, he gradually changed from being a restless, professional revolutionary and became a settled, hard-working employee in the private sector, though some believe he still maintained ties with the clandestine Communist Party.[68] His arrest in 1930 put an end to what had been, to all appearances, a quiet, politically non-active life.[69]

Pishevari spent the next ten years in prison, where he came to know the younger generation of Marxists, popularly referred to as "The Fifty-Three", and with whom he did not always see eye to eye. Indeed, he adopted a condescending attitude towards them in view of what he took to be their protected bourgeois background and lack of political experience. This critical attitude was to colour his future relations with the Tudeh Party.[70] By 1940, his prison sentence was commuted to internal exile in Kashan. A year later, however, he was back in Tehran preparing the ground for his next newspaper, *Azhir*.[71]

Pishevari attended the gathering at Soleyman Mirza's house on 29 September 1941, when the new Tudeh Party was founded,[72] but he declined to join the Party on that occasion. According to Iraj Eskandari, although Pishevari's hesitation to join the Tudeh Party was not to last long, the period of his party membership did not last very long either. Iraj Eskandari records that the Tudeh Party's First Congress took the decision to evict Pishevari from the party on the grounds that "he was not committed to the party's principles", which was apparently a reference to Pishevari having published his condolences on the occasion of the ex-Shah's death.[73]

The controversy over the facts of Pishevari's life is not confined to the his early career. The manner of his death has occasioned heated disputes among the old guard of the ADF, as well as among scholars of Soviet history who are specialists on Stalin's period. Pishevari's death occurred in Soviet Azerbaijan in 1947, one year after the fall of the autonomous government of Azerbaijan and the flight of the ADF leadership. The Soviet authorities officially reported his death as the result of a car accident. There are, however, well-informed sources which maintain that Pishevari was murdered by agents of Stalin-Baqirov in the hospital where he was taken after the car accident.[74]

Hajj Mirza 'Ali Shabestari was born in 1898 in Shabestar, a city north-west of Tabriz. After finishing his studies at the *maktab-khaneh*, the traditional religious school, he began to work as a small-scale merchant in the bazaar, just as his father had done. He took part in Khiyabani's revolt and eventually fled to Soviet Azerbaijan where he lived until 1941.[75] Following his return to Iran in October 1941, Shabestari founded the Azerbaijan Society and, one month later, began publishing *Azerbaijan*, a daily newspaper in the Azerbaijani language. In February 1942, he joined the Azerbaijan anti-Fascist Society and, two months later, appeared as a member of the early core of the Tudeh

Party in Azerbaijan. His membership in the Tudeh Party, however, was short-lived. By 1943, he had withdrawn from the party. Although Shabestari never held an executive office, his position as head of the *Azerbaijan Milli Majlisi* (the National Assembly of Azerbaijan) made him a very influential figure in the ADF.

Sadeq Padegan was born in Tabriz in 1899. After finishing the *maktab-khaneh*, he left for Russia, where he lived as a merchant until 1938.[76] On his return to Iran, he continued to work as a merchant in the bazaar of Tabriz and soon after the formation of the Tudeh Party in Azerbaijan, he began his political career in the same city.[77] It did not take long for Padegan to demonstrate his *apparatchik* capabilities and he quickly rose to become the head of the Azerbaijan Provincial Committee of the Tudeh Party. When the amalgamation of the ADF and the Tudeh Party took place, Padegan became Pishevari's under-secretary in the ADF, an office which he retained even after the ADF leadership had fled to the Soviet Union.[78]

Salamollah Javid (formerly Madadzadeh) was born in Khalkhal in 1898. When he was ten years old, he moved to Baku where he began to study at the *Ettehad-e Iraniyan*, a school which had been set up by the Iranian Social Democrats. In 1916, he joined the Caucasian Moslem Students Society and organized the first Iranian Students' Corps in Baku.[79] After making the acquaintance of Heydar Khan 'Amoghlu, Javid became a member of the *Ferqeh-e 'Edalat* (the Justice Party) and was later sent as a delegate of the *Ferqeh* to Tabriz to establish contact with Sheykh Mohammad Khiyabani. However, his arrival in Tabriz coincided with the suppression of Khiyabani's revolt.[80] Javid was still in Tabriz when Lahuti instigated his revolt. He joined the revolt but after its collapse fled to Baku. For the next nine years Javid remained in Baku, studying medicine at Baku University and pursuing his career as a revolutionary within the newly born Communist Party of Soviet Azerbaijan.[81] In 1929, six months after his return to Iran, he was arrested by Reza Shah's secret police and spent the next two years in prison. He was then kept in Kashan in "internal exile" until his definitive release in 1941.[82] Javid never joined the Tudeh Party but after the founding of the ADF, he became a member of the latter's executive committee. His office of Minister of Internal Affairs in the autonomous government was later changed by the central government to that of Governor of Azerbaijan. Following the fall of the autonomous government, Javid resided in Tehran and pursued his second profession as a medical doctor.

Ja'far Kaviyan, the future Minister of the *Khalq Qushuni* (the People's Army) in the autonomous government of Azerbaijan, was born in Tabriz in 1900. His military career goes back to Khiyabani's revolt when he was appointed as head of a paramilitary group. When the revolt was suppressed, Kaviyan turned his attentions to the trade union movement and founded a labour organization known as the *Hezb-e Kargaran* (the Labour Party),[83] "which would only accept labourers as members".[84] Together with Javid, he took part in Lahuti's revolt and, after the revolt's swift collapse, fled to Soviet Azerbaijan. In 1927, after a short stay in Baku, he returned to Iran and formed a new leftist circle as a result of which he was arrested and sentenced to seven years imprisonment.[85] During the years which followed, he was kept in "internal exile" in Zanjan where he opened a bakery. He only returned to Tabriz when the Allies invaded Iran.[86] Like Javid, he was never a member of the Tudeh Party but became one of the chief architects of the ADF.

When talking of the ADF or the autonomous government of Azerbaijan, it is quite common for Iranians to think immediately of two names, Pishevari and Gholam Yahya. Gholam Yahya Daneshiyan was born in 1906 in Sarab, a city west of Tabriz. By 1918, he left Sarab to join his father who was then living in Baku and working in the oilfields of Balakhan. After the establishment of the Soviet Government in Azerbaijan, he joined *Komsomol* and attended the "cadre preparatory courses" given at the Institute attached to the Communist Party of Soviet Azerbaijan. Later, he became head of the Committee of the Communist Party in Sabunchi, a district close to Baku. He held this post for fifteen years until his return to Iran in 1937.[87]

Daneshiyan was arrested soon after his return and spent the next six months in prison. By 1941, he attempted to organize some displaced landless peasants who had risen up against the landlords in the district of Sarab.[88] Later, he moved to Miyaneh, a city south-west of Tabriz, where he joined the local branch of the Tudeh Party and its associated labour organization.[89] When the ADF was founded, he did not hesitate to join the new party and soon became one of the chief organizers of the *Feda'iyan* paramilitary forces.

The tragic aspect of any failed political enterprise often comes to be associated with the person of one or two of the chief protagonists who are seen as victims of the attendant historical circumstances. In the case of the autonomous movement in Azerbaijan, Biriya is certainly such a figure. Mohammad Biriya (Hajj Gholam Oghlu) was born in Tabriz in 1914.[90] His father earned his living as a carpenter. By 1930, Biriya had fled to Soviet Azerbaijan and was pursuing his studies in Baku.[91] Later, he returned to Iran and worked as a labourer for the Tabriz Municipality and then for the Iranian Railways.[92] After the Tudeh Party was founded, Biriya became a member and was soon very active in the party's associated Labour Organization. On the eve of the ADF-Tudeh fusion, he held the office of First Secretary of the Azerbaijan Central Union of Workers and Toilers.

Besides having talent as an *apparatchik*, Biriya was also a believing Muslim and a poet. His poetry, in Azerbaijani and Persian, has been characterized as "rude but with some literary merit", while the British consul in Tabriz has referred to him as "the Tudeh Party lampoonist".[93] In the autonomous government, Biriya was appointed Minister of Culture and served as under-secretary to Pishevari. He held both these posts while continuing to function as First Secretary in the Labour Union. However, he did not serve as under-secretary to Pishevari for very long. Just before the fall of the autonomous government when Pishevari was absent, Biriya was appointed head of the ADF, though he only held this position for a few days.[94]

With regard to the language issue, Nasrollah Jahanshahlu Afshar has pointed out that, as a protégé of Mirza Ibrahimov, Biriya soon made it clear that he was "one of the fanatic supporters of the Azerbaijani language". Jahanshahlu Afshar has also noted that: "On a few occasions he even publicly advocated the idea of a Greater Azerbaijan, by which he obviously meant that Iranian Azerbaijan should separate from Iran and join with Soviet Azerbaijan".[95] After the fall of the autonomous government, Biriya, having stayed on in Tabriz, was attacked by a pro-central government crowd and was seriously injured. This incident caused some eyewitnesses, including R. Rossow, the American vice-consul in Tabriz, to imagine that Biriya had been killed.[96] In reality, Biriya survived and fled to Soviet Azerbaijan where he then spent the most difficult period of his life. He only managed to return to Iran after the Islamic Revolution in 1979, and died in Tabriz in 1985. Biriya began his life in exile as the editor of *Azerbaijan*, the ADF's official newspaper, which was published in Baku. He was also in charge of a propaganda radio program that was broadcast to Iran from Soviet Azerbaijan. However, after living for two years in Soviet Azerbaijan, he requested permission to return to Iran in 1948. Unfortunately, he apparently misjudged the reaction of the Soviet authorities. He was accused of having secret ties with the Iranian government and condemned to exile in Siberia.

Over the years that followed, Biriya's ideological attitude changed completely and he reverted to being a committed Muslim. Most of the poetry he wrote during this period is in praise of the Prophet Mohammad, the Imam 'Ali and Reza Shah. After Stalin's death and the beginning of some degree of de-Stalinization in 1955, Biriya was rehabilitated and allowed to return to Baku. However, Biriya, this time as a committed Muslim, got into trouble once again with the Soviet authorities. Having become involved with charitable activities, in particular feeding some poor young boys, he was eventually arrested on a trumped up charge of pederasty and sentenced to five years' imprisonment. He in fact served seven years in prison. On his release, he again settled in Baku where he lived until 1979 when he was able to return to Iran.

The core of the ADF leadership, i.e. the seven most influential figures whose careers and backgrounds I have considered above in some detail, all came from a lower middle class or working class background. Likewise, they were all of Azerbaijani ethnic origin but born in Iran. At the time of the ADF's formation, the average age of the group was forty-four. It is also noteworthy that every one of them had spent some years in Russia or what came to be the Soviet Union. Of the seven, five had been actively involved with the *Jangalis*, Khiyabani or the early Communist movement. On the eve of the ADF's formation, only three of them were members of the Tudeh Party.

If we look at Table 2, it is clear that of the larger group of twentyfive ADF leaders whose vital statistics are presented, everyone, with the sole exception of 'Abedin Nava'i, is of Azerbaijani origin and was born in Iran. Their average age is thirty-nine. Thirty-six per cent of them were from lower middle class or working class families, forty-eight per cent from middle or upper middle class families, and sixteen per cent from the Qajar or tribal nobility. While some eleven per cent or so had enjoyed the benefits of higher education, the rest had only finished the *maktab-khaneh*, the traditional religious school, or completed a few years of secondary studies. What is significant about these percentages is the increasingly important role which the lower and middle layers of society were coming to play in Iranian political life.

TABLE 2[97]

Social and Political Background of the Leaders of the ADF
and the Autonomous Government of Azerbaijan[98]

Name	Place of birth	Date of birth	Ethnic Origin	Class Origin	Education	Occupation before joining the ADF	Residence	Previous Politics
Pishevari	Khalkhal	1892	Azerbaijani	Working class	High school	Journalist	Tehran	CP*, Jangali
Shabestari	Shabestar	1898	Azerbaijani	Urban middle class	Primary school	Merchant/Journalist	Tabriz	Khiyabani
Padegan	Tabriz	1899	Azerbaijani	Urban middle class	Primary school	Merchant	Tabriz	Tudeh
Javid	Khalkhal	1898	Azerbaijani	Urban lower class	Medicine	Medical doctor	Tehran	CP
Kaviyan	Tabriz	1900	Azerbaijani	Working class	Primary school	Baker	Tabriz	CP, Khiyabani
Daneshiyan	Sarab	1906	Azerbaijani	Working class	Primary school	Metalworker	Miyaneh	Tudeh, LU†
Biriya	Tabriz	1914	Azerbaijani	Working class	Primary school	Labourer	Tabriz	Tudeh, LU
Qiyami	Tabriz	1891	Azerbaijani	Urban upper middle class	Law	Governor of Azerbaijan	Tabriz	CP, Khiyabani, Tudeh
Kabiri	Maragheh	1889	Azerbaijani	Qajar nobility	High school	Civil servant	Tabriz	None
Jahanshahlu Afshar	Tehran	1913	Azerbaijani	Tribal nobility	Medicine	University lecturer	Tehran	Fifty-Three, Tudeh
Shahin	Tabriz	1916	Azerbaijani	Urban middle class	High school	Civil servant	Tabriz	Fifty-Three, Tudeh
Shamideh	Khalkhal	1914	Azerbaijani	Working class	High school	None	Tehran	CP, Tudeh, LU
Chashm Azar	Tabriz	1920	Azerbaijani	Urban lower middle class	Primary school	None	Tabriz	Tudeh
Panahiyan	Tabriz	1904	Azerbaijani	Urban middle class	Military	Colonel	Tehran	Tudeh
Vela'i	Tabriz	1911	Azerbaijani	Rural middle class	Primary school	None	Tabriz	Tudeh
Ebrahimi	Astara	1918	Azerbaijani	Urban middle class	Law	None	Tabriz	Tudeh
'Azima	Tabriz	1911	Azerbaijani	Urban middle class	Law	Judge	Tabriz	Tudeh
Elhami	Tabriz	1904	Azerbaijani	Urban upper class	Political science	Mayor of Tabriz	Tabriz	None
Azar	Mashhad	1903	Azerbaijani	Military	Military	Colonel	Tehran	Tudeh
Muhtash	Osku	1912	Azerbaijani	Rural middle class	Veterinary	Head, Dept of Agriculture	Tabriz	Tudeh
Orangi	Tabriz	1910	Azerbaijani	Urban middle class	Medicine	Head, Dept of Health	Tabriz	None
Nava'i	Tehran	1906	Persian	Urban upper middle class	Military	Colonel	Mashhad	Tudeh
Rasuli	Tabriz	1904	Azerbaijani	Urban upper middle class	High school	Civil servant	Tabriz	None
Pishnamazi	Sardrud	1905	Azerbaijani	Rural lower class	High school	Merchant	Tabriz	Tudeh
Rafi'i	Tabriz	1886	Azerbaijani	Qajar nobility	Primary school	Civil servant	Tabriz	Tudeh

*Communist Party   †Labour Union

TABLE 3
Position of the Leaders of the Autonomous Government of Azerbaijan and their Subsequent Careers

Name	Function in the ADF and the autonomous government (a.g.)	Subsequent Career
Pishevari	Chairman of ADF; Prime Minister of a.g.	Killed in Soviet Azerbaijan
Shabestari	Member, Executive Committee of ADF; President, National Assembly	Retired from politics; remained in Iran
Padegan	Under-sec of ADF; Member, Executive Committee of ADF	Died in Sovier Azerbaijan
Javid	Minister of Interior of a.g.; Member, Executive Committee of ADF	Retired from politics; remained in Iran
Kaviyan	Minister of Armed Forces in a.g; Member, Executive Committee of ADF	Died in Soviet Azerbaijan
Daneshiyan	C-in-C of *Feda'iyan*; chairman of ADF in exile	Died in Soviet Azerbaijan
Biriya	Minister of Culture in a.g.; Member, Executive Cimmittee of ADF	Returned to Iran; died in Tabriz
Qiyami	Head, Legal Tribunal in a.g.; Member, Executive Committee of ADF	Died in Soviet Azerbaijan
Kabiri	Minister of the Post in a.g.; Member, Executive Committee of ADF	Executed in Tabriz after fall of a.g.
Jahanshahlu Afshar	Under-sec'y of Prime Minister of a.g.; Member, Executive C'ttee of ADF	After long stay in Soviet Union, fled to the West
Shahin	Chief Secretary to Prime Minister of a.g.; Governor of Urumiyeh under a.g.	Historian at Academy of Baku
Shamideh	Chairman, Miyaneh Committee of ADF	Historian at Academy of Baku
Chashm Azar	Chief Adviser to Prime Minister of a.g.	Chairman of ADF in exile
Panahiyan	Commander of *État-Major* in a.g.	Died in Moscow
Vela'i	Chairman, Tabriz Committee of ADF	Died inSoviet Azerbaijan
Ebrahimi	Public Prosecutor in a.g.	Executed in Tabriz after fall of a.g.
'Azima	Minister of Justice in a.g.	Fled to the West from Iran
Elhami	Minister of Finance in a.g.	Died in Soviet Azerbaijan
Azar	Commander of *État-Major* in a.g.	Returned to Iran and died
Mahtash	Minister of Agriculture in a.g.	Returned to Iran
Orangi	Minister of Health in a.g.	Remained in Iran
Nava'i	Head, Finance Department of Armed Forces in a.g.	Returned to Iran
Rasuli	Minister of the Economy in a.g.	Remained in Iran
Pishnamazi	Officer in armed forces of a.g.	Died in Soviet Azerbaijan
Rafi'i	Member, Exec C'ttee of ADF	Remained in Iran

The ADF and the autonomous government also recruited their members and personnel from those who had worked in the preceding administration. Besides seventy or more military officers who had previously served in the Iranian Army, there were some high-ranking civil servants, including a former governor and two heads of ministerial departments, who came to hold positions in the autonomous government.

When one considers the political background of our larger group of ADF leadership, it is clear that the ADF could not have been successful as a political party without having amalgamated with the local Azerbaijani branch of the Tudeh Party. Although the central core of the ADF, as mentioned above, only included a small percentage of former Tudeh members, some sixty-eight per cent of the leadership in the autonomous government had either been a member of the Tudeh Party or had been associated with the party's labour union. These ex-members of the Azerbaijani branch of the Tudeh Party did not maintain close ties with Tudeh Party headquarters. They did not feel they had strong interests in common with the Tudeh Party which many of them now saw as pursuing political goals tinged with a "Western" flavour or mentality.[97]

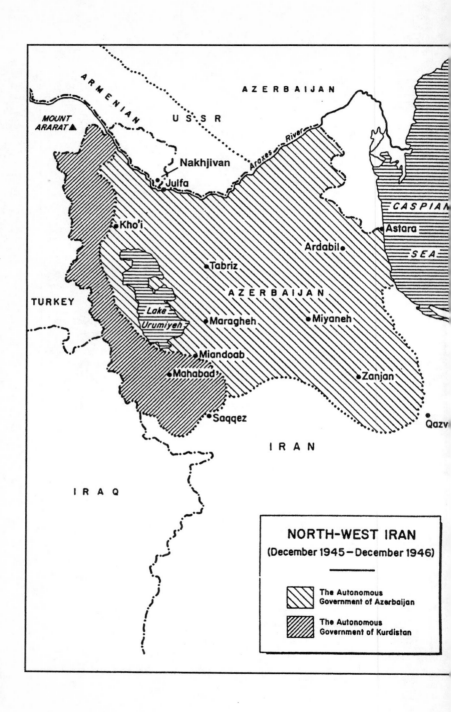

NORTH-WEST IRAN
(December 1945 – December 1946)

The Autonomous
Government of Azerbaijan

The Autonomous
Government of Kurdistan

6

The Autonomous Government of Azerbaijan

Democratization might automatically help to solve the problem of how states and regimes could acquire legitimacy in the eyes of their citizens, even if these were disaffected. Naturally the state would use the increasingly powerful machinery for communicating with their inhabitants, above all the primary schools, to spread the image and heritage of the nation and to inculcate attachment to it and to attach all to country and flag, often inventing tradition or even nations for this purpose.

E.J. Hobsbawm,
Nations and Nationalism since 1780, p. 89.

Establishing Autonomy

What only a few months earlier appeared to be no more than a fantastic dream had, by the end of the autumn of 1945, turned into a reality. On 12 December of that year, the *Azerbaijan Milli Majlisi* (the National Assembly of Azerbaijan), with seventy-five of its one hundred and one deputies present, was officially opened. Of these one hundred and one elected deputies, sixteen were labourers and artisans, twenty-six were farmers, twenty-four were from among the intelligentsia (teachers, journalists, medical doctors, engineers, etc.), and there were thirteen civil servants, two factory owners, seven merchants, eleven landlords and two members of the Muslim clergy.[1] Hajj Mirza 'Ali Shabestari, who was forty-seven years old at the time and one of the deputies, was elected President of the *Majlis*. After electing a president, the *Majlis* voted for members of a body which was to function as a parliamentary chairing committee and would replace the recently elected *Hay'at-e Milli* (the National Board).[2] The next step of the *Majlis* was to create the structure of the executive power.

Azerbaijan Milli Hükumati (the National Government of Azerbaijan) was the name which the *Milli Majlis* officially adopted to designate the totality of the governmental offices of executive power in the province. This complex of executive powers, which included the military as well as the political substructure, was defined as "entirely separate from the legislative power", the latter being embodied in the National Assembly of Azerbaijan.[3]

This executive power was exercised by a *Dowlat* (State) which was known as the *Azerbaijan Milli Mökhtar Dowlati* (the National Autonomous State of Azerbaijan). Subsequently, plans for a *Hay'at-e Dowlat* (Cabinet) were formulated which would be made up of twelve ministers who were the representatives of the *Milli Mökhtar Dowlati*. The ten ministers who formed the cabinet were to be the ministers of the Interior, Finance, *Khalq Qushuni* (the People's Army), Justice, Agriculture, Health, Road-PostTelegraph and Telephone, Trade and Economy, Labour and Toil (*Ish va Zahmat*), and Culture. At their head was the *Bash Vazir* (the Prime Minister).[4] It is significant that in the decrees of the *Milli Majlis* there was no reference to creating a Ministry of Foreign Affairs. This is an indication of the Democrats' recognition of the central government's authority in that domain and demonstrates that "the autonomy for which they asked was not equivalent to independence".[5]

Pishevari was appointed by the *Majlis* as *Bash Vazir* (Prime Minister) and invited to form a cabinet and propose it to the *Majlis* for their approval. The members of the cabinet he formed were: Javid (Interior), Kaviyan (People's Army), Mahtash (Agriculture), Biriya (Culture), Orangi (Health), Elhami (Finance), 'Azima (Justice), Kabiri (Roads/Post/Telegraph and Telephone) and Rasuli (Trade and Economy).[6] Furthermore, Pishevari appointed Qiyami as Chief Justice of the Supreme Court of Azerbaijan and made Fereydun Ebrahimi

Prosecutor General of Azerbaijan.[7]

Out of the eleven members of Pishevari's cabinet, seven had held posts in the previous administration. Moreover, two of these seven actually retained their former offices, only now with the title of Minister rather than "Head of the Department". Again, of the eleven ministers seven had previously been active in politics, five of them being ex-members of the Tudeh Party. Commenting on the eleven new ministers, the British consul in Tabriz remarked that not all of them "were well-known public figures" and added: "Of the whole cabinet the only two of any noticeable ability were the Prime Minister and the Minister of Culture, Mohammad Biriya."[8]

Once the National Government of Azerbaijan was established, it went on to publish a program containing twenty separate articles. After reiterating its "commitment to Iranian independence and territorial integrity" and its desire "not to act to the detriment of Iran's sovereignty", the National Government of Azerbaijan went on to declare its intention to carry out a series of changes and reforms in Azerbaijan, the most important of which were the following:

– laying the groundwork for electing members of the provincial councils.
– purging undesirable elements from the gendarmerie and the police department.
– revising the current tax assessment and preparing the annual budget of the province.
– working out an appropriate, centralized organization of the People's Army and the *Feda'iyan*.
– introducing Azerbaijani as the official language to be used in the school system.
– implementing the necessary measures to systematize the relations between landlords and peasants.
– decreeing a comprehensive labour law.
– encouraging private investment by capitalists and establishing security for capital.[9]

What the new government called for was certainly more far-reaching than what is usually understood by the term "local autonomy", especially with regard to the reorganization of the country's armed forces. Likewise, there were occasional references in the program of the National Government of Azerbaijan to certain demands which had been voiced by reformist circles in Iran ever since the abdication of Reza Shah, notably demands to do with land reforms. However, the government was consciously seeking broad support throughout the province and attempted to present a *moderate* program which would not alienate any particular social group. While calling for a comprehensive labour law and promising reforms affecting land tenure, the National Government of Azerbaijan made it clear it would respect private property and only introduce changes equitable to both landlords and peasants.

Although the Democrats' political strategy was geared to insurrection, there was no trace of any intention to do away with the previous administrative structure and replace it with a wholly new one. As the American consul in Tabriz remarked: "In general the old structure of internal administration was kept, and most of the minor civil servants appear to have stayed on in obedience to Pishevari's appeal",[10] namely to "stay calm and to function as before".[11]

In contrast to taking charge of the civil administration, securing control over the military proved to be less of an easy task for the autonomous government. Although, within two weeks, "the gendarmerie was overpowered and control was assumed by the Democrats in a zone stretching from Sarab, through Miyaneh to Miyandoab, cutting across all the lines of communication between Tabriz and the rest of Persia",[12] when the Democrats attempted to take control of the military garrisons in Reza'iyeh (Urumiyeh), Ardabil and Tabriz, they met with some difficulties.

The capitulation of the Tabriz garrison was officially announced on 13 December. After a few weeks of disputes and confusion, a joint statement was issued by Colonel Derakhshani, the commander-in-chief of the Tabriz garrison, and Pishevari, who referred to himself throughout the negotiations as the "head of the Internal Government of Azerbaijan", to the effect that the surrender of the garrison would take place on the following conditions:

– All the guns and artillery of the garrison would be handed over to the internal government.
– The internal government would provide all the necessary measures for the safe withdrawal of any officers who did not wish to remain in

Azerbaijan.

– Those members of the military personnel who wished to co-operate with the new government would be accepted, provided they took an oath of allegiance to the internal government.[13]

The garrison at Urumiyeh held out longer before surrendering and there were even armed clashes between the soldiers in the garrison and the *Feda'iyan*. After the capitulation of the Tabriz garrison, the commander-in-chief of the Urumiyeh garrison and acting governor-general of western Azerbaijan, Colonel Zanganeh, actively resisted the Democrats. However, after a week of skirmishing, his military supplies were running low. Even more important was the continuous Soviet pressure. According to the British consul's account, although there was "no evidence that they were in action, ... there seemed little doubt that their presence contributed to the *Feda'iyan*'s victory".[14] When the Urumiyeh garrison finally did surrender to the autonomous government, the commander-in-chief, Colonel Zanganeh was arrested and transported to Tabriz where he stood trial and was sentenced to ten years imprisonment.[15] The surrender of the Urumiyeh garrison on 21 December 1945, removed the last barrier preventing the autonomous government from exercizing full authority throughout Azerbaijan.

The reaction of the Azerbaijani people to the establishment of the autonomous government was apprehensive rather than enthusiastic. While most of the reforms promised by the Azerbaijan National Government's program were welcomed by many Azerbaijanis,[16] the methods which the Democrats used to achieve them were alarming. However, whatever their views were towards the Democrats, the more politically conscious elements of the population were outspoken in their condemnation of the central government's behaviour. It was a widely held opinion that the central government was chiefly responsible for the recent events. As one eyewitness recorded:

> complaint was made by every native of the province with whom I talked, even those who are bitterly opposed to the Democrats and their present program. It was the unanimous opinion of all such that the central government has largely itself to blame for presenting the insurgents with a cause of just complaint.[17]

Therefore, when they boldly took the necessary steps to grasp power, the Democrats counted, at least in part, on the widespread discontent which the central government had aroused throughout the province – a tactic which is commonplace enough in the realm of politics.

While the Democrats set about consolidating the autonomous government's power throughout Azerbaijan, the central government in Tehran, besides categorically denouncing the ADF's undertakings, decided to appoint a prestigious, trusted figure to the post of governor-general of Azerbaijan, in the hope that this might convince the Democrats to give up their early gains and abandon their insurrection. Hakimi, who had come to power once again on 25 October 1945, following the fall of the Sadr government, by mid-November designated ex-Prime Minister Bayat as the new governor-general of Azerbaijan. The appointment of Bayat was intended by Hakimi as an opening gesture of goodwill in an attempt to end the hostility which prevailed between Tehran and Tabriz.

Upon arrival in Tabriz, Bayat, who "appeared concerned but was definitely optimistic", issued a memorandum indicating "his readiness to hear complaints and proposals to the central government and assuring the people of his conciliatory intentions".[18] However, Bayat's initial mood of optimism did not last long. After his second meeting with the ADF leaders Pishevari, Shabestari and Biriya, he confessed to the American envoy in the city that "he was no longer in control of the situation in any sense of the word and that a solution could only occur on the very highest level".[19] In view of this situation Bayat had no choice but to leave Azerbaijan. On 11 December, after almost a month of unsuccessful attempts, he admitted that his mission of reconciliation was a failure and left for Tehran.[20]

Bayat's remark that a solution to the problem could only be implemented "on the very highest level" was in fact an indirect indication that the central government's authority in Azerbaijan could only be re-established if the matter were dealt with on an international, rather than a national, level. Indeed, after the failure of Bayat's mission, Hakimi, in a "communication" to the American Ambassador in Tehran, did not hesitate to blame the Soviets for what had happened in Azerbaijan. In the said "communication" Hakimi asserted:

> The people of Azerbaijan already enjoy 'democratic rights' as provided in the Iranian Constitution and Supplementary Code.

> The insurgents have no popular support but have so terrorized the populace that local opposition is rendered difficult.

And he maintained that:

> If Iranian forces in Azerbaijan had enjoyed freedom of movement, they would easily have suppressed the uprising, and Soviet interference in the movement of Iranian security forces is in violation of the Tripartite Treaty.

He concluded by demanding that the Soviets:

> refrain from interfering in the internal affairs of Iran, and that they also withdraw their forces from the country.[21]

On 19 January, Hakimi asked the Iranian delegation to the United Nations to bring the matter before the Security Council. Hasan Taqizadeh, the well-known veteran Azerbaijani constitutionalist, and at the time the head of the Iranian delegation to the United Nations, submitted a letter to the acting secretary-general which called for "an investigation of Russian interference in Iran's internal affairs".[22] Five days later, in a bitter reply, Andrei Vyshinsky, the chief of the Soviet delegation to the United Nations, repudiated the substance of Taqizadeh's accusation, and, while justifying the Soviet military presence in Iran by referring to the Irano-Soviet Treaty of 1921[23] and the Tripartite Treaty of 1942, "denied that Soviet troops had any connection with events in Azerbaijan, and asserted that Iran's appeal was unfounded". To this he added that negotiations between the two governments had taken place "with satisfactory results".[24]

Obviously, Hakimi had not been a consulted party in the so-called negotiations to which Vyshinsky was referring. In fact, one of the main reasons for Hakimi's fall was his failure to establish negotiations with the Soviets. Ironically, the most likely candidate as a negotiator with the Soviets was Hakimi's rival, Qavam, who had already begun to lay the foundation for his future premiership,[25] and who proved to be the only one the Soviets were ready to negotiate with.[26]

On 21 January 1946, after some three months in office, Hakimi tendered his resignation to the *Majles*. His departure was welcomed by almost all parties in the country's political spectrum. Even the court supporters in the *Majles* who had never concealed their fear that if Hakimi resigned, Qavam, who had a reputation for not getting along with the shah, would stand a good chance of being elected prime minister, did not hesitate to withdraw their support from Hakimi during his last days in office. Hakimi's unpopularity is best demonstrated by the results of the routine election which followed, for the office of prime minister. The *Majles* arranged to hold elections for a new prime minister on 26 January, and despite his having resigned, Hakimi was once more nominated for the office, along with Qavam and Pirniya. Rather embarrassingly, Hakimi received only one vote out of the hundred and four votes cast, while Qavam came out on top with fifty-two, followed by Pirniya who received fifty-one votes.[27]

While, in the capital, the different political parties and the press were pleased at Hakimi's resignation, their reactions to the establishment of the National Government in Azerbaijan were varied. From late November 1945, the right-wing parties, some of which were aligned with the court, launched a campaign to discredit the activities of the Democrats in Azerbaijan. Their tactics followed the traditional pattern of defamation when they accused the Democrats of being:

> alien agents who could only cross the border and enter Azerbaijan because the central government exercised no control over the country's northern borders.

And the necessary corollary to the above assertion was:

> The so-called Azerbaijan National Government neither has any legitimacy, nor any popular support in the province, and it has merely been set up by unfriendly neighbours.

Furthermore, some right-wing delegates demanded that the central government:

> take every possible measure to bring the terrorizing activities of the Democrats to an end and to reinstate the long-standing prosperity of the province.[28]

On the other hand, contrary to what one might expect, the early reaction of the left-wing and liberal parties and the press to the

Democrats' actions in Azerbaijan was rather cool and stand-offish. Various newspapers associated with the Tudeh Party at first refrained from making direct comments on events in Azerbaijan. The Tudeh Party leadership was aware that there was a strong sense of discontent among the Party intellectuals with regard to the "self-sacrificing" act by which the Tudeh Party's Azerbaijan branch abolished itself in order to join the *Ferqeh*. [29] Consequently, the party leadership, at least publicly, showed little interest in the creation of the *Milli Majlis* and the *Milli Hükumat* in Azerbaijan. In referring to current events in Azerbaijan, the left-wing press limited its news coverage to citing from local Azerbaijani newspapers or from foreign radio broadcasts. A second factor contributing to the Tudeh Party's markedly cool attitude was that the Tudeh Party still considered itself a constitutionalist party committed to the maintenance of law and order throughout the country, and party leaders would have found it difficult, if not impossible, to justify legally all the actions undertaken by the Democrats in Azerbaijan.

Whereas the Tudeh Party, with its reputation as a left-wing, pro-Soviet party, found it difficult at first to formulate its position with regard to events in Azerbaijan, liberal elements in Iran were more outspoken in demonstrating their concern. They admitted that there were good reasons behind the present attempts in Azerbaijan. None the less, a newspaper like *Iran-e Ma*, which had close ties with the liberal factions in the *Majles*, was quick to manifest its criticism of the "destructive measures" taken by the Democrats in "challenging the central government" – this despite the ADF's "just demands".

In an article entitled "The Reactionary Camp Is Ready to Benefit from the *Azadikhahan*'s [Partisans of Liberty] Shortcomings", the newspaper *Iran-e Ma* began by praising the "Azerbaijani compatriots" as:

> always having been devoted to the liberty and glory of Iran, and now, due to their geographic location, being beyond the reach of the bayonets of tyranny, are enjoying some freedom of movement.

But the article goes on to warn the Azerbaijanis:

> not to forget their compatriots who are still living under bayonets in Fars or other parts of the country, and not to

commit certain mistakes which would cause great and serious problems for them.

Furthermore, the newspaper, while urging moderation, basically expressed sympathy and support for the Democrats:

> If the Azerbaijani Democrats do not go to extremes in insisting on the language issue and the question of autonomy (which, after all, is provided for in the articles of the Constitutional Code concerning the provincial and district councils), then they will surely win the sympathy of almost eighty per cent of the Iranian people.[30]

When news of the establishment of the National Government reached Tehran, once again *Iran-e Ma* displayed its enthusiastic support, this time in the following terms:

> The question of Azerbaijan and the movement which has come into being and established itself there is a question which will constitute one of the distinguished phases of Iran's history. The enemies of this movement and members of the ruling clique and reactionary elements may say and do whatever they wish. None the less, history will confirm the truth that the present day movement in Azerbaijan is a glorious movement which, despite any faults or shortcomings it may have, will play the chief role in assuring the comfort and happiness of the deprived and unfortunate classes of Iran and in bringing society in Iran closer to true freedom and independence and closer to the civilization of present day humanity.[31]

With regard to developments in Azerbaijan, Mosaddeq, who at this time represented a loose parliamentary coalition of thirty deputies known as the *Fraksiyon-e Monfaredin* (the Caucus of Individuals),[32] presented his reaction before the *Majles* in no uncertain terms. After reviewing a long list of complaints he had received from different groups in Azerbaijan to illustrate the causes of the Democrats' revolt, Mosaddeq informed the *Majles* at great length of his disapproval of the way events were progressing in Azerbaijan:

I do not maintain that an autonomous state does not exist in some countries like the United States and Switzerland, but I maintain that an autonomous state must be formed by a general referendum. Today our Constitutional Code does not allow such a state. It is possible to hold a referendum. If the nation so votes, then Iran, like the United States and Switzerland, may become a federation. It is not possible to say that in one country one part is federal and another part is the central government. The Constitutional Code is a social contract (*contrat collectif*). As long as this *contrat collectif* is not amended or abolished, it is enforceable. I myself am not at all opposed to Iran becoming a federated state. Perhaps it would be better to have a federated state in which every province had a degree of internal autonomy and would then coordinate with the central government, while the central government dealt with international relations. However, any change, even a partial change, to the Constitutional Code must be done by means of a general referendum.[33]

Meanwhile, back in Azerbaijan the situation appeared to be encouraging for the Democrats. The reservations or outright condemnation of politicians in Tehran were not publicized in the highly controlled local press. The autonomous government was now ready to exercise its newly won executive powers.

The Days of Optimism

On the eve of the new year, 1946, the Democrats had every reason to believe that a new era was about to begin, an era in which they would be unhampered in their exercise of absolute power in Azerbaijan. Generally speaking, the people of the province were tired of the economic and political instability they had experienced over the previous four years. Moreover, there was a prevalent feeling that Azerbaijan's specific needs had been neglected by the central government based in Tehran. People longed for a series of far-reaching reforms which they hoped would put an end to political stagnation and the economic recession. As for any role the central government could

play in fulfilling these local aspirations, it was generally perceived that
the central government was impotent to extend its power beyond the
periphery of the capital, while the *Majles* was too divided to be able to
agree on co-ordinated national policies. Furthermore, the shah appeared
to be totally ineffective. He was described as being "so accustomed to
taking action on the advice of others, that it [was] hard [for him] to
make an independent decision".[34]

Also contributing to this atmosphere of optimism among the
Democrats was the fact that they felt that they enjoyed, on the international level, the support of the "strongest power on the Asian-European
Continents".[35]   By the end of World War II, the Red Army was
installed all over Europe from Berlin to Sofia, as well as being in
control of Manchuria and North Korea in the far east. The Soviet Union
seemed, more than ever, committed to change the pre-war political map
of the world, especially in Europe, and thus to end the era in which
there was "socialism in one country only". It therefore came as no
surprise that when commenting on the establishment of the National
Government in Azerbaijan, the Soviet Union declared that it had been
done:

> in accordance with the wishes and aspirations of the
> Azerbaijani people.[36]

During these early days of optimism within the autonomous
government, besides directing their attention to winning greater popular
support on the home front, the Democrats also had to concern themselves with the opposition being generated by the government in
Tehran.

In the days before he assumed the office of prime minister, Qavam
had presented an image of himself as the only candidate for the
premiership who was capable of finding a solution to the mounting
crisis within the country. And the most important of all the problems
facing Iran at the time was "the crisis of Azerbaijan". In a political
context where there was virtually no chance whatsoever of co-operation
between the *Dowlat* (State) and the hopelessly divided *Majles*, the only
way to live up to such an image and effectively tackle the crisis was to
eliminate the *Majles*.

Conveniently, the official term of the Fourteenth *Majles* was due to
come to a close in mid-March 1946. However, there was a group of

deputies in the *Majles* who were in favour of extending the closure date of the existing *Majles*. This group, headed by Seyyed Zia Tabataba'i, was prepared to take every possible measure to accomplish their aim, whereas the other factions within the *Majles*, especially the Tudeh caucus, were strongly opposed to Seyyed Zia and his supporters.

The Tudeh Party whole-heartedly welcomed Qavam as prime minister and described him as "the last alternative for carrying out a peaceful solution to the country's crisis".[37] Confident that it would win more seats for its deputies in the next *Majles*, the Tudeh Party launched a vigorous campaign to defeat Seyyed Zia's plan to prolong the current *Majles*. Whatever different motives the Tudeh Party may have had, it was ultimately successful in consolidating support for the Prime Minister. Following a series of scandalous demonstrations, meetings and even occasional street fighting, the plan for prolonging the *Majles* was defeated and on 11 March 1946 the Fourteenth *Majles* was officially dissolved.[38]

While the Tudeh Party proved successful on the home front in mustering political support for Qavam, the latter soon set about establishing direct negotiations with the Soviet Union with the intention of "resolving the problems which have arisen in the relations between the two countries".[39] On 19 February 1946, Qavam began his nineteen day visit to Moscow. Although, on the eve of his return to Iran, it seemed that Qavam's visit to the Soviet Union had been a total failure, in early memoranda exchanged during negotiations, both parties set forth what would be the necessary pre-conditions for any further negotiations. On the question of Azerbaijan, the Iranian delegation stated its position in unambiguous terms:

> The province of Azerbaijan always was and still is an inseparable part of Iran and the Turkish language has never been more than a local language. Whatever exists in the way of culture and literature in Azerbaijan, from olden times until now, has been in the Persian language. In Azerbaijan poets, men of letters, all administrations and books, have recognized Persian as their mother tongue. Therefore, maintaining Iran's independence and territorial integrity depends on those people who have undertaken actions detrimental to the independence and territorial integrity of Iran desisting from this way of thinking. It is clear that the state will undertake every form

of assistance and self-sacrifice for the sake of reforms in Azerbaijan, and will adopt every possible reformatory proposal to improve the administration of the province, and will make an adequate effort to apply the law concerning the provincial and district councils and attend to the needs of the people in Azerbaijan.[40]

The Soviet response to the Iranian government's stated position with regard to Azerbaijan was formulated with caution and restraint. While the Soviets recognized that any political developments in Azerbaijan were clearly part of Iran's "internal affairs" and as such under the jurisdiction of the Iranian government, they did not hesitate to propose some changes in the province. However, the Soviet proposals, as it turned out, were more moderate than what might have been expected:

> With regard to Iranian Azerbaijan, which is an internal matter and a concern of the state of Iran, it is recommended that arrangements be made to give full attention to carrying out social, economic and cultural reforms in the province. The name of the National Assembly should be changed to the provincial and district council, and the local prime minister of Azerbaijan should be the provincial governor of the central government of Iran. Twenty-five percent of the local revenues should be given to the central government and the rest should be spent on economic, social and cultural reforms there in the province. There should be no local Ministry of War and Ministry of Foreign Affairs but these two ministries should belong to the area of competence of the central government.[41]

The position adopted by the Soviets on Azerbaijan was characterized by two opposite tendencies. On the one hand, there was a clear reluctance to become directly involved in Iran's internal affairs. On the other hand, the Soviets did not conceal their real concern over future political developments in Azerbaijan. Soviet reluctance to become involved in Iran can best be understood against the backdrop of the mounting international pressure being brought to bear on the Soviet Union because of the degree of her involvement in Europe. However, the Soviets' concern for future developments in Iranian Azerbaijan may be traced to the power-sharing structure in the Soviet Union's Communist Party. The Baqirov caucus was, at the time, able to exert considerable influence within the Soviet Communist Party. Baqirov, the First Secretary of the Communist Party of Soviet Azerbaijan, had frequently displayed serious interest in developments in Iranian Azerbaijan. Moreover, Baqirov's attitude had gradually evolved beyond the early stage of aiming at establishing an autonomous government in Azerbaijan.

Besides the question of autonomy in Azerbaijan, there were two other issues concerning which Qavam had to negotiate with the Soviet authorities, namely the longstanding demand on the part of the Soviets for an oil concession in the north of Iran, and the crucial issue of Soviet military withdrawal from Iran. Concerning the oil concession, both parties soon agreed to settle for a compromise which was to consist of the formation of a Iranian-Soviet joint-stock company. However, the question of Soviet military withdrawal proved to pose a more complex problem.

Following the invasion of Iran by Allied forces (British and the Soviet) in August 1941, a Tripartite Treaty of Alliance was signed by Britain, the Soviet Union and Iran in January 1942. According to Article Five of this Treaty:

> Allied armed forces shall be withdrawn from Iranian territory not later than six months after all hostilities between the Allied powers and Germany and her associates have been suspended by the conclusion of an armistice or armistices or on conclusion of peace between them, whichever date is earlier.[42]

In view of the capitulation of the Third Reich on 7 May 1945, and the Japanese surrender on 2 September of the same year, the six-month interval allowed for the Allies' military withdrawal was due to run out on 2 March 1946. Whereas the United States and Britain pulled their troops out of Iran before the completion of the set time limit,[43] on 1 March Moscow Radio announced that Soviet troops would evacuate certain designated areas (Khorasan, Shahrud and Semnan) by the following day, but that other regions of northern Iran would remain under occupation until the local political situation had been clarified.[44]

When the Soviets announced that they would only be withdrawing part of their occupying forces from Iran, there was a great uproar among Iranian politicians. Mosaddeq, in a speech he gave before the *Majles*, declared that: "The issue of evacuation is a closed matter and the Iranian government has no right to negotiate concerning that."[45]

Mosaddeq's passionate speech on the issue of Soviet military withdrawal, as was to be expected, was received by the great majority in
the *Majles*, whether conservatives or liberals, with "an unusual outburst
of applause and excitement". Consequently, Qavam, who was still
engaged in negotiations with the Soviets in Moscow, felt that the stand
he was taking was reinforced by the wide spectrum of political support
he could count on in Iran.[46]

On his return to Iran, while waiting for the Soviets to formulate their
final proposals, Qavam continued the policy of his predecessors and
exerted pressure on the Soviet Union by bringing the dispute before the
eyes of the international community. On 18 March, Hoseyn 'Ala, who
was closely associated with the shah's court and now the head of the
Iranian delegation to the United Nations, presented Iran's second formal
complaint to the Security Council.[47] In response, Andrei Gromyko, the
Soviet Ambassador to the United Nations, asked the Security Council
to postpone treating the question until 10 April, since "preparations
were underway to deal with the matter through the ordinary channels".
In his recently published memoirs, Andrei Gromyko recalls chairing the
Soviet delegation to the United Nations when the question of Soviet
troop withdrawals from Iran was on the agenda and comments:

> At the end of the war, the USSR felt it could not withdraw its
> troops before a number of questions had been settled, princi-
> pally, the continued existence of British bases in Iraq and
> India, and the large number of US bases around the perimeter
> of our frontier, to say nothing of British naval forces in the
> Persian Gulf. Therefore, the USSR declared it would keep its
> troops in Iran for the time being.
>
> A murky wave of anti-Soviet feeling at once rose up and a
> question was tabled at the Security Council - which was what
> Washington and London wanted. I received the following
> instructions from Moscow: If the question is tabled, say that
> our troops are being kept in Iran because of unforeseeable
> circumstances.[48]

The expression "ordinary channels" which Gromyko had employed was
a reference to the joint communiqué that had been signed in Moscow
before Qavam's departure. According to this communiqué, "the
negotiations had been conducted in a spirit of friendship" and

negotiations "would be continued through the newly appointed Soviet Ambassador to Iran".[49]

On 20 March 1946, Sadchikov arrived in Tehran with a package of proposals. Two weeks later, on 4 April, a joint proclamation was published by Prime Minister Qavam and the Soviet ambassador, announcing that the following points had been agreed upon:

– The Red Army, which had begun withdrawing its troops on 24 March 1946, would complete its with-drawal within one and a half months.

– An agreement for the formation of a joint IranoSoviet oil company would be presented to the Fifteenth *Majles* for ratification, no later than seven months after 24 March.

– The problems concerning Azerbaijan being an internal Iranian matter, conciliatory arrangements would be made between the Iranian government and the *ahali* of Azerbaijan, with the intention of carrying out reforms in accordance with existing Iranian law and in a spirit of goodwill.[50]

The agreements reached on 4 April proved to be a milestone in the Iranian government's attempts to deal with the Azerbaijan question. Qavam had made a concession to the Soviets which the as yet non-existent Fifteenth *Majles* was supposed to guarantee. In return for this, the central government had won the Soviet Union's acknowledgement that the problems relating to Azerbaijan were "an internal Iranian matter". Indeed, the Soviets appeared to be offering Qavam exactly what he needed to accomplish his "long march" on the road to Azerbaijan.

On 22 April, the Iranian government published its proclamation along with the Council of Ministers' "decision on Azerbaijan". The proclamation stated:

> In accordance with the principles of the Supplement to the Constitutional Code concerning the provincial and district councils in Azerbaijan:
> – The heads of agriculture, commerce, industry, transportation, culture, health, the police, the Justice Department, and finance will be elected by the provincial and district councils, and in conformity with regulations their official authority will be issued by the government in Tehran.

– The designation of the governor, with due account being taken of the views of the provincial councils, will rest with the government, and the appointment of commanders of the armed forces and the gendarmerie will be carried out by the government.

– The official language of Azerbaijan, like other parts of the country, will be Persian, and the business of local administrative offices and the business of the Justice Department will be carried out in Persian and Azerbaijani. However, teaching in the five classes of elementary school will be carried out in Azerbaijani.

– When the taxes and credits of the country's budget are fixed, the government, with regard to Azerbaijan, will take into consideration the welfare and prosperity of the cities and improvements affecting cultural affairs, health, etc.

– The activities of democratic organizations in Azerbaijan, as well as unions, etc., like in the other parts of the country, will be free.

– With regard to supporters and employees of the autonomous government of Azerbaijan, there will be no penalties applied to them because of their participation in the democratic movement in the past.

– It is agreed that there will be an increase in the number of Azerbaijan's parliamentary representatives in accordance with the province's real population. At the beginning of the fifteenth legislative session, the necessary proposal with regard to this matter will be presented to the *Majles*, and when it is approved, the numerical deficiency will be made up by elections for that same session.[51]

After publishing the above proclamation the central government took the initiative to invite a delegation from Azerbaijan to Tehran in order to take "the preliminary steps towards the final settlement of the dispute concerning Azerbaijan". Subsequently, on 28 April 1946, a seven- man delegation of Democrats, headed by Pishevari, arrived at Qaleh Morghi airport in Tehran with the intention of beginning the first official talks with the central government.[52]

While conservative circles in Tehran were very sceptical of Qavam's way of handling the problems concerning Azerbaijan, the left-wing and liberal caucuses considered his negotiated settlements to be a "nation-wide victory" in their "long-standing struggle to establish democracy in Iran". In an editorial article entitled "Establishing Democracy Is the Answer to the Azerbaijan Question", *Zafar* (Victory), the newspaper of the most important labour union in Iran, urged the government to apply the same measures it was proposing to carry out in Azerbaijan to the rest of the country:

> We are partisans of the non-partitioning of our country and wish to see all our fellow countrymen enjoying peace and prosperity while clasped in the embrace of democracy. Therefore, as every Iranian thinks, whether he is from Azerbaijan or from Kerman, and as the leaders of the *Ferqeh-e Democrat* have repeatedly declared, we must be united and as one, and make the whole of Iran into a true constitutional country.[53]

As one might expect, the Tudeh Party's reaction was broadly similar to that expressed by the labour union in *Zafar*. Anvar Khameh'i, in an editorial in *Rahbar*, while insisting that the Azerbaijanis be referred to as *mardom* or *ahali* (people) and not as a *mellat* (nation), presented the Tudeh Party's views on the government's proclamation. His main criticisms were, firstly, that the government had not provided any executive structures which would guarantee that its proposed reforms would be carried out; and secondly, that the government had ignored the existence of a People's Army in Azerbaijan and failed to provide for its protection.[54] Despite these negative points, in order to put more pressure on the government, three days later Khalil Maleki, in another editorial in the same newspaper, adopted a provocative stance and called upon all Iranians to support their Azerbaijani compatriots in their struggle to apply the Constitutional Code in Iran:

> The present situation in Azerbaijan is the result and conclusion of a widespread national and democratic mass movement which has come into existence in the context of a serious, long-term struggle. The people of Azerbaijan, as a result of this united struggle and the organizing of men of progress within a powerful national party, have been able to win those rights which the spirit of the Constitution and the Constitutional Code of Iran demands. If [other] provinces and

districts wish to take Azerbaijan as their model, they must travel down this very same road.[55]

In contrast to the Tudeh Party's radical stance, the Iranian liberals adopted a rather moderate and cautious attitude towards the government's political manoeuvres in Azerbaijan. In its official organ, *Jebheh* (The Front), *Hezb-e Iran* (the Party of Iran), which had the reputation of being closely associated with the Mosaddeq faction within the *Majles*, expressed its appreciation of the fact that Qavam's government represented "the will of the people" and consequently welcomed his proclamation dealing with the Azerbaijan question. However, the Party of Iran did not conceal its concern for the possible effects which the government's concessions to autonomy might have on the future political development of Iran:

> A national government means that a nation has the right to participate in shaping its destiny by appointing representatives to the national assembly and the provincial councils. However, an autonomous government and separation from the centre in such a form that a province is in practice not under the authority of the centre, is not in the country's interest because Iran is a small country and a nation with a small population. If every one of her provinces, on the basis of having a local language and local customs, were to form an autonomous government, such action would, in my opinion, not be to the country's advantage.[56]

Nonetheless, what both the left and the liberals had in common with regard to Qavam's proposed package of reforms was a desire to see these reforms applied throughout the whole country.[57]

Meanwhile, in Azerbaijan itself the autonomous government was fully absorbed in dealing with local matters, such as mobilizing the peasants to take part in the first National Conference,[58] organizing supplementary military forces to repulse the continuous attacks of the Iranian army and the tribal militia on the eastern front,[59] and endeavouring to remove the road blockade which the central government had set up just outside Zanjan to stop the flow of trade between Tehran and Tabriz.[60] As for Qavam's proclamation, to begin with it did not receive much attention locally. In fact, it was not even published in the ADF's official newspaper *Azerbaijan*. What was noticeable, however, was a rather sudden shift of emphasis in the Democrats' political rhetoric. They adopted a softer, less absolute tone, and presented their struggle in the light of the struggle of the *mellat-e Iran* (the nation of Iran) for democracy:

> Azerbaijan is the standard-bearer for the whole nation of Iran. The nation of Iran knows that its freedom is bound to the freedom of Azerbaijan.[61]

An Interlude of Reforms

By way of winning popular support in Azerbaijan, the *Milli Hükumat* set about putting into effect a series of reforms, many of which the ADF had promised in its early program. The most important of these were land reforms.

According to estimates produced by the Democrats, until December 1945 some 80 per cent of the total of productive land in Azerbaijan was owned by large-scale landowners, while 12 per cent belonged to *khaleseh* (the government estates). The remaining 8 per cent of the land was owned by small-scale landlords.[62] On 16 February 1946, the Presidium of the National Assembly of Azerbaijan, acting on behalf of the Assembly, passed two bills specifically aimed at appeasing the landless peasants. According to the first bill, all lands and waters (rivers, springs and *qanats*) of those landowners would be confiscated:

– who had fought to oppose Azerbaijan attaining its freedom or fought against the establishment of the National Government of Azerbaijan, whether the said person is an Azerbaijani or not.
– who had left Azerbaijan for Tehran or elsewhere in order to take part in propaganda directed at undermining Azerbaijan's freedom and the National Government of Azerbaijan.
– The lands confiscated for the above reasons were to be distributed among the poor peasants.[63]

The second land reform bill which was passed concerned the distribution of the *khaleseh* land. The bill stipulated that:

All lands and water rights (rivers, springs and *qanats*) owned
by the government will be donated to the peasants who live
on those lands. Furthermore, all the meadows on these lands
will be for the communal use of all the inhabitants.[64]

As a result of implementing these two bills, the land of 437 villages
which had formerly been owned by individual landlords, together with
that of another 373 villages which had belonged to the government, was
– at least on paper – distributed among more than one million peasants.
In this manner, a total of 380,000 hectares of land was designated to be
given free of charge to new peasant owners. Consequently, by the
autonomous government's enacting these bills every family in
Azerbaijan would supposedly come to possess three to five hectares of
land.[65]

Another important bill brought in by the autonomous government
aimed at reforming the old established method of share cropping. In
Iran, share cropping was traditionally based on a system of five *nasaq*
(an "input" unit). The five input units consisted of land, water, labour,
seed and oxen, and the crop, once harvested, was divided up between
the peasant and the landlord according to the number of *nasaq* each of
them had contributed. However, in practice, due to his providing land,
water, seeds and sometimes even the oxen, the landlord usually claimed
three to four of the five shares of the crop. The new bill which the
Democrats passed changed the system. Instead of a five share system,
the new system was based on seven shares. Water no longer counted as
a share, whereas labour was made equal to three shares. The oxen now
counted as two shares and the seed and the land counted as one share
each. This way the minimum share of the crop guaranteed to the
peasant rose from 20 per cent to 43 per cent.[66]

One issue which was part of the Democrats' original program and
which still maintained its momentum was the importance they had
accorded to the question of the Azerbaijani language and the place it
should occupy in the province's education system. One of the early bills
passed by the *Milli Hükumat* declared that the Azerbaijani language was
not only to be the "official state language" in Azerbaijan, but that the
use of any languages other than Azerbaijani in the "official local administration", as well as for "education and trade", was "strictly
forbidden".[67] A decree "was issued by the Minister of Culture for
Azerbaijan" which stipulated that a "special commission" was to be

appointed whose task would be to provide the necessary school books in the Azerbaijani language.[68]

Besides taking measures to assure the Azerbaijanis that they had a prosperous future to look forward to, the autonomous government, like any new government born of an insurrection, was desperately concerned to present itself as a legitimate government with popular support. To this end, the *Milli Hükumat* introduced a series of electoral reforms to encourage more people to participate directly in day-to-day politics.

As early as 8 January, 1946, the National Assembly of Azerbaijan passed bills which regulated the electoral procedure affecting the provincial, district, regional and municipal councils.[69] According to these bills, for the first time in Iranian history, women had the right to stand for office in an election. After these bills were passed, a vigorous propaganda campaign was launched by the autonomous government which urged all Azerbaijanis "to participate in determining their destiny by going to the ballot box". According to Pishevari, hundreds of thousands of voters took part in the ensuing elections which went on for ten days.[70] None the less, Robert Rossow, the American vice-consul in Tabriz, commented that this enormous turn-out of voters was "utterly meaningless".[71] Moreover, he characterized the proceedings as a "corrupt election" which, far from being an innovation of the Democrats, was "an old Persian custom".[72]

Another measure which the Democrats took in order to win the support of the religious elements was to lift the ban on certain religious practices which had been forbidden since the early days of Reza Shah's assuming the imperial crown. These practices included such popular traditional religious customs as *Sineh-zani* (beating the breast) *Zangirzani* (self-flagellation), *Qameh-zani* (wounding oneself with a dagger) and the *Ta'ziyeh* (performance of a religious drama), especially during the mourning procession of *Muharram*, the month of Imam Hoseyn's martyrdom. Moreover, the right of women to wear the veil, which Reza Shah had made illegal in the 1930s, was once more guaranteed. The American press attaché, who was visiting Tabriz at this time, noted in one of his reports that:

> It is of corollary interest to note that the Democrats are encouraging the free return to religious celebrations and customs. At the present time they are taking part in the Muharram mourning demonstration.[73]

The Democrats' stand on religious tolerance was clearly a gesture on their part to appease the religious hierarchy which had never concealed its dislike of the Democrats. Nevertheless, by recruiting a few mullahs and guaranteeing that traditional religious practice would be unhampered under the autonomous government, the Democrats attempted to open the door to compromise with the theologians.[74]

Having inaugurated these changes and reforms, the Democrats desperately needed a period of political calm and stability in order to implement their program. On the other hand, what was puzzling to many ordinary Azerbaijanis at the time was the degree of social and economic upheaval which this experiment in reform was causing. In short, they were shocked at the price they were being forced to pay to put their ideals into practice.

The Kurdish Challenge

Almost simultaneously with the activities of the Azerbaijani Democrats, the Iranian Kurds launched their own campaign for establishing an autonomous state in Iranian Kurdistan.[75] In view of the deeply rooted tribal nature of society in the region, the campaign for autonomy in Kurdistan was based more on ethno-tribal loyalties than a purely ethnic identity as in Azerbaijan. Consequently, the somewhat tribal nature of the Kurdish movement, if anything, added to the already aggravated relations between the Kurds and the Azerbaijanis.

Azerbaijan and Kurdistan being neighbouring provinces, there had occasionally been some incidents of ethnic conflict between the two peoples, especially around the problem of landownership in regions where the two communities lived side by side. Likewise, in the past, religious differences between the two communities, the Azerbaijanis being Shi'ites, and the Kurds Sunni Muslims, had contributed towards exacerbating these conflicts.

Following the formation of the Democrat Party of Kurdistan on 25 August 1945,[76] the Kurdish Democrats went on to publish a manifesto which contained seven articles. Article 6, it is interesting to note, state that:

> The Democrat Party of Kurdistan will make efforts to establish complete fraternity with the people of Azerbaijan and the minorities living there.[77]

The first official step the Kurdish Democrats took to display their "fraternity" with their Azerbaijani fellow Democrats was to send a Kurdish delegate to be present at a ceremony which was held in Tabriz on 3 September 1945, to celebrate the "merger" of the Tudeh Party with the ADF.[78] Likewise, on the very same date a separate delegation was sent to Tabriz to attend the official opening of the National Assembly of Azerbaijan. However, to their great disappointment the Kurdish delegates found that they were regarded as deputies representing a district within the province of Azerbaijan, rather than a delegation from a friendly neighbouring province.[79] Upon their return to Mahabad, the Kurdish Democrats, being discontent with the actions of the Azerbaijani Democrats, launched a new, vigorous campaign to set up their own Kurdish autonomous government. On 22 January 1946, the Kurdish autonomous government was officially established.

Moreover, relations between the autonomous government of Azerbaijan and the autonomous regime in Kurdistan, which paradoxically called itself the Republic of Kurdistan, were not to remain fraternal for long.[80] Both parties laid claim to areas with mixed populations to the west and south-west of Lake Urumiyeh. By mid-February 1946, tension between the two neighbouring provinces was close to breaking-point and it was feared that an armed conflict would take place.[81] However, thanks to Soviet mediation both sides agreed to lay down their arms and seek a peaceful solution to their problems through negotiation.[82]

On 23 April 1946, after a series of negotiations, a Treaty of Friendship and Alliance was signed by high-ranking representatives of "the National Governments of Azerbaijan and Kurdistan". According to the terms of this rather vague agreement, which had obviously been signed under pressure from the Soviets, both sides, having declared their "willingness to co-operate in seeking peace and prosperity in the region", acknowledged that there were minority groups of Azerbaijanis in Kurdistan and groups of Kurds in Azerbaijan. The treaty called on both regimes to consider the areas with minority enclaves as self-ruling.[83] However, the most important aspect of the treaty did not concern relations between Kurds and Azerbaijanis but both parties' relations with the central government. Out of fear that Qavam would adopt a policy of "divide and rule", the Treaty of Friendship and Alliance called for both autonomous governments to form a joint delegation to undertake future negotiations with Tehran.[84]

The Days of Pessimism

The Democrats' mission to Tehran participated in negotiations which lasted for two weeks. In a speech delivered at Tabriz airport on the occasion of his departure for Tehran, Pishevari warned the central government in militant words:

> No one will be able to take away from us the freedom which has been won by force of arms by the *Feda'iyan*. At that time we could have come to Tehran and abolished the reactionary government of Tehran in order to free the whole of Iran. But international circumstances caused Azerbaijan to refrain from this.[85]

However, when Pishevari met with the government authorities in Tehran and discussions began concerning Azerbaijan's specific problems, he soon came to realize that he had greatly underestimated the intensity of Tehran's opposition to all "centrifugal" tendencies. Wherever such tendencies arose in the country and whatever shape and form they took, the central government was determined to fight tooth and nail to preserve its overriding authority which it believed was indispensable to guarantee Iran's survival as a sovereign nation.

The proposals put forward by the Democrats, which consisted of thirty-three articles, sought to establish powers for the government in Azerbaijan which went far beyond what, by anyone's definition, could rightly be called the powers of an autonomous region.[86] The Democrats aimed at making Azerbaijan a sovereign state within Iran, with the autonomous government being in charge of all regional affairs, including the running of the locally based army. The central government would only deal with foreign relations. And the Democrats justified these demands by referring to the Atlantic Charter rather than the Iranian Constitutional Code.[87]

On the other hand, the central government, to begin with, negotiated on the basis of its proclamation concerning Azerbaijan which Qavam had signed,[88] and which has been described above. However, early on in the negotiations the government accepted some of the Democrats' demands, in particular, certain of the land reforms, as well as the increase of their military forces in Azerbaijan. In exchange, the Democrats significantly modified their position, more or less limiting their demands to what was provided for by the Constitutional Code. Likewise, they agreed to call the National Assembly the Provincial Council of Azerbaijan, and to change the name of the Council of Ministers to the Council of Directors, and the Local Ministers were renamed the Local Directors of the Governmental Departments. Nonetheless, the two obstacles to a final settlement were the questions of land reform and military reorganization in the province.

When, on 10 May, Qavam took a preliminary draft of an agreement before his cabinet, the majority of the ministers voted against it and urged the prime minister to stand by the stipulations in his previously published proclamation. A few days later, the Democrats' mission was informed that: "Irresponsible elements in the government and the commander-in-chief of the country's armed forces [a reference to the shah] were to blame for the failure of the negotiations, since they had taken every possible measure to frustrate the government's efforts to settle the dispute."[89]

In the view of the Democrats, the land reforms proposed by the autonomous government in Azerbaijan, and in particular the recent distribution of lands belonging to the government and in some cases to private landlords, were already settled and could not be reversed. All that remained was for the central government to ratify the reform bills which dealt with this issue. However, the government position on this question was two-fold. It approved of government lands being distributed among the peasants who lived on them but, where private landlords' land was concerned, it maintained that the Fifteenth *Majles* (yet to be formed) should have the jurisdiction to decide the matter. As for building up the military in Azerbaijan, the central government was willing to accept the *Feda'iyan* as having parallel military functions alongside the country's national army, the gendarmerie and the police force. The Democrats, on the other hand, refused to allow the old armed forces back into the province unless a specific set of reforms was first carried out within the army's structure.[90]

By 13 May 1946, it was clear that the negotiations had ended in failure. Nevertheless, the central government soon appointed a mission to Tabriz to resume negotiations with the Democrats. The failure of the Democrats' mission to Tehran marked an important stage in the history of the autonomous government of Azerbaijan, a stage which heralded a growing atmosphere of complication and uncertainty. It was now six months since the Azerbaijani Democrats had established their autonomous government and already they were becoming aware that the golden period of their exercising absolute power in the province was coming to an end, and they were about to enter upon a new, more precarious phase of political life.

On the local level in Azerbaijan itself, the Democrats were faced with an anxious, impetuous population which, while appreciating the reforms promised by the autonomous government and being "materially somewhat better off than they were seven months earlier",[91] was gradually showing signs of being alienated by what some eyewitnesses took to be "the more harsh and unpopular actions of the Democrats".[92]

On the national level, they had to reckon with a central government which had an adequate understanding of how to juggle national as well as international political forces, and was constantly on the look-out to take advantage of any opportunity to disarm its political rivals.

The Democrats also had to manage with less direct encouragement and support from the Soviets who were gradually realizing where their international priorities lay and were prepared to make some concessions as the price to be paid for their presence in Eastern Europe.

By mid-1946, the Soviet Union realized that it could not sustain its early post-war policy in the Middle East in general and in Iran in particular. If, in the spring of 1946, the Soviets were gazing on the Middle east "as an artichoke whose leaves are to be eaten one by one",[93] by the summer of that year they were on the point of abandoning the artichoke to other superpowers and limiting themselves to what was on their plate in Eastern Europe. Likewise, whereas previously politics in Tehran had been dominated by staunch pro-British politicians, by the end of 1945 figures such as Qavam and Firuz, who were on good terms with the Soviets, were shaping the policies of the central government. This new state of affairs made it all the easier for the Soviets to revise their attitude towards the autonomous government of Azerbaijan.

Almost one month after the failure of the first round of talks between the Iranian government and the Azerbaijani Democrats, through the mediation and indeed the pressure of Sadchikov, the Soviet ambassador to Tehran, the second round of negotiations was resumed on 11 June 1946, in Tabriz. The central government's delegation was headed by Mozaffar Firuz, the under-secretary to the prime minister, and otherwise consisted of two high ranking army officers and seven senior civil servants. At the other end of the negotiating table were Pishevari, Shabestari, Jahanshahlu Afshar and Mohammad Qazi, the head of the Kurdish autonomous government.[94]

Aware that the government had been unsuccessful at reaching an agreement during the first round of negotiations with the Democrats because of the opposition of pro-court elements in the cabinet, the newly appointed envoys delayed their departure for Tabriz until they had secured the approval of the entire cabinet. Thus, anticipating that no difficulties would be raised by the *Majles* and that the court would abstain, if only temporarily, from interfering, Qavam launched his second campaign to reach a satisfactory settlement with regard to the question of Azerbaijan.

Indeed, the process of negotiation did not take long and on the eve of 13 June 1946, a final agreement between the *Dowlat* (State) and the *Azerbaijan Numayandalari* (the Representatives of Azerbaijan) was announced. The next day, a new agreement was drawn up, based on the preliminary agreement which had been reached a month earlier in Tehran. It is interesting to note that the document bore the seals of Mozaffar Firuz and Pishevari, though they both abstained from using their official government titles which presumably might have provoked disagreement as to a mutually acceptable terminology.[95]

Also noteworthy, with regard to the agreement, is what one might call Qavam's by now familiar *inshallah* (if God wills) policy, which in the context of Iranian culture is an expression used to denote the vaguest of promises. Qavam had successfully employed the same tactic when negotiating with the Soviets. In exchange for their immediate military withdrawal from Iran, he promised to raise the question of an oil concession before the Fifteenth *Majles* (as yet unformed) and, *inshallah*, the *Majles* would grant the concession to the Soviets. Now in negotiating a treaty with the Azerbaijani Democrats, whenever he realized that his Azerbaijani counterparts would not make a compromise, he deferred the disputed point, indicating that it would be dealt with in some unspecified future negotiations.

With regard to land reform, the central government maintained its previous stance. According to the Agreement, which contained fifteen articles, the central government approved of distributing government lands among the peasants living on them; but when it came to the private lands expropriated by the autonomous government, "proper compensation" would have to be given to the original landlords. And as for the other touchy point in the negotiations, the reorganization of the military, the agreement's provision was no more definite than that "a joint commission consisting of representatives of the central government and the provincial councils" would be appointed to study the future function of the local armed forces and consider a possible merging of the *Feda'iyan* with the former gendarmerie of Azerbaijan.

The reaction of many Democrats to the agreement, rather than being enthusiastic, was that too many concessions had been made, while there were some who even considered the agreement to be a capitulation. In a "historical address" broadcast by Tabriz Radio, Pishevari attempted to play down the idea that there had been any form of capitulation on the part of the Democrats. None the less, it was apparent that he was concerned about the criticism which the agreement would inevitably evoke among ADF supporters, as well as his opponents:

> At present, all manner of talk and false rumours exists. There are those who say Mr Qavam os-Saltaneh has tricked the Democrats. Others attempt to maintain that Mr Qavam os-Saltaneh, in order to preserve his government, threw himself at the feet of the Democrats and sought refuge in Azerbaijan. We ought not to pay the least attention to these words. Neither has Mr Qavam os-Saltaneh put one over on us, nor are we out to trick him. All this talk is sheer nonsense! There are even those who have interpreted the signing of a treaty on our part as an act of capitulation. Some, perhaps in order to show off, also claim to have conquered Azerbaijan. For our part, we laugh at these statements and consider those who make them to be fools. Here no one has surrendered to anyone, and, furthermore, no one has conquered Azerbaijan.[96]

Having concluded the agreement, there was nothing else left for the autonomous government to do but adapt itself to the new state of affairs and resign itself to being a provincial administration under the central government. Consequently, the *Milli Majlis*, with Shabestari as its president,[97] changed its name to the "Provincial Council of Azerbaijan". Likewise, the old ministers of the autonomous government were now considered as heads of the local departments of the central government.[98] Meanwhile, in a proclamation issued by Qavam, Salamollah Javid was appointed as the new governor of Azerbaijan. However, Pishevari preferred to remain the first secretary of the ADF, and not to accept a governmental office.[99]

In contrast to his Azerbaijani counterparts, Qavam had every reason to consider the signing of the Azerbaijan agreement as a victory for the central government. In an address broadcast by Tehran Radio, he described the "Azerbaijan dispute" as "the most serious problem" he had to contend with "since coming to power", and thus characterized the agreement reached with the Azerbaijani Democrats as "a step in the direction of liberty and Iranian national unity".[100] In anticipation of likely negative criticism from his opponents, Qavam called on all *Azadikhahan* (Partisans of Liberty) to rally around him in full support of his wide-ranging campaign against the *Kohneh-Parastan* (Hyper-Conservatives) and the *Mortaje'in* (Reactionaries).[101]

Qavam's call for support soon received an enthusiastic response not only from the Tudeh Party, but from the liberals as well. The liberal press dubbed him *"Naji-ye Mellat"* (the Saviour of the Nation) and *"Nakhost Vazir-e mahbub ol-qolub"* (the prime minister beloved of everyone).[102] Consequently, Qavam found himself more and more aligned with the liberals and the left, while the conservatives presented an increasing opposition to his policies. In mid-June 1946, when his popularity had nearly reached its peak, he decided to form his own political organization, *Hezb-e Demokrat-e Iran* (the Democrat Party of Iran). Abrahamian notes that Qavam had two "implicit and paradoxical reasons for establishing the new organization. On the one hand, he intended to use it, together with the Interior Ministry, to defeat royalist and pro-British candidates in the forthcoming election, and thereby pack the Fifteenth *Majles*", and "on the other hand, he hoped to use it to mobilize non-Communist reformers, steal the thunder from the left and hence build a counterbalance to the Tudeh". Likewise, "the Party label tried to give the organization the appearance of being both the heir of the old Democrat Party and the rival of the Democrat Party of Azerbaijan".[103]

Once the Democrat Party had been founded, Qavam went further with his pro-left policy by enacting a series of measures which had long since been demanded exclusively by the liberals and the left. The most important of these measures were: a labour bill; the creation of a Ministry of Labour; drafting plans for the distribution of crown lands; putting certain pro-British political figures under house arrest; and, finally, appointing some politicians who were known to be pro-Soviet to high government positions.[104]

However, Qavam was to go further yet in co-operating with the liberals and the left. In August 1946, he formed a coalition cabinet with members from the Democrat Party, the Tudeh Party and the Party of Iran. The three Ministries of Trade and Industry, Health, and Education were assigned to Iraj Eskandari, Morteza Yazdi and Fereydun Keshavarz respectively – all three men being members of the Tudeh Party. Likewise, Allahyar Saleh from the Party of Iran was appointed Minister of Justice. One of the chief motives of the Tudeh Party in joining this coalition government, as Iraj Eskandari has remarked, was to block the power of the Azerbaijani Democrats more effectively.[105]

By reserving the post of Minister of the Interior for himself, Qavam maintained direct control over negotiations affecting the question of Azerbaijan. None the less, as a gesture of co-operation to his fellow ministers, he invited an envoy from Azerbaijan to come to the capital to continue talks concerning the various points which still remained to be settled.

On 21 August, the Azerbaijani delegation, with Shabestari at its head, arrived in Tehran. The delegation included other prominent Democrats, men such as Padegan, Javid and General Panahiyan.[106] The main topics of discussion on the agenda were the future function of the *Khalq Qushuni* (the People's Army) and the fusion of the *Feda'iyan* with the gendarmerie. However, it soon became clear that, having in the meantime acquired a high degree of confidence in itself, the government was not prepared to make any concessions to the visiting Democrats. Indeed, in a talk with the US Ambassador to Tehran a few weeks earlier, Qavam had been outspoken in stating his determination to have his way and had added that: "If negotiations broke down, he might have to use force to bring Azerbaijan back into the Iranian nation".[107] Moreover, he is reported to have remarked on that occasion that: "The reason he had been so overly conciliatory to Azerbaijan and the Tudeh Party up to the present was his lack of confidence in the Iranian army, but he had that confidence now."[108]

The new round of negotiations came to an end with a verbal agreement as to the following arrangements:

– Ten thousand Azerbaijanis will be incorporated into the Iranian army and stationed in Azerbaijan. Likewise, four thousand former members of the Azerbaijani *Negahban* (the old gendarmerie) will be chosen and stationed in Azerbaijan.

– The commander of the Azerbaijan Division will be an officer from Tehran who will be chosen by the provincial council of Tabriz from among three candidates nominated by Tehran. The commander's chief of staff will be General Panahiyan, who was the current Azerbaijan Commander of the Tabriz garrison. General Daneshiyan, who was the current commander of the *Feda'iyan*, will hold the office of under-secretary of the *Negahban* forces.

– The Azerbaijani forces will evacuate Zanjan and in return they will be given Sardasht and Takab in Kurdistan.

– All revenues are to be centralized in the *Bank-e Melli* (the National Bank), and the deposits of all government agencies will be kept there.

– Thirty-five per cent of the customs revenues will belong to Tabriz and sixty-five per cent to Tehran.[109]

In the end, however, the agreement remained an oral one and was not committed to writing and signed. The Azerbaijani delegation departed for Tabriz on the understanding that Javid, the Governor of Azerbaijan, who was now on good terms personally with Qavam, would conclude the negotiations in the immediate future.[110]

By the summer of 1946, the previous period of inactivity of the country's conservative alliance appeared to be coming to an end. As part of a strategy to offset the recent successes of their political rivals, in particular the Tudeh Party, the conservatives were willing, at least for the time being, to abet regional conflicts and encourage other regional autonomous movements, in the hope that the fissiparous trend thus created would destabilize the political atmosphere in Iran and, in the end, lead to the downfall of Qavam and his allies in the Tudeh Party.

Two days after the conclusion of the agreement between Pishevari and Firuz, *Anjoman-e Iyalati-ye Khuzestan* (the provincial council of Khuzistan) sent a telegram to Qavam demanding the same rights of autonomy as had been granted by the central government to the Azerbaijanis.[111] The "Khuzistani call" was quickly followed by identical demands from the *Komiteh-e Iyalati-ye Demokrat-e Fars* (the provincial Democratic Committee of Fars).[112] Likewise, on 18 May, two Qashqa'i khans visited the US Embassy in Tehran "to discuss the dangerous political situation" and to manifest their discontent with the Tudeh Party's activities in Khuzistan, which province borders on the Qashqa'i region. Furthermore, with regard to "the demands of the Azerbaijani government" which they thought "were not unreasonable", the Qashqa'i khans declared that: "If wide concessions were made to Pishevari, they would insist on receiving the same treatment".[113]

After consulting with the chiefs of the Bakhtiyari tribe, the Qashqa'i khans launched an extensive military campaign against the Tudeh Party and its associated labour unions in the southern regions of Iran. Simultaneously, by way of challenging the authority of the central government, the Qashqa'is published a proclamation which included the following demands:

– the removal of the Tudeh Party ministers from the cabinet and replacing the incompetent chiefs in the army.
– allowing the administrative affairs of Fars, military as well as civil, to be run by the people of Fars themselves.
– the formation of provincial and district councils in the capital of the province and in the districts.
– increasing the number of representatives in the *Majles* in proportion to the population.
– designating a sufficient sum of money for local development, culture and health care.
– revising laws which are detrimental to the interests of the Constitutional Code.
– extending the central railroad to Shiraz and Bushehr, and surfacing the roads with asphalt.[114]

Qavam had always been on good terms with the Qashqa'i khans.[115] On 13 October, without consulting his cabinet, Qavam sent General Zahedi as a special envoy to Fars to attempt to settle the dispute with the southern tribes. After discussions which lasted three days, the government gave in to all the minor demands of the chiefs, but insisted that the Tudeh Party ministers would not leave the cabinet, there would not be changes in the leadership of the army, and the civil and military administration of Fars would not be transferred to local Farsis.[116]

As was to be expected, Qavam's willingness to enter into negotiations with the tribal khans was not welcomed by his ministers in the cabinet. On the other hand, whatever may have been the real motives behind the Qashqa'is' proclamation at this time, their demands could be interpreted as a direct response to the call sounded by Khalil Maleki who urged all Iranians to follow the example of their Azerbaijani fellow countrymen in demanding what he described as "the rights provided for by the Iranian Constitutional Code".[117] A few months after these events, in an interview with *Iran-e Ma*, Naser Qashqa'i commented that:

> Since the government of the Democrats in Azerbaijan presented a real threat to Iran's independence and the central government was in practice controlled by the left and the radical parties, despite the fact that we had no scientific or cultural basis for justifying our action, we launched the Southern movement, purely as a political manoeuvre.[118]

On one occasion, the shah, during a meeting with Javid, the governor of Azerbaijan, pretended to be puzzled by what he called the Tudeh Party's "double standard" with regard to regional autonomy. When the shah asked Javid how the Tudeh Party explained this apparent inconsistency, Javid's answer was based more on political concerns than on a purely legal assessment:

> There is no doubt that we want a democratic movement for the whole of Iran, but it must be seen whether the demands which have been made in Khuzistan are on the part of the people of Khuzistan and the democratic organizations there, or whether they are on the part of a few reactionary landowners who, by this means, will possibly arm themselves against democracy.[119]

To manifest their extreme discontent with the fact that the prime minister had not consulted with them but had made a wholly independent decision concerning the "Southern Crisis", the Tudeh Party members in the cabinet voted to abstain from attending any cabinet meetings.[120] Counting on "the prime minister's amity", they were confident that he would soon give in to their point of view and repeal the Southern Agreement. In fact, Qavam reacted in quite the opposite way. On 17 October, Qavam submitted the cabinet's resignation to the shah who accepted the resignation and immediately authorized Qavam to form a new government.

The coalition cabinet, which lasted just seventy-seven days, had furnished Qavam with the breathing space he desperately needed in order to accomplish the first phase of his political scenario. On the national level, Qavam had successfully established his credibility as a liberal-minded Constitutionalist. Furthermore, by introducing certain radical reform measures, though still only on paper, he had broken the monopoly which the Tudeh Party had secured for itself with regard to social change and political reform. Likewise, by inviting the Tudeh Party to participate directly in the executive power, he deprived them of the somewhat more comfortable "holier than thou" position which they had occupied as the political opposition. Finally, by winning the support of the urban middle classes and the trust of the liberals and the left, Qavam was able to limit the influence of the court.

On the international level, by implementing his positive equilibrium policy with regard to oil concessions, Qavam was able to secure at least some degree of support from all three of the major world powers (US, Britain and the Soviet Union). His manner of handling the oil dispute, as well as the Azerbaijan "crisis" even made a sceptical observer, such as the US Ambassador to Iran, conclude that:

> If anyone can steer this ship of state through the dangerous waters it is now traversing, Qavam is the most likely instrument for the purpose.[121]

In Azerbaijan, the Democrats' reaction to Qavam's obvious victory was a mixture of ambivalence and despair. The fact that the Azerbaijani delegation returned home empty handed from the negotiating table made it all the more clear to the Democrats that the days when they had posed a serious challenge to the authority of the central government were over. Indeed, they realized that there were now other forces at work in the country's political scene – besides the government – which posed a threat to their existence.

The Democrats' Enduring Dilemma

One of the major hindrances which the Democrats faced while they were in power was the religious establishment whose influence reached into every corner of the province. In a predominantly Muslim society presided over by a well-defined Shi'ite hierarchy, the religious opposition focused on the fact that the majority of the Democrats had the reputation of being revolutionary Marxists, and consequently, whatever they might say to the contrary, any government which they were involved in setting up must by definition, it was argued, be a Marxist ideological state. Furthermore, what the religious establishment particularly feared was any change in the prevailing social structure which the Democrats had been attempting to modernize since the abdication of Reza Shah. Since the clergy's main source of income was the diverse religious taxes and tolls collected from individuals, especially from the landowners in the province, the religious hierarchy was to a large extent directly dependent on the existing system of land ownership in Azerbaijan.

The early measures adopted by the Democrats which aimed at guaranteeing the freedom of religious practices and the right for women to return to the veil was, indeed, a gesture on the part of the Democrats to draw attention to their religious tolerance and thereby to appease the religious establishment. However, despite these undertakings and even the autonomous government's having recruited a few mullahs, the door to compromise with the theologians was never opened. On the contrary, from the very first day that the Democrats began to exercise power, the religious leaders openly declared their categorical rejection of what they referred to as the *ahl-e kofr* (infidels).

In a letter addressed to "the President of the United States of America" and "the Prime Minister of Britain", two prominent religious leaders, Seyyed Mohammad Behbehani and Hajj Seyyed Mohammad Imam Jom'eh, condemned the political developments in Azerbaijan as:

> untimely incidents and sinister rumours which have spread throughout Azerbaijan ...

The letter went on to describe the situation in the following terms:

> The integrity of our country which has been individually and
> jointly guaranteed by the governments of the United States,
> Soviet Russia and Britain, is under threat, and every day
> innocent people in this country are losing their lives.

The two religious leaders called for:

> the immediate evacuation of the [Allied] forces from Iran in
> order to alleviate the Iranian people's anxiety and concern,
> and setting free the central government so that it may occupy
> itself with internal improvements and the re-establishment of
> public security in the country.[122]

There were also some religious figures who were prepared to go further
in castigating the autonomous government. The high-ranking mullah
Seqat ol-Eslam accused the Democrats of not being true Iranians[123]
and declared that the central government should "take every necessary
measure to eliminate them". Seqat ol-Eslam's pronouncements carried
a certain amount of weight among the populace, due to the fact that his
father was considered to have died a martyr's death at the hands of the
tsarist authorities when they occupied Tabriz in 1911.

By the early summer of 1946, it was no longer an easy task for the
Democrats to maintain their original revolutionary image even among
their own rank and file party members, let alone among the people at
large. During the early days of their coming to power, they enjoyed the
illusion of having replaced the old political power structure with an
utterly new system. Now, however, having returned from Tehran
empty- handed, they realized there was almost no chance of them
implementing any significant reforms with regard to the old established
social and political structures.

Nevertheless, to maintain the revolutionary momentum, the Democrats felt the need to intensify their campaign of cultural propaganda.
On 7 April for the very first time, a radio broadcasting service was
founded, the *Azerbaijan Milli Hükumatinin Sasi* (the Voice of the
National Government of Azerbaijan) which broadcast daily programs in
Azerbaijani, Kurdish and Persian.[124] Likewise, they increased the
number of Azerbaijani language newspapers and periodicals to a total
of sixteen, while newspapers previously published in Persian or with a
bilingual (Persian-Azerbaijani) format all disappeared. For instance,

Azerbaijan, which had always been the Democrats' most influential newspaper with a circulation of 10,000,[125] was originally published with a bilingual format but, following its designation as the ADF's official organ, it abandoned its bilingual format and adopted the exclusive use of Azerbaijani.[126]

Furthermore, by the summer of 1946, the six-volume work entitled *Vatan Dili* (Language of the Homeland) was published for use in the local schools. It is significant that throughout the six volumes of this work, whereas Azerbaijan's history and culture are frequently dealt with in great detail, there is no reference to Iran's history or Iran's social and cultural ties with Azerbaijan.[127]

Contrary to their expectation, the Democrats' new cultural campaign, and the emphasis which they placed on the Azerbaijani language as a means of consolidating local ethnic identity, did not succeed in rallying the entire population under the government's banner, but actually caused most people to believe that their ties with the rest of Iran were about to be severed for good. Furthermore, there was a steadily growing fear that the new destiny which awaited the people of Azerbaijan was eventually to become appended to the neighbouring Caucasus, and to be governed by the Soviet Union.[128] Consequently, as a reaction to the government's measures, a noticeable change in attitude towards Persian speakers took place on the part of Azerbaijanis. Even in the rank and file of the Democrat Party, the minority group of Persians now came to enjoy more sympathy from the people, compared with their Azerbaijani counterparts, especially those known as *Muhajir* (Immigrant). This increased sympathy could at times lead to clashes between the Persian rebel officers known as the *Fars Afsarlari* (the Persian officers), who had deserted from the Iranian army and gone over to the autonomous government's *Khalq Qushuni* (the People's Army), and the native *Feda'iyan* militia.[129]

Besides these disturbing local reactions produced by the Democrats' new cultural campaign, there were also important implications on the national level, namely the danger that the gap which already existed between the Democrats and the liberal political spectrum throughout the country might widen even further. Consequently, having followed political developments in Tehran, the Azerbaijani Democrats now perceived that it was in their interest to have closer ties with the other Iranian opposition groups, and towards that end they decided to distance themselves from Qavam and join the governmental opposition. Until then, the autonomous government, while enjoying the support of some political parties in Tehran, had pursued a policy of abstaining from political alliances and had limited its relations with Tehran to a purely governmental level.

Now, however, renouncing their early calls for secession, the Democrats decided to emphasize their commitment to Iran's territorial integrity, and at the same time they indicated a willingness to co-operate with other political parties throughout the country. On 29 October 1946, the ADF, together with the Democrat Party of Kurdistan and the rather minor *Jangali* Party, were affiliated under the name *Jebheh-ye Mo'talef-e Ahzab-e Azadikhah* (the United Front of Progressive Parties).[130] The United Front of Progressive Parties had originally been founded by the Tudeh Party and the Party of Iran, in Tehran in June 1946. Although this act on the part of the Democrats was welcomed enthusiastically by the liberals and the left-wing caucuses of the country, by that stage it was the prevailing view in political circles throughout Iran that it was too late to re-establish the lines of co-operation which the Azerbaijani Democrats had cut more than a year before.

The Collapse

The political storm clouds were gathering and all signs indicated that the Democrats' days in power were numbered. None the less, the *Ferqeh* was preparing to celebrate the first anniversary of its forming a government in Azerbaijan. While the province was busy harvesting "the most extraordinary bumper crop in recent memory",[131] Pishevari called on all Democrats to close ranks and rally around him for a triumphant victory in the elections for the Fifteenth *Majles*.[132] Indeed, despite the grave difficulties facing them, at the time no one among the Democrats could have foreseen that in less than a month their government would collapse and they would be swept out of power never to return.

By mid-autumn 1946, that Qavam's political authority had increased was undeniable, even by those who were outspoken in opposing his policies. Having secured the shah's *farman* to hold elections for the Fifteenth *Majles* and feeling confident in the backing of the newly consolidated Iranian Army, Qavam now thought the time was right to implement the second phase of his political scenario.

In late November 1946, the central government launched its final attack against Azerbaijan. In accordance with the earlier verbal agreement made in Tehran, the provincial council of Azerbaijan (formerly the *Milli Majlis*), in a session held on 11 November, concluded that Zanjan would be ceded to the central government.[133] The decision to have the *Feda'iyan* evacuate the city, a process which in the event took ten days, was by no means an easy one to take. Besides the resentment it aroused among the more radical elements of the *Feda'iyan*, the Democrats had to consider the serious threat of eventual reprisals against their supporters in the city.[134] In a region with a longstanding tradition of social as well as political retaliation, the city's Democrats had good reason to be alarmed by the news from Tehran that large-scale preparations for a final military take-over were under way in the capital.

However disquieting the news of "the capital's large-scale military preparations" was, there were other indications, as well, of the government's aggressive intentions with regard to Azerbaijan. On 12 November Qavam left Tehran, ostensibly to take a vacation on his tea plantation in Gilan. His departure from the capital at the very moment when the political crisis in the country seemed to be coming to a head made one journalist comment that: "Qavam, by leaving Tehran, was indeed avoiding any possible confrontation with foreign powers".[135] Likewise, nine days later the Iranian army, under the shah's command, carried out manoeuvres outside Tehran.[136] And that same day the government initiated its censorship campaign against the opposition press by closing down the offices of *Jebheh*, the Party of Iran's influential newspaper.[137]

Finally, on the eve of 23 November, the date agreed upon for the surrender of Zanjan to the central government, the Iranian army made a sudden attack on the remaining *Feda'iyan* in the city and occupied all the municipal government offices.[138] The impact of the Iranian army's actions was devastating as far as the political position of the Democrats was concerned. As the US consul at Tabriz commented:

Whatever the psychology of it may have been, this was the blow that cracked the Democrats' armour. Here for the first time they were defeated on their home ground. [139]

News of *Zanjan faji'ahsi* (the Zanjan disaster) came as an overwhelming shock to the populace and the Democrats in Tabriz. In an atmosphere of "uncertainty and desperation", the government was accused of "occupying a city according to agreement, then trying to make people think it has won a great military victory".[140] Furthermore, "the Tabriz Radio announcements became more unrestrained and the newspaper articles more violent".[141] *Azad Millet*, for instance, in a lead editorial published after the attack on Zanjan warned Qavam that "there will be armed resistance waiting for the government troops", should he persist in his new policy of aggression:

> Together with all partisans of liberty, we will resist reactionaries with our last drop of blood ... Let Tehran know that we will not stand by quietly in face of their reactionary conspiracies.[142]

With the central government's troops installed behind the walls of Zanjan, Prime Minister Qavam declared in a manifesto concerning "preparations for a rapid election" that:

> Since it bears full responsibility *vis-à-vis* the National Consultative Assembly [*Majles*] to see that the elections run smoothly, the government is obliged to devote its complete concern to maintaining order and security, and to send sufficient forces of *Negahban* [the gendarmerie] to all the election locales and, in case of need, forces from the army. The government will send troops from Tehran. This precaution will be carried out throughout all parts of Iran without exception.[143]

The government manifesto was clear and explicit. None the less, Javid, the governor of Azerbaijan, sent a telegram to Qavam asking him directly if he intended to send government troops to Azerbaijan as well.[144] Qavam, who was apparently waiting to be asked just that question, replied promptly in the affirmative and added that his only motive in undertaking such a measure was "to conform to the rules, and grant equal electoral rights to everyone all over the country".[145]

The Democrats' reaction to the government's declaration was by no means uniform. Indeed, increasingly there were signs of a possible split developing among them. As the confrontation with the government proceeded, two camps of Democrats began to form. On the one side, there was the ADF leadership, as well as the rank and file of the local armed forces, especially the *Feda'iyan*. In the second camp were the members of the provincial council and those in the local administration.

Since the publication of the June agreement, the ADF had tried to dissociate itself from provincial government affairs. Pishevari, still the chairman of the ADF, specifically declined to hold any post in the autonomous government by way of demonstrating his aloofness from government functions. By contrast, the former *Milli Majlis* deputies who now sat on the provincial council, and the ex-ministers who now functioned as heads of local governmental departments, considered themselves, if not the direct agents of the central government, none the less, as civil servants.

Consequently, the reactions of these two groups of Democrats to the *"Zanjan faji'ahsi"* (Zanjan disaster) were by no means identical. Pishevari, for instance, in an editorial entitled *"Ney-ichun Galillar?"* (Why Are They Coming?), gave full vent to his anger and accused Qavam of being:

> a deceiver, who for the last six months, had been carrying out a policy of double-crossing Azerbaijan, that is, while promising a peaceful solution to the dispute, had been making preparations for a military option.[146]

Pishevari then went on to threaten Qavam, warning him "not to play with fire", since:

> Our people have sworn an oath to preserve, at whatever cost, the liberties which they have won ... We have stood by our word, and those who wish, by force of bayonets, to trample our freedom under foot, whoever they may be, will be pounded by the strength of the people's biceps and driven back. This is my final word: *Ölmak var, dönmak yok!* [Death, but no retreat!][147]

However, in sharp contrast to Pishevari, the provincial council adopted a moderate, rather conciliatory stance *vis-à-vis* the central government. In reply to Qavam's proclamation that he intended to send government troops to Azerbaijan, Shabestari, the president of the provincial council, pointed out that this ought not to be necessary since, according to the "June Agreement", the local armed forces of Azerbaijan had been recognized as "part of the Iranian army". He then went on to suggest:

> Since their arrival would disrupt public security in Azerbaijan, we do not consider it advisable to send government troops. If His Excellency really has good intentions, he might despatch inspectors and so perform his duty in accordance with Article Thirty-Eight of the Electoral Law.[148]

Shabestari's telegram to Qavam was intended to be a piece of well-meaning advice. In any case, Shabestari never received a reply from the prime minister. Instead, Qavam sent a telegram to Javid in which he not only disregarded everything the provincial council had to say, but categorically stated that the council had no authority to interfere in the matter:

> The matter of sending armed forces has nothing to do with the provincial council's approval or disapproval ... The present forces of Azerbaijan do not at this time inspire trust and confidence in accordance with all the regulations, nor has their organization been consolidated. Consequently, the government does not consider them to be sufficient for the task and will send the necessary forces to Azerbaijan in order to assure the smooth running of the elections.

To this Qavam added the tough-sounding warning that:

> As long as the government's decision is met with good will, there will be no manner of misunderstanding or cause for concern ... But should there be any resistance offered to the government forces, the serious consequences and the responsibility thereof will lie with the officials in charge of the province's affairs.[149]

It was now obvious that the door to any future compromise was firmly closed and that a military confrontation was inevitable. On 7 December, the central committee of the ADF, in a declaration signed by Pishevari, officially stated that they were at war with the central government. In the ADF's public declaration, which was addressed to all Iranian *hamvatanan* (fellow countrymen), Pishevari proclaimed that he was prepared to fight with determination:

> We have openly said that no one in Azerbaijan wants war. However, if Mr Qavam os-Saltaneh speaks to us out of the mouth of a cannon, we will defend our liberty.

And Pishevari called on all "Iranian brothers ... to stand up and fight to safeguard liberty and democracy in the country". He promised "to crush the attack of the reactionaries" in order to "make it possible for the Iranian *Mellat* to liberate itself". The declaration ended with a series of patriotic exclamations:

> Long live the freedom and independence of Iran!
> Long live the Front of the Partisans of Freedom!
> Long live the glorious name of Azerbaijan, the pioneer of Iran's freedom movement!
> Long live the freedom-loving *Feda'iyan*, soldiers and officers who are defending our freedom and that of the whole of Iran in blood-stained entrenchments![150]

Though his "Iranian brothers" did not rise up and answer Pishevari's call to arms, which could have made all the difference in the conflict at hand, the Azerbaijani Democrats did not sit down and passively accept defeat. As part of their preparations for armed resistance, the Democrats formed a military division known as *Babak* which was added to the still existing *Qizilbash* and *Feda'iyan* army units.[151] According to the report of the US consul in Tabriz who was an eyewitness of events in the city:

> During the last days of the Democrat government, there was a great deal of whistling in the dark, but there was also a great deal of effective preparation. Civilians were trained in the city square, even to the ludicrous extent of having women clutching a gun in one hand while the other hand held a veil across their face. Supplies, especially small arms and ammunition, were moved in large quantity. Grain was brought into the Tabriz silo. There was every evidence of a long and costly siege.[152]

But, significantly, the US consul remarks:

> What was lacking was the spirit and confidence which the
> leaders tried to instill with their repeated cries of fighting to
> the last drop of blood.[153]

However, the increasing state of disarray within the ranks of the
Democrats' leadership during these last days made it virtually impossible for them to shed their "last drop of blood" in defense of
Azerbaijan. When, on 10 December, Qavam signed the final *farman* in
which he ordered the Iranian Army to advance into Tabriz[154], the
leaders of the ADF convoked their last deliberative meeting. Among
those present, Shabestari and Javid voted for total capitulation, whereas
other party members such as Pishevari and Badegan vigorously opposed
the motion.[155] In the end, through the mediation of Quliev, the
military attaché of the Soviet consulate in Tabriz, Biriya was elected as
the first secretary of the ADF and Pishevari, Badegan and Jahanshahlu
Afshar were advised to leave Iran for Soviet Azerbaijan.[156]

The next day, in what was to be its last issue, the newspaper
Azerbaijan published a declaration concerning the final submission of
Tabriz:

> Relying on the good intentions of Mr Qavam os-Saltaneh and
> the decree of the provincial council of Azerbaijan, the
> following has been decided:
>
> – In order to avoid fraternal bloodshed, when the government
> security forces enter the city of Tabriz, there shall be no form of
> hostile demonstrations and they shall be received with complete
> self-control.
> - The Democrat Party of Azerbaijan, as in the past, is a
> supporter and defender of Iran's territorial integrity and
> independence, and the happiness of the people.
> – All the organizations of the *Ferqeh*, such as the trade
> unions, will carry on their daily work as previously.
>
> Long live the independence of Iran![157]

On 12 December 1946, just one year after it had been established, the Democrats' rule in Azerbaijan came to an end. Ironically, this was the date on which the anniversary celebrations were set to take place in commemoration of "the glorious day when the government of the province had been placed in the hands of the people". The Iranian army had prepared itself to face stiff resistance from the Democrats over an extended period of time,[158] but, to everyone's surprise, the army did not encounter any serious barriers to establishing its authority in the province. There were only a few isolated cases of Azerbaijani armed resistance.[159] However, according to some descriptions, what was supposed to be "the army of emancipation, was a savage army of occupation".[160] As a result, during the early days of chaos which followed upon the arrival of government troops in Azerbaijan, a great number of lives were lost and a mass migration to Soviet Azerbaijan took place.[161] Whereas on the eve of the collapse of the autonomous government only a few of the ADF leaders were advised to leave the country, in the days that followed there was a mass exodus of upwards of 15,000 people.

The End of a Venture

The sudden and complete submission on the part of the Democrats has caused some observers, as well as historians, to speculate that what really brought the Azerbaijan "crisis" to an end were pressures exerted by the great foreign powers.[162] In this connection, mention has frequently been made of the pressure the US President, Harry S. Truman, is supposed to have put on the Soviets to change their policy in Iran, so that the latter, in turn, by pressurizing the Azerbaijani Democrats, put a seal to the last page of the autonomous government's history. There have even been references to Truman's having given the Soviets an "ultimatum" in this regard.

The so-called ultimatum was in fact no more than a letter Truman sent to the Soviet authorities demanding that they honour their commitments as defined in the Tripartite Treaty of Alliance and withdraw their troops from Iran by the agreed date.[163] However, the term "ultimatum" which Truman himself employed in a press conference on 24 April 1952, has led to a great deal of confusion in this matter.[164]

Finally, in 1969, after seventeen years of controversy, the US State Department officially announced that: "There is no document in the departmental archive concerning a United States ultimatum to the Soviet Union."[165] None the less, despite the fact that there was never any solid evidence for the existence of such an "ultimatum", several politicians and academic scholars have maintained that the hypothetical "ultimatum" was the "decisive factor" in bringing about the Democrats' fall from power in Azerbaijan.[166]

Postulating an "Eastern retreat" on the part of the Soviets as the only reason for the sudden and total collapse of the Democrats' regime in Azerbaijan is as inadequate as taking for granted the existence of "Western pressure". Undoubtedly, since the early days of their coming to power, the Democrats did enjoy the moral support of the Soviets, but this moral support never translated itself into significant material terms. As George Allan, the US Ambassador to Iran, remarked:

> The Soviet help to the Azerbaijan regime during the past year was rather niggard and accompanied by close bargaining. The Soviets made Azerbaijanis pay high prices in wheat and other commodities for such supplies as were accorded. While a considerable amount of automatic rifles, ammunition, and light equipment were furnished, no heavy armament was included.[167]

What appears to have been much more crucial than "Western pressure" or the "Eastern retreat" in bringing about the downfall of the Azerbaijani Democrats was the lack of popular support with which they increasingly had to cope. Indeed, the speed with which their regime collapsed and the virtual absence of any form of popular armed resistance to the central government's troops are signs of the Democrats' of the Democrats, rather than the real strength of their opponents. And yet, no attempt at a balanced view of the Democrats' position should ignore the widespread popularity of some of their political measures. As the US Consul in Tabriz noted:

> The Democrats had the wisdom of modern politics. They did things that appealed to the people. They were also wise enough to emphasize tangible results. They built roads and paved streets, things that people could see. And things that

the Tehran government had not bothered to do for years and years. They emphasized education, revamping the schools entirely and thereby showed a true instinct for perpetuating their control.[168]

However, what did go wrong from the beginning was that the Democrats were unable to mobilize support in the province by means of an inspiring socio-political movement. Their attempts to formulate such a movement always remained ambiguous. Pishevari strove to legitimize his position by calling for the restoration of the Iranian Constitution and by championing the rights which the Constitution guaranteed. None the less, his day-to-day actions made it clear that his idea of "autonomy" went far beyond what was stipulated in the country's Constitutional Code concerning the right of the people in the provinces to form their own provincial and district councils. Moreover, he did not hesitate to stress his commitment to the ideals of the early Bolsheviks by referring to "the right of nations to self-determination, the right to secede and to form an independent national state".

Indeed, on a few occasions when Pishevari was hurling threats at the central government, he had no qualms about openly referring to Azerbaijan seceding from Iran:

> Azerbaijan is capable of administering her own affairs. If the swindlers in Tehran ... persist in eradicating freedom, we will be forced to take one step further and cut our ties with them ... If Tehran chooses the reactionary road, well then, good-bye! That will be without Azerbaijan. This is our final word![169]

And on another occasion, Pishevari was even more explicit:

> Rather than ending up as a prisoner with the rest of Iran after the manner of an India, Azerbaijan prefers to become a free Ireland.[170]

Rhetoric of this kind, with its distinct secessionist tone, was not only abhorrent to the central government in Tehran, but could arouse antagonism in political circles in Tabriz as well. None the less, it was only during their last days in power that the Democrats operated a manifest shift in their political discourse by abandoning their secession-ist attitude, i.e. by renouncing their insistence on a people's right to self-determination and to setting up their own nation-state. The form which this shift in discourse took consisted of no longer merely emphasizing the advantages to be had by Azerbaijan breaking away from the control of the central government, but of the Azerbaijani Democrats beginning to portray themselves as the champions of the Constitutional Code on behalf of all Iranians. By defending the Constitutional Code and promoting the implications of decentralized government which this entailed, the Democrats claimed to represent the progressive democratic political line for all Iran to follow. However, the tragic final outcome of their endeavours confirmed that the adoption of this new theme into their repertoire unfortunately came too late.

7

Epilogue

National consciousness, the sense of belonging to a political and social community which constitutes – or wishes to constitute – a nation organized as a state, is the fundamental basis of the cultural or political nation. In principle, national consciousness is independent of the existence of a national state; without national consciousness, however, a national movement would be doomed to failure.

P. Alter, *Nationalism*, p. 18.

To Hegel's remark that history tends to repeat itself, Marx added ironically that events first occur in a tragic form, and then as a comedy. Whatever validity this view may have with references to some historical occurrences, in the case of the autonomous movement in Iranian Azerbaijan the notion is clearly not applicable. During the twentieth century, two major revolts have taken place in Iranian Azerbaijan with the aim of limiting the central government's authority in the region and thereby instituting a new power structure based on a greater measure of local participation. Both these attempts ended in complete failure. Moreover, the circumstances which led to the disastrous conclusion of the second attempt, i.e. Pishevari's career and the downfall of the autonomous government of Azerbaijan in 1946, although somewhat more complex in form, were identical with those of the first attempt, which brought about the tragic end of Khiyabani's revolt in 1920.

Khiyabani, a radical reformist preacher, lived for a time under the rule of Tsarist Russia. Nonetheless, he was much more strongly influenced by social ideas, which originated in Western Europe in the eighteenth century than by the ideas, which were current during his formative years in the social milieu under Russian colonial administration. Although he was staunchly opposed to the centralized administration of Iran, nevertheless, with a view to preserving the territorial integrity of Iran, he was committed to the idea of an Iranian nation-state, rather than to the establishment of independent or even autonomous rule in Azerbaijan. In this area, his political demands did not go beyond seeking a fair distribution of executive powers between the central government and local authorities throughout Iran.

Indeed, undertaking to introduce political reforms throughout the country from the capital, as compared with more regional initiatives, was one of the main issues dividing the Iranian nationalist-reformist camp. If Khiyabani and his comrades, by launching their campaign for reform from Tabriz rather than Tehran, were playing down the central government's functions, others in the reformist camp of the day wholeheartedly felt that any initiative which decreased the role of the capital would directly or indirectly weaken and thereby endanger the country's sovereignty. The two sides were so divided on this issue that even Khiyabani's independent stand and his outright refusal to seek any support from foreign powers did not prove adequate in persuading the entire reformist camp to unite under his banner.

Twenty-five years later, Pishevari, a revolutionary Communist, while maintaining that he had learned a lesson from Khiyabani's tragic end, was prepared to lead another regionally based movement in Azerbaijan. As a Marxist-Leninist who had spent years in the revolutionary Communist movement, Pishevari not only considered Iranian Azerbaijanis to be a separate nation, but also insisted on championing the Leninist rallying cry of "the right of nations to self-determination, the right to secede and form an independent state". Pishevari's understanding of autonomy clearly went beyond merely demanding a greater degree of local participation in regional legislation and administration, while remaining within the borders of an established sovereign state. Furthermore, Pishevari belonged to the generation of Communists who not only believed in the right of the Communist camp to intervene internationally in the internal affairs of associated political parties, but also never hesitated to seek direct assistance from the Communist camp. In Pishevari's eyes the Soviet Union, as the leading power in the Communist camp, was apparently not in the same category as other big powers such as Britain or the United States. Pishevari did not look upon the Soviet Union with what had become standard Iranian mistrust of any foreign intervention in Iran's internal affairs.

Undoubtedly, not everybody within the political spectrum of liberals, not even all Communists, shared these attitudes with Pishevari. Since the beginning of the nineteenth century, foreign intervention in Iran's internal politics had been a constant threat. To be identified with a foreign power, in the long run at least, worked against a statesman's chances of political success. Thus, even for many members and cadres of the Tudeh Party, it was difficult to give their unconditional support to the measures of Pishevari's Democrat Party. Consequently, in view of what was perceived to be Pishevari's unambiguous involvement with, and dependence on, the Soviet Union, one is obliged to question to what extent the autonomous movement was wholly indigenous. Of course, there were numerous local grievances which have been referred to in previous pages, but such grievances alone would never have been an adequate cause for the autonomous government to employ such menacing, provocative language in its dealings with the central government or to adopt such drastic measures as it did – to the extent of even breaking off all ties of any kind with Tehran.

Far from what Pishevari had expected, Soviet backing of the Azerbaijani Democrats' call for autonomy had, in the end, rather negative consequences. The existence of the then Soviet Socialist Republic of Azerbaijan – a republic bearing the same name as Iranian Azerbaijan – made many Iranians wary that what really lay behind the Soviet policy was nothing less than the desire eventually to annex Iranian Azerbaijan. In the face of this lurking suspicion, many politically active Iranians who were, generally speaking, in favour of allowing greater autonomy to the provinces were reluctant to lend their unconditional support to the Azerbaijani Democrats. In their minds, Pishevari's call for regional autonomy was associated with the nightmare scenario of Azerbaijan's secession from Iran. Furthermore, the fact that the Azerbaijani Democrats in many cases adopted an imprecise terminology with regard to autonomy and ethnic issues only added to the confusion and ambiguity, which surrounded their policies in the public's eyes.

Similarly, on their home ground in Azerbaijan, the Democrats' policy of relying on Soviet support appears to have gradually alienated the Azerbaijanis from their autonomous government. Here, too, the spectre of secession engendered widespread anxiety that for the foreseeable future all ties with Iran would be cut, leading to irreversible economic and cultural losses for Azerbaijan. Consequently, despite the government's implementation of many attractive reforms – educational, electoral, and especially the large-scale reforms involving land – their policy makers clearly did not manage to win and hold onto genuine popular support, as is attested by the autonomous government's swift collapse when challenged militarily by Tehran.

If there was a lesson to be learned from the defeat of Khiyabani's revolt, it had to come from an explanation of why his revolt gradually lost its popular support. When the central government sent armed forces into Azerbaijan, and not even a very large number of them at that, not only did they not meet with any serious resistance, but also most of the local inhabitants appear to have welcomed their arrival. Was the package of reforms introduced by Khiyabani not adequate to meet the demands of the people? On the contrary, given the socio-economic conditions in Azerbaijan at the beginning of this century, the program proposed by Khiyabani was very advanced for what one could realistically expect from a reform campaign at that time. In view of the weak military pressure, which the central government brought to bear, and the fact that Khiyabani's reform programme was so popular, it is only natural to seek some other reason or reasons for his revolt having been so easily defeated.

During the nineteenth and twentieth centuries, the world witnessed the emergence of a considerable number of state-nations, as distinct from nation-states. In such cases, the usual preconditions of a state, the necessary historical and cultural bonds, were created or virtually invented. New countries, whose borders were arbitrarily drawn in the rapid process of decolonisation and whose ethnic and cultural make-up was very mixed, or which even included mutually hostile ethnic elements, suddenly appeared on the map as modern nations. Likewise, during the same period there were historical nations which developed their modern state on the basis of new political institutions, some of them having accommodated many ethnic groups under one sovereign who exercised varying degrees of authority throughout the country at different times. If, in the first case, creating a nation by bringing together different ethnic groups with different cultural backgrounds and reducing the inherent centrifugal tendencies is a difficult, if not impossible task, in the second circumstance, the different ethnic groups within a nation may be so integrated with one another and mutually dependent that any attempt to lessen the ties, especially the economic and cultural/religious ones, is bound to meet with understandable resentment.

Moreover, in the last century, most of the secessionist movements worldwide, in one way or another, originated in the peripheral areas by calling to obtain greater autonomy from the centre or the central government. The clash of centre and periphery often evolved into some sort of armed confrontation, when the periphery with the help of some international recognition, held the banner of an independent state.

Considering the centre-periphery relation, one should realize that Iran has never enjoyed – for any lengthy period of time – a single city as her permanent centre of political power; unlike such cities as Constantinople or St. Petersburg with a long history of being the seats of imperial strength, no single city in Iran can claim a similar history. In the four hundred years since A.D. 1500, Iran has had to contend with a number of capital cities. The inter-changeability of capitals and centres of power has been attributed to the "preconditions of their creation, on similar bases of their social and political structure and on comparable economic foundations of their economy".[1] The development of the powerful centralized state of the Safavids first began in a city in the North-Western of their empire. The city, Tabriz, was located on the cross-road of ethnic and cultural blending between Iran and the Ottoman Empire. Moreover, Tabriz was – and still is – the capital of Iran's largest ethnic minority, i.e. the Azerbaijani Turks. After Tabriz, the city of Qazvin, with a Turko-Persian ethnic composition, became the capital city of the Safavids. Later, from Qazvin the capital was moved to the city of Isfahan, in the South-West of the Safavid Empire with the majority of Persian-speaking population. Following the fall of the Safavid dynasty, under the short-lived rule of Nader Afshar (1732–1747), Mashhad, in the North-East Iran, enjoyed a brief status as Iran's capital. However, when Karim Khan Zand (1747–1790) founded his dynasty, he favoured the city of Shiraz as the centre of his dominion. Finally, with the rise of the Qajar dynasty, the then insignificant town of Tehran was named as the new capital in 1792.

The immediate consequence of a city being named as the capital was the spectacular rise of its political, social and economic status. This in part contributed to a significant rise in the city's population and its ethnic composition. Here, in this context, Mashhad might be a noteworthy example. As a result of Nader's decision to elevate this city to the role and function of a capital, the city's population increased by a quarter of a million inhabitants.[2]

Contributing factors to the tremendous and sudden rise of the urban population were "the fact that not only the royal family, but its huge entourage of administration and bureaucrats, military personnel and religious leaders filled the capital cities. Second, the majority of the national nobles and notables i.e. landlords and tribal chiefs seem to have gathered around the crown. Third, however, the Shahs themselves ordered the resettlement and sedentarisation of large tribal groups as well as that of ethnic and/or religious minorities in close neighbourhood to the royal residences. All these factors had immediate impacts both on the development of the capital city and spatial structures within the empire as a whole."[3]

The policy of population dislocation by means of forced migration and sedentarisation of the nomadic groups had a tremendous homogenizing effect on the ethnic as well as religious composition of the empire's subjects. For example "Safavids population policy of forced migration included the resettlement of approximately 100,000 Turkic nomadic families, not to speak of at least 20,000 Armenians and Georgians settled in the southern precincts of Isfahan. The short rule of Nader Shah affected about 150,000 families. The Zands, finally caused approximately 40,000 tribal families to be removed from their traditional areas closer to Shiraz. Resettlement was accompanied by genuine population policy: new villages were founded, existing villages enlarged and cities were transformed by the addition of new *mahalleh* (quarters)."[4]

Although the inner-urban quarters were separated along ethnic and religion demarcations, the inhabitants of these quarters regularly interacted peacefully with each other across socio-economic barriers. It may be argued that growing cosmopolitan cities which contained a mixed and fluid population of a diverse ethnic and socio-economic background, at times encouraged an individual sense of neighbourliness, fidelity, allegiances, and most importantly, attachment to territory. In the history of Iranian cities, dissatisfaction, discord, and bloody episodes between minorities were not uncommon, but not a single city has ever disintegrated because of ethnic or religious diversity. Furthermore, the phenomena of bi-lingualism (or even multilingualism) had a negative effect on the spread of linguistic nationalism, with its homogenizing policies.

The rise of one city as the new capital had some impact on the decline of the previous capital, especially its population, however, the new capital was never capable of causing a "dramatic decay of the predecessor", as has been perceived by some scholars.[5] Each former national capital remained the administrative centre of its respective province; hence it was able to retain much of its economic role and function. Qajar Iran was divided into four large *iyalats* (provinces) of Azerbaijan, Khorasan, Fars and Kerman-Siystan, each with its own *vali* (governor) and numerous *velayat* (districts). Later, with the reshuffling of the old provinces, a new province was formed with Tehran as its centre. 19th century Iran saw the prospering of Mashhad and Tabriz, two cities which functioned, sometimes more effectively than Tehran. Mashhad had a special role as a Shi'a centre of sanctuary and pilgrimage and Tabriz was a gateway for European as well as Russian economic penetration into the interior of the country. Indeed, during the reign of the Qajar dynasty (1790–1925), Tabriz flourished as the predominant commercial centre, as the country's granary, and as the country's second most politically important city and the official place of residence of the Qajar Crown Prince's court, Dar al-Saltaneh. Tabriz, during this period, proved to be more receptive to outside influences and was a breeding ground for progressive political thinkers, many of whom became leaders of the Iranian constitutional movement of 1905–1911.

Furthermore, prior to 1900 Iranian borders were predominantly elastic. The Safavids attempt to introduce greater political unity through centralization and institutionalization of Shi'ism, created for Iran a new defensive identity in relation to those who lived beyond their borders. For the subjects of Safavid Persia the notion of self-identification was not by reference to their own "national" characteristics, but rather by local exclusion, i.e. through a negative definition, comparing themselves with their immediate Sunni Muslim neighbour. Whatever the case may be for the rise in self-identification and dynastic allegiance in Safavid Persia, the emergence of Persia, as a territorial entity stretching from the Caspian Sea to the Persian Gulf took on a more concrete shape in the 17th and 18th centuries, with the first semi-modern European maps of the country. The mapping of Iran as such, which was mainly based on the Safavids, territorial achievements, was different from the ancient design of the Persian Empire.

In the pre-modern period, the Ottoman expansionist threat made the European powers concerned about the boundaries of their hated neighbour. Indeed, it was with reference to such mapping that Nader in 1736, following the fall of the Safavids when the Ottomans successfully claimed the North and North-West of Iran, began to demand the return of those territories and insist on the persistence of Iran's legitimate frontiers. Indeed, it was not only Nader who referred to Iran's legitimate frontiers. Safavids' territorial Persia indeed turned to become a standard reference for all following rulers. Karim Khan Zand and Aqa Mohammad Khan Qajar came also with the similar call. During the early 19th century and following the confrontations Iran faced with the Russian and the British, and as result of two consecutive wars with Russia and the peace treaties signed in 1813 and 1828, Iran lost part of its Northern territory and was squeezed into its present frontiers. The fate of the people in the north, though the majority were Shi'ite Muslims, then became far more intimately connected with the Russians and the Muslim people of the Russian Empire than with Iran. It was only during the final days of the First World War that the people of Nakhjivan, by signing a petition, induced the Iranian government to reunite them with Iran. Nonetheless, this unfeasible and naïve call was drowned in the post-War uproar.

Furthermore, in Iran, the network of social interaction has been articulated and coordinated within a unique characteristic form. Such a pattern of interaction can be found to exist in the institution of, what has been called, arbitrary rule. The framework of arbitrary rule has also ensured political unity, despite the heterogeneous nature of Iranian society.

During the First World War, and in the absence of a powerful state, one might well have expected that Iran, like the Ottoman Empire, would disintegrate into a number of smaller states. Yet Iran managed to preserve its territorial integrity after the war. With the gradual establishment of Pahlavi's rule, the Reza Shah's policy of pseudo-modernization during 1920s and 1930s with its motto – "one country, one nation", – was not too dissimilar to attempts by previous monarchs to rewrite the parameters of ethnic identity in Iran. Forced migration and resettlement of nomadic tribes continued with even greater force, this time in order to eradicate the power of tribal chieftains who posed a threat to Reza Shah's modernization program. Encouraging a homogeneous urban society was seen as the formula for modelling the image of a modern Iranian citizen. Constructing the modern nation-state was based on the assumption of unity and homogeneity and the nation-state itself turned to become a viable entity.

Furthermore, the well-known enduring social mobility, a characteristic feature of Iranian social dynamic, remained in place alongside growing anti-ethnic/anti-tribal social polices, contributing to a rapid growth of economic mobility in society. Therefore a new meritocracy gradually formed in Iran. Every citizen regardless of his ethnic origin enjoyed the right of personal achievement in the new-born administration, as long as he appreciated the state definition of Iran as a modern integrated nation-state. Individual Azerbaijanis, promoted through their own merits, often managed to attain the highest ranks within Iran's military and administrative apparatus. Whereas society in Iran may be described as tribal up until the reign of Reza Shah, with the concomitant possibility of ethnic groups temporarily allying themselves with one another against the central power, once Reza Shah established the modern centralized state, it became difficult for the old routine process of power struggle to continue. The move towards total integration of regional economies in Iran increased the degree of interdependence of the different provinces throughout the country.

The country's cultural unity was considered to be paramount in Reza Shah's brand of nationalism. As a result of the Shah's educational reforms, the traditional religious *maktab-khaneh* was transformed into modern primary schools with their curriculum taught in Persian, now the official language of Iran. Meanwhile, it was not permitted to publish books and newspapers in any language other than Persian. As a result a new Iranian "high culture" – to use Gellner's phraseology – was gradually recast. Here too, the influence of economic imperatives determined cultural and national norms. As Gellner remarks:

> "A modern economy depends on mobility and communication between individuals at a level that can only be achieved if these individuals have been socialized into high culture [i.e. the official culture of the state and its ruler], so as to be able to communicate properly. This can only be achieved by a fairly monolithic educational system. Thus, culture, not community provides the inner sanctions. The requirements of a modern economy inevitably result in the new idea of the mutual relationship of modern culture and state."[6]

The outbreak of the Second World War and the abdication of Reza Shah in 1941, expanded the public space in the Iran. The general call for greater public participation in the political life in some provinces was furthered with calls for limiting the central government's authority in the provinces and granting a greater measure of local participation. Indeed, Pishevari in his endeavour to form his "Autonomous Government of Azerbaijan" was referring to this call. Following the fall of the Azerbaijan Autonomous Government of 1945–1946, and in the years proceeding the Second World War, with the importance of Iran's geopolitical location and national resources, which made the West become aware of her territorial integrity, Iran went through a major socio-economic transformation. The process of rapid urbanization and industrialization caused some degree of ethnic dislocation throughout the country. In the capital, Tehran, as in almost all the country's big cities, Azerbaijanis formed a strong community, dominating the local economy. Furthermore, the expansion of the educational and communication system for the most part contributed to a more homogeneous culture in Iran. This tendency towards homogeneity on the social, political and cultural level may be seen to have culminated in the Islamic Revolution of 1979 and during the years, which followed. Except the Kurdistan call for regional autonomy within Iranian frontiers, one could not find a serious political challenge with either an ethnic or religious flavour.

At the turn of millennium and with the world coming out of the Cold War, the international political setting has been altered. On the other side of Iran's northern frontiers, instead of a great Czarist/Soviet power, which Iran had been used to be living with for the previous two hundred years, a number of small independent states have emerged. Some of these newly independent states accommodate a majority population whose corresponding ethno-linguistic groups live within Iranian territory. The calls for unity of the people who share a common language but live under different national flags are occasionally heard. In the newly formed Republic of Azerbaijan, there are some political groups and intellectual circles that have initiated a campaign advocating the establishment of a greater Azerbaijan. To attain this goal, once again the call has been raised for the province of Iranian Azerbaijan to secede from Iran and to unite with the Republic of Azerbaijan.

In June 1989, during a congress held in Baku, bringing together some academics, artists as well as some trade unionists, the "*Azerbaijan Khalq Jebhesi*" (The People's Front of Azerbaijan-PFA), was formally established. In a programme, which was adopted during the party founding congress, reference was given to the PFA's chief goal as to abolish all political barriers obstructing the development of cultural and economic ties with Iranian Azerbaijan:

> The people's Front supports the restoration of ethnic unity of Azerbaijanis living on both sides of the border. The Azeri people should be recognized as a united whole. Economic, cultural, and social ties between our divided nations should be restored. All obstacles to the creation of direct human contacts (visits to relatives and friends) should be abolished.[7]

While the ethnic violence spreading throughout the Caucasus, and the crisis of Nagorna-Karabagh leaving the Azerbaijanis with a mixed feeling of being ignored or rather humiliated by Moscow, the call for solidarity between all Turkic people of the region, particularly the Azerbaijanis, became the main item in the PFA's agenda. The political air was even more exited when Gorbachev decided to send the Soviet Army to the Caucasus in order to bring the pieces of the empire's jig-saw together. The PFA in its weekly gathering in *Mydan* (square, the largest square in Baku, once an area of official parades, known as Lenin Square) often invited individual Azerbaijanis from the south to the stony podium to address the huge crowds about the bitter pages of their history when they were divided and to express their heartfelt longing to change the status quo and join one another again. Repealing the Tukmenchay Treaty of 1828, which by introducing the Araxes River as the new border between Iran and the Czarist Russia, divided the north and south of the province, became one of the most popular mottos during these congregations.

The call for unification was somehow realised during the last days of 1989, when a crowd of Azerbaijanis from the Nakhjivan province, by dismantling the frontiers posts and installations, crossed the border dividing them form Iranian Azerbaijan. On the Iranian side of the border, the event was observed with caution and the enthusiasm and compassion remained confined to the frontiers settlers who had some family ties in the north. Nevertheless, for some circles in Baku, the event was explicit enough in order to analogise it with the recent fall of the Berlin wall. In the West the event of crossing the border received wide media coverage and for a few days, the whole world through the international television networks became acquainted with the euphoric crowds, burning the frontiers' military installations and clipping barbed wire. In the other corner of Azerbaijan, in the Lenkaron region, the Azerbaijanis also adopted the Nakhjavani practice. Free passage through the Iranian border soon became a common exercise. So far, the Iranian government reaction was nothing other than caution. While the Shi'ite brothers and sisters from the north were most welcomed, nevertheless, they endeavoured to impose a religious dimension to the situation rather than an ethnic one. On the other hand, Moscow by dispatching some provocateurs and agitators in the region and distributing pictures of Ayatollah Khomaini, attempted to pave the way for the justification of its long march towards Azerbaijan in order to bar the spreading of "fundamentalist Islam" within its border.

The Soviet Army's assault on Baku on January 1990, although it was successful to halt the rapid political change in Azerbaijan, nevertheless, was unable to turn the clock back. In September 1990, while country still under martial law, an election for a new Supreme Soviet was conducted. During the election campaign, the PFA, though more cautiously, referred to the question of unity between two Azerbaijans. In its electoral programme, it called for closer cultural as well as economic contacts with "southern Azerbaijan".

In the Caucasus, the economic hardship of the last year of the Soviet rule was mingled with the wide-ranging ethnic conflicts. The most momentous of these conflicts then became the quarrel between two neighbours, Armenia and Azerbaijan concerning the autonomous region of Nagorna-Karabagh, a quarrel that eventually developed into an open military confrontation. As a result of Armenia military successive offensive on the Azerbaijan frontier cities, the ill-equipped Azerbaijani troops suffered a chain of humiliating defeats. While Moscow was standing next to her historical ally, Armenia, the Azerbaijani turned to neighbouring countries for seeking help. However, neither Iran nor Turkey were willing to jeopardise their relations with Moscow.

The failure of the August 1991 coup in Moscow left the former local Communist power elite led by president Ayaz Mutallibov in total confusion and disarray. The late August call for independence was formally ratified on 18 October 1991, with Mutallibov still acting as president. Nevertheless, the political chaos, which was spreading all over the country, forced the president to resign and a new presidential election was held in June 1992. Abulfazl Elchibäy, a former dissident and political prisoner, was elected as the first elected president of the independent Azerbaijan Republic.

Although the term of presidency of Abulfazl Elchibäy did not last more than a year, nevertheless, his programme that included opposition to Azerbaijan's membership in the Commonwealth of Independent States (CIS), close relations with Turkey, ignoring Tehran and exhibiting a desire for extended links with the Azerbaijanis in Iran, caused some mistrust and power re-alignment in the region. For many Iranians, his pro-Turkish nationalistic stand and sincere aspiration to form a greater Azerbaijan which often revealed in his rhetoric that he considers the Republic of Azerbaijan as a place of succour and a harbour for the Iranian Azerbaijan's struggle to secede from Iran and joining the north, was nothing less than the replication of the old Soviet-style scenario. Besides some small nationalist circles of the Azerbaijani in diaspora, Elchibäy's call for a greater Azerbaijan was not enthusiastically received in Iranian Azerbaijan. Yet, however abhorrent the idea of breaking away from Iran and therefore, and being denied access to a potentially huge market, one should still notice the effect which a neighbouring country might have on a bordering province, especially when the people of both regions enjoy a common language and culture. The call for enjoying more cultural rights, right of having a bi-lingual national colloquium in Azerbaijai as well as in Persian, increasingly has become more marked in Iranian Azerbaijan.

The new-born Republic of Azerbaijan, during the one year period of Elchibäy's rule faced wide-spread economic as well as military problems. Unable to address the worsening military situation in Nagorno Karabakh and the declining domestic economy in Azerbaijan, left Elchibäy with no alternative rather than leaving the capital for his birth place, Karaki, a small village in the east of Nakhjivan.

The tragic end of Abulfazl Elchibäy's short rule in Baku was simultaneously marked with the rising of Heidar Aliev to the throne in June1993. Amongst the factors that eased the return of Heidar Aliev to power, one could certainly refer to the disillusionment that the Azerbaijanis observed with Elchibäys's pro-Turkey's policy while in power. At the end, Turkey's competency of helping Azerbaijan turned out to be much less than the emotional liaison.

Contrary to his predecessor, Heidar Aliev from the early days of holding his office, unequivocally displayed his displeasure with any "greater Azerbaijan" scenarios. Even before holding his new presidential post, during his office as president of the Autonomous Republic of Nakhjivan, he made a visit to Iran and paid pilgrimage to the shrine of the Imam Reza in Mashhad. His restrained policy towards Azerbaijan's neighbouring countries, somehow mitigated his predecessor's actions, nevertheless, the mistrust, which was instigated during the short-lived rule of Abulfazl Elchibäy, turned to be more durable and profound than one could expect.

To conclude this epilogue, I recall the final question that Carroll Bogert in one of her interviews for *Newsweek* asked me: "can one expect that one day the dogs of ethnic strife begin to bark in Iran?"[8] My immediate reaction was that so far twentieth-century Iran has succeeded in avoiding the fate which befell the Ottomans, Czarist and later the Soviet empires and the different ethnic groups in Iran, have all got along. Nevertheless, one should not fail to notice that in twenty-first-century Iran the question of ethnicity and territorial integrity, may be more than any other factors associated with sweeping reforms in the country's political structure, in securing the gradual development of a more functional society where the individual as well as the collective rights are observed. Or else, nothing is eternal.

Appendix

The Agreement Between the Iranian Central Government and the Representative of Azerbaijan (13 June 1946)*

Subsequent to negotiations carried on between the State (*Dowlat*) and the representatives of Azerbaijan and as a result of an exchange of views during which the sevenpoint proclamation (*eblaghiyeh*) put forward by the *Dowlat* on 2nd *Ordibehesht* 1325 and accepted by the aforesaid representatives was taken into consideration, it has been agreed that the following explanatory and complementary articles should be drawn up and put into force.

Article 1. It is agreed that the following sentences shall be added to Article 1 of the Government's *eblaghiyeh*: "The Director of Finance also shall be appointed on the proposal of the Provincial Council and his appointment confirmed by the Government."

Article 2. As it is laid down in Article 2 of the Government's *eblaghiyeh* that the Governor-General shall be appointed by the Government after ascertaining the views of the Provincial Council, in order to give effect to this principle it is agreed that the Ministry of the Interior shall elect a Governor-General from among a few individuals proposed by the Provincial Council and shall recommend him to the *Dowlat* for confirmation of his appointment.

---

* The rather clumsy, literal translation of the Agreement is quoted from the F.O. 371/52740, Tabriz Diary, June 1946. By cross-checking with the original text published in *Azad Millat*, no. 51, 16 June 1946, Persian terms have been added to indicate the original terminology.

Article 3. Taking into consideration the recent changes in Azerbaijan, the *Dowlat* will recognize the present *Milli Majlis* [the National Assembly] in place of a Provincial Council. After the convening of the Fifteenth *Majles* and the passing of a new Provincial and District Councils law to be proposed by the *Dowlat*, the election of an Azerbaijan Provincial Council on the basis of the approved law will be immediately begun.

Article 4. The conscript army which was raised as a result of the reform and uprising in Azerbaijan shall become with the signing of this Agreement a part of the Iranian Army, and it is agreed that in order to establish the foundation of this [Azerbaijan] army and its commanders, there shall be formed a commission composed of representatives of the *Dowlat* of Qavam os-Saltaneh and of representatives of the Azerbaijan Provincial Council which will submit proposals for an early settlement of the question.

Article 5. It is agreed that 75 per cent of the revenues of Azerbaijan shall be devoted to local expenditure and 25 per cent shall be sent to the Central Government as a contribution to the general expenses of the Kingdom.

Note 1. The income and expenditure of the Post and Telegraph, the Customs, the Railway and the Lake of Urumiyeh Boat Service pertain entirely to the Central Government and the *Dowlat* will have sole control of them, while it is understood that the Provincial and District Councils and the Government Departments shall have the right to send telegrams free of charge.

Note 2. The *Dowlat* is responsible for the building and repair of the main roads, while the Provincial Council is responsible for the modernization and repair of the secondary and local roads.

Note 3. In recognition of the great services the Azerbaijani people have rendered to the Iranian Constitution and in appreciation of the sacrifices made by the zealous people of Azerbaijan in establishing freedom and democracy, the *Dowlat* agrees that 25 per cent of the customs revenue of Azerbaijan shall be allocated to meet the expenses of the University of Azerbaijan.

Article 6. The *Dowlat* agrees that the extension of the railway between Miyaneh and Tabriz shall be begun forthwith and completed with all speed. It is understood that in this work Azerbaijani workmen and technicians shall have priority of employment.

Article 7. The volunteer forces which are known as *Feda'iyan*, shall be converted into a Gendarmerie and it is agreed that in order to define the functions of these regular forces and likewise for the purpose of appointing their commanders there shall be formed, in Azerbaijan, a commission composed of representatives of the *Dowlat* of Qavam os-Saltaneh and representatives of the Azerbaijan Provincial Council shall submit proposals for the rapid settling of this question.

Note 1. Since in recent years as a result of a number of improper acts the name of "*Amniyeh*" or Gendarmerie arouses general aversion in Iran and particularly in Azerbaijan, and since of late, the Head of Government has personally assumed control of this force and it is expected that reforms and a purge of undesirable elements will be carried out in this department, it is agreed that the general feeling about the Gendarmerie and particularly the feeling of the people of Azerbaijan shall be brought to the notice of head of the *Dowlat* so that the name of this Force may be changed and the necessary decision taken to choose a more suitable name.

Article 8. As regards the lands which were distributed among the peasants as a result of the democratic uprising in Azerbaijan, since the *Dowlat* accepts the principle of the distribution of State lands among the peasants throughout the Kingdom, it sees no objection in the execution of this matter in Azerbaijan as far as the State lands are concerned and will take the first opportunity to put before the Grand National Assembly a law to sanction this measure. As regards the other lands which were distributed among the peasants as a result of the late changes in Azerbaijan, it is agreed that in order to make good the losses suffered by the landlords or to compensate them for their properties, there shall be set up a commission composed of representatives of the *Dowlat* of Qavam os-Saltaneh and representatives of the Azerbaijan Provincial Council which will submit proposals for the settling of this question.

Article 9. The *Dowlat* agrees that as soon as the Fifteenth *Majles* opens it will present to the *Majles* a law for the holding of elections on a free and democratic basis, that is to say, universal, secret, direct, proportional, equal and including women, and the *Dowlat* will request the immediate approval of this law. The *Dowlat* likewise agrees that on the opening day of the Fifteenth *Majles* it will present a law providing for the increase of the number of Deputies from Azerbaijan and other parts of the Kingdom so as to bring the number of Deputies into proportion with the population and will request the passing of this law with double urgency so that after the approval the remaining Deputies from these districts may be elected and sent to the *Majles*.

Article 10. The Province of Azerbaijan shall consist of the Third and Fourth Provinces (*Ostans*).

Article 11. The *Dowlat* agrees that for better conduct of affairs in Azerbaijan there shall be set up a Departmental Council (*Edareh-e Showra*) composed of the GovernorGeneral, the Head of Departments and the Presiding Committee of the Provincial Council, and this Departmental Council shall carry out its task under the supervision of the Provincial Council.

Article 12. As the meaning of Article 3 of the Government's *eblaghiyeh* of the 2nd *Ordibehesht* 1325 concerning the organization of middle and high schools is obscure, the following sentence is added: "In the middle and high schools instruction both in the Persian and Azerbaijani languages shall be carried out on the basis of the Ministry of Culture's reforms corresponding to contemporary and local conditions and democratic principles and on the basis of a program drawn up in suitable form. "

Article 13. The *Dowlat* agrees that the Kurds living in Azerbaijan shall enjoy the advantages of this Agreement and in accordance with Article 3 of the Government's *eblaghiyeh*, instruction up to the Fifth elementary class in their schools shall be in their own language.

Note 1. Minorities living in Azerbaijan, such as Assyrians and Armenians, shall have the right to use their mother tongue for instruction in their schools up to the Fifth class.

Article 14. The *Dowlat* takes note that it will present for approval to the Fifteenth *Majles* a new Town Council Law for all Iran based on democratic principles, i.e. providing for elections by universal, secret, direct and equal suffrage, and as soon as this law is passed the election of Town Councils will begin in Azerbaijan and all other parts of Iran. Until the passing of this law and the holding of new elections the Town Councils at present existing in Azerbaijan will continue to discharge their functions.

Article 15. This Agreement has been drawn up and exchanged in two copies and will be put into force after ratification by the cabinet and the Azerbaijan Provincial Council.

Tabriz, dated 23.3.1325 (13 June 1946)

Mozaffar Firuz-Pishevari

Notes

Introduction

1. As an example, see: *Azerbaijan Tarikhi*, 3 vols., Baku, Azerbaijan Academy of Sciences, 1958–1962.
2. Thomas H., *Armed Truce. The Beginning of the Cold War 1945–1946*, London, Sceptre, 1988, p. 562.
3. Ladjevardi, H., *Labour Unions and Autocracy in Iran*, Syracuse University Press, 1985, p. 287.
4. Beyhaqi, Abolfazl Mohammad, *Tarikh-e Beyhaqi*, Fayyaz, A. (ed.), Mashhad University Press, 1971, pp. 221–2.

Chapter 1: Origins of the Azerbaijanis

1. Markaz-e Amar-e Iran, *Iran dar Ayeneh-e Amar*, 1365, no. 6, Tehran, 1988, p. 276.
2. Kasravi, A., *Azeri ya zaban-e Bastan-e Azerbaijan*, 2nd print, Tehran, Taban, 1938, p. 8.
3. Yaqut al-Hamavi, *Kitab Mu'jam al-Buldan*, Wüstenfeld, F. (ed). vol. 1, Leipzig, Brockhaus, 1866, p. 17.
4. Ibn Faqih, Abu Bakr Ahmad b. Mohammad b. Eshaq Hamedani, *Kitab al-Buldan*, Tehran, Bonyad-e Farhang-e Iran, 1970, p. 128.
5. Anonymous, *Hodud al-'Alam men al-Mashreq ela al-Maghreb*, Sotudeh, M. (ed.), Tehran, Daneshgah-e Tehran, 1962, p. 50.
6. Ibn Hawqal, *Surat al-Arz*, Sho'ar, J. (ed.), Tehran, Bonyad-e Farhang-e Iran, 1966, p. 82.
7. Al-Muqaddasi, Shams al-Din b. Abi Abdollah Mohammad b. Abi Bakr al-Banna al-Sami al-ma'ruf beh al-Beshari, *Ahsan al-Taqasim fi Ma'rifat al-Aqalim*, de Goeje, M.J. (ed.), Leiden, Brill, 1906, p. 259.
8. Yaqut al-Hamavi, *op. cit.*, p. 183.

198

9. Mohammad b. Khalaf Tabrizi motakhalles beh Borhan, *Borhan-e Qate'*, Mo'in, M. (ed.), vol. 1, 2nd print, Tehran, Ebn-e Sina, 1963, p. 41.

10. Al-Istakhri, Abu Ishaq al-Farsi, *Kitab al-Masalik wa-l-Mamalik*, de Goeje, M.J. (ed.), Leiden, Brill, 1927, pp. 191–2.

11. Al-Mas'udi, *Kitab al-Tanbih wa-l-Ishraf*, de Goeje, M.J. (ed.), Leiden, Brill, 1894, pp. 77–8.

12. Yaqut al-Hamavi, *op. cit.*, p. 173.

13. Frye, R.N. (ed.), *The Cambridge History of Iran*, vol. 4, Cambridge, Cambridge University Press, 1975, p. 238.

14. Boyle, J.A. (ed.), *The Cambridge History of Iran*, vol. 5, Cambridge, Cambridge University Press, 1968, p. 44.

15. *Ibid.*, pp. 349–56.

16. Jackson, P. (ed.), *The Cambridge History of Iran*, vol. 6, Cambridge, Cambridge University Press, 1986, p. 162.

17. Kasravi, A., *op. cit.*, p. 25.

18. Rumlu, Hasan Beg, *Ahsan al-Tavarikh*, Navai, A. (ed.), Tehran, Babak, 1978, p. 87.

19. Avery, P., Hambly, G., Melville, C. (eds.), *The Cambridge History of Iran*, vol. 7, 1991, p. 45.

20. Seton-Watson, H., *Nation and State, An Enquiry into the Origin of Nations and the Politics of Nationalism*, Boulder, Westview Press, 1977, p. 5.

21. Gellner, E., *Nations and Nationalism*, Oxford, Blackwell, 1983, p. 15.

22. Connor, W., "A Nation is a Nation, is a State, is an Ethnic Group", *Ethnic and Racial Studies*, vol. I, no. 4, p. 381.

23. Anderson, B., *Imagined Communities, Reflections on the Origin and Spread of Nationalism*, 3rd print, London, Verso, p. 16.

24. Connor, W., "A Nation is a Nation, is a State, is an Ethnic Group, ...", op. cit.

25. Stalin, J., *Marxism and the National Question*, New York, International Publishers, 1935, cited in Connor, W., *The National Question in Marxist-Leninist Theory and Strategy*, New Jersey, Princeton University Press, 1984, p. 121.

26. Anderson, B., *op. cit.*, p. 15.

27. *Ibid.*

28. Andrews, P., *Ethnic Groups in the Republic of Turkey*, Wiesbaden, Ludwig Reichert Verlag, 1989, pp. 17–18.

29. Oscanyan, C., *The Sultan and His People*, vol. 2, New York, Derby & Jackson, 1857, p. 409, cited in: Davidson, R., "Nationalism as an Ottoman Problem and the Ottoman Response", in Haddad, W.W. and Coshenwald, W. (ed.) *Nationalism in a Non-Nation State*, Columbus, Ohio State University Press, 1977, p. 34.

30. Safi Alishah, *Zobdat al-Asrar*, Tehran, Safi 'Alishah, 1962, p.363.
31. Berkes, N., *The Development of Secularism in Turkey*, Montreal, McGill University Press, 1964, p. 197.
32. Lewis, B., *The Emergence of Modern Turkey*, London, Oxford University Press, 1962, p. 330.
33. Davidson, R., *op. cit.*, p. 33.
34. "Napoleon à Nasser-ed-din Schah, Palais de Tuilerie, 12 Avril 1858", in: Nateq, H., *Iran dar Rah-yabi-ye Farhangi, 1834-1848*, London, Payam, 1988, p. 142.
35. Nateq, H., *op. cit.*, p. 257.
36. Moshiri, M., *Sharh-e Ma'muriyat-e Ajudanbashi*, Tehran, Ashrafi, 1977, p. 226.
37. *Ibid.*, p. 342.
38. Adamiyat, F., *Fekr-e Azadi va Moqaddameh-e Nahzat-e Mashrutiyat*, Tehran, Sokhan, 1961, p. 186.
39. *Ibid.*
40. Mostashar od-Dowleh, Y., *Resaleh-e Mosumeh beh Yek Kalemeh*, Paris, no publisher given, undated, p. 14.
41. *Ibid.*, p. 39.
42. *Ibid.*, p. 8.
43. *Ibid*, p. 12.
44. Mostashar od-Dowleh to Crown Prince Mozaffar od-Din, cited in Nazem ol-Islam Kermani, *Tarikh-e Bidari-ye Iraniyan*, new edition, Tehran, Agah and Novin, 1983, pp. 176-7.
45. Adamiyat, F., *op. cit.*, p. 197.
46. Rahimi, M., *Qanun-e Asasi-ye Iran va Osul-e Demokrasi*, 3rd edition, Tehran, Amir Kabir, 1978, pp. 213-22.
47. Sani' od-Dowleh, *Rah-e Nejat*, Tehran, Farus, 1907.
48. Kelekiar, D., *Turc-Francais Dictionnaire*, Istanbul, Mehran Matb'asi, 1911, p. 122.
49. Safa'i, E., *Rahbaran-e Mashruteh: Sani' od-Dowleh*, Tehran, no publisher given, 1964, p. 5.
50. Anonymous, *Haqq-e Daf'-e Sharr va Qiyam bar Zedd-e Zolm*, no publisher given, undated, p. 17.
51. "*Mellat Kist va Hoquqash Chist?*", a nocturnal leaflet distributed on 30 March 1909, reprinted in the memoirs of Sharif Kashani, M.M., *Vaqe'at-e Ettefaqiyyeh dar Ruzegar*, vol. 1, Tehran, Nashr-e Tarikh-e Iran, 1983, p. 314.
52. *Maram-nameh-e Jam'iyat-e Sosyal-Revolusiyoner-e Iran*, Tehran, Matba'eh-e Dowlati, undated, p. 4.
53. *Ibid.*

54. Hovanissian, R.G., *The Republic of Armenia*, vol. 1, Berkeley, University of California, Press, 1971, pp. 25–8.

55. Carr, E.H., *The Bolshevik Revolution 1917–1923*, vol. 1, London, Macmillan, 1950, p. 342.

56. Hovanissian, R.G., *op. cit.*, p. 31.

57. *Ibid.*

58. *Ibid*, p. 288.

59. Akçuroğlu, Y. (ed.), *Türk Yili, 1928*, Istanbul, Yeni Matba'eh, 1928, p. 483.

60. Mohammad Amin Rasulzadeh to Taqizadeh, 15 March 1924, *Ayandeh*, vol. 4, nos. 1–2, 1988, pp. 57–9.

61. For a detailed study on the history of Russian Azerbaijan, see: Kazemzadeh, F., *The Struggle for Transcaucasus (1917–1921)*, New York, Philosophical Library, 1951. Swietochowski, T., *Russian Azerbaijan 1905–1920, The Shaping of National Identity in a Muslim Community*, Cambridge, Cambridge University Press, 1985. Sumbatzadeh, A.S. *Azerbaidzhanskaia Istoriografia XIX–XX vekov*, Baku, 'Elm, 1987. Altstadt, A., *The Azerbaijani Turks, Power and Identity under Russian Rule*, Stanford, Hoover Institute Press, 1992.

62. The Azerbaijan Republic (Soviet Socialist Republic, SSR, until 1991) comprises 86,600 square kilometres. According to the Soviet general census of 1989, the population of the Soviet Azerbaijan was 7,029,000, of which Azerbaijanis made up some 75 per cent of the total. See: *USSR Census '89*, Moscow, Novosti Press, 1989.

Chapter 2: Genesis of the Autonomous Movement in Azerbaijan

1. Mokhber os-Saltaneh Hedayat, M., *Khaterat va Khatarat*, 3rd edition, Tehran, Zavvar, 1982, p. 143.

2. The six categories of the electorate were: Qajar princes, 'ulama and mullahs, nobles, merchants, landlords and guild members.

3. Kasravi, A., *Tarikh-e Mashruteh-e Iran*, vol. 1, 14th edition, Tehran, Amir Kabir, 1978, p. 224.

4. Taqizadeh, H., *Khetabeh, Tarikh-e Ava'el Enqelab va Mashruteh-e Iran*, Tehran, Bashgah-e Mehregan, 1959, p. 46.

5. In his memoirs, Ehtesham os-Saltaneh, who was the head of the *Majles*, gives the details of his visit with the Shah, and describes how the Shah had hesitated to ratify the Supplementary Laws. See: Ehtesham os-Saltaneh, *Khaterat*, 2nd edition, Tehran, Zavvar, 1988, pp. 610–11.

6. Kasravi, A., *Tarikh-e Mashruteh-e Iran, op. cit.*, p. 165.

7. Nateq, H., "Anjoman-ha-ye Showra'i dar Enqelab-e Mashruteh", *Alefba*, no. 4, Paris, 1983, p. 55.

8. F.O. 371/301, Spring Rice to Grey, 27 May 1907.
9. *Ibid.*
10. "Ma-ra Che Bayad Kard", *Anjoman*, 2nd year, no. 29, 6 June 1908.
11. *Jarideh-e Melli*, 1st year, no. 1, 19 October 1906.
12. Ehtesham os-Saltaneh, *op. cit.*, p. 594.
13. Nateq, H., "Anjoman-ha-ye Showra'i dar Enqelab-e Mashruteh", *op. cit.*
14. Adamiyat, F., *Fekr-e Demokrasi-ye Ejtema'i dar Nahzat-e Mashrutiyat-e Iran*, Tehran, Payam, 1975, p. 34.
15. See for example: *Anjoman*, no. 66, 17 April 1907.
16. Kasravi, A., *Tarikh-e Mashruteh-e Iran*, *op. cit.*, pp. 214–15.
17. *Ibid.*, pp. 584–6. *Anjoman* has published this declaration too, although there are some minor differences in *Anjoman*'s version from that published by Kasravi, see: *Anjoman*, no. 30, 11 June 1908.
18. *Anjoman*, no. 31, 13 June 1908.
19. Malekzadeh, M., *Tarikh-e Enqelab-e Mashrutiyat-e Iran*, vol. 4, 2nd edition, Tehran, 'Elmi, 1984, p. 706 and pp. 748–60. See also, Kasravi, A., *Tarikh-e Mashruteh-e Iran*, *op. cit.*, pp. 631–57.
20. Open letter to the Prime Minister, Moshir os-Saltaneh, Dutch Archives, Archief van de Nederlandse Legatie te Teheran, Politieke Zaken, 25 June 1908.
21. Malekzadeh, M., *op. cit.*, p. 936–7.
22. Kasravi, A., *Tarikh-e Mashruteh-e Iran*, *op. cit.*, p. 236.
23. Kasravi, A., *Tarikh-e Mashruteh-e Iran*, *op. cit.*, p. 216.
24. Kasravi, A., *Tarikh-e Mashruteh-e Iran*, *op. cit.*, p. 355. The English translation is taken from Abrahamian, E., *Iran Between Two Revolutions*, Princeton University Press, 1982, p. 98.
25. Malekzadeh, M., *op. cit.*, p. 937.
26. Kasravi, A., *Tarikh-e Mashruteh-e Iran*, *op. cit.*, p. 676.
27. Malekzadeh, M., *op. cit.*, p. 969.
28. Telegram to Tehran from Tabriz, 16 May 1909, Sharif Kashani; M.M., *op. cit.*, p. 308.
29. *Ibid*, p. 943. See also: Mokhber os-Saltaneh, M., *op. cit.*, p. 174.
30. Kasravi, A., *Tarikh-e Mashruteh-e Iran*, *op. cit.*, p. 628.
31. Letter of the Sa'adat Society to the Minister of Foreign Affairs of Holland, Dutch Archives, Archief van de Nederlandse Legatie te Teheran, Politieke Zaken, 15 July 1909.
32. Kasravi, A., *Tarikh-e Mashruteh-e Iran*, *op. cit.*, p. 726.
33. Hoseyn Aqa Feshangchi, Memoirs, in: Rezazadeh Malek, R., *Heydar Khan 'Amoghlu*, Tehran, Ruzbeh, undated, p. 145.
34. Taherzadeh Behzad, K., *Qiyam-e Azerbaijan dar Enqelab-e Mashrutiyat-e Iran*, Tehran, Eqbal, 1963, p. 45.

35. A number of interesting letters exchanged between the Tabrizi Social Democrat, Chalangariyan, and Karl Kautsky throw light on the position which the Iranian Social Democrats felt they had to adopt with regard to the Constitutional Revolution. They document an early stage in the development of political concepts and social attitudes which to this day have played a major role in Iranian political life. Archives of the International Institute for Social History, Amsterdam. Also see: "Asnad-e Tazeh dar Bareh-e Goruh-e Sosiyal-Demokrat-e Tabriz", *Donya*, vol. 12, no. 4, Winter 1971. Kambakhsh, 'A., "Dar Bareh-e Sosiyal-Demokrasi-ye Enqelabi", *Donya*, vol. 3, no. 2, Summer 1962.

36. For details on this Agreement, see: Ramazani, R., *The Foreign Policy of Iran (1500–1941)*, University Press of Virginia, 1966, pp. 88–94.

37. F.O. 371/956, Annual Report on Persia, 1909, p. 8.

38. For a detailed study on the formation of the political parties in Iran, see: Ettehadieh, M., *Peydayesh va Tahavvol-e Ahzab-e Siyasi-ye Mashrutiyat*, Tehran, Gostareh, 1982.

39. Atabaki, T., "Two Programmes of the Communist Movement in Khorasan in the Early 1920's", *Utrecht Papers on Central Asia*, Utrecht, University of Utrecht, 1987, p. 146.

40. Ra'in, I., *Heydar Khan 'Amoghlu*, vol. 2, Tehran, no publisher given, 1979, p. 265.

41. *Donya*, vol. 4, no. 3, Autumn 1963, p. 89.

42. Anonymous, "Sanad-i Nashenakhteh dar Bareh-e Hezb-e Sosyal-Demokrat-e Iran", *Donya*, vol. 7, no. 2, Summer 1966, pp. 99–103.

43. For a detailed discussion on the formation of *Hemmat* and the early Iranian Social-Democrat movement see: Ravasani, S., *Sowjetrepublik Gilan: Die sozialistische Bewegung in Iran seit Ende des 19JH. bis 1922*, Berlin, no publisher given, undated.

44. Letter to Taqizadeh from Pilosiyan cited in Afshar, I., *Owraq-e Tazehyab-e Mashrutiyat* Tehran, Javidan, 1980, p. 228.

45. Mahmud Mahmud, as a founder of the party, in his memoirs names these eight members. See: Adamiyat, F., *Fekr-e Azadi, op. cit.*, p. 334

46. Pilosiyan to Taqizadeh, 30 February 1910, Afshar, I., *Owraq-e Tazehyab-e Mashrutiyat, op. cit.*, p. 220

47. *Kaveh*, vol. 3, no. 29/30, 15 July 1918, pp. 6–8. Bahar, a prominent Democrat, gives the number of Democrat deputies at the *Majles* as twenty-eight. See: Bahar, M., *Tarikh-e Mokhtasar-e Ahzab-e Siyasiye Iran*, vol. 1, Tehran, Jibi, 1978, p. 9.

48. Abrahamian, E., *Iran Between Two Revolutions, op. cit.*, p. 103.

49. *Maram-nameh-e Ferqeh-e Siyasi-ye Demokrat-e Iran ('Amiyun)*, 4th edition, Tehran, Matba'eh-e Dowlati, 1911.
50. *Iran-e Now*, vol. 1, no. 134, 16 February 1919.
51. Browne, E.G., *The Press and Poetry of Modern Persia*, Cambridge, Cambridge University Press, 1914, pp. 27–153.
52. *Ibid*, p. 52.
53. Adamiyat, F., *Fekr-e Demokrasi-ye Ijtema'i dar Nahzat-e Mashruteh-e Iran*, *op. cit.*, pp. 96–7.
54. Rasulzadeh, M.A., *Tanqid-e Ferqeh-e E'tedaliyun ya Ejtema'iyun E'tedaliyun*, Tehran, Farus, 1910.
55. Abrahamian, E., *Iran Between Two Revolutions*, *op. cit.*, p. 102.
56. For the details of the ultimatum see: Kasravi, A., *Tarikh-e Hejdah Saleh-e Azerbaijan*, vol. I, 9th edition, Tehran, Amir Kabir, 1978, pp. 235–40.
57. Ramazani, R. *op. cit.*, pp. 103–8.
58. Blucher, W.V., *Zeitenwende*, Persian Translation: *Safar-nameh-e Blucher*, Tehran, Khwarazmi, 1984, p. 37.
59. Ramazani, R.; *op. cit.*, p. 115.
60. *Ibid.*, p. 117.
61. *Kaveh*, *op. cit.*, pp. 9–10.
62. For details of these ethnic and communal conflicts see: Kasravi. A., *Tarikh-e Hejdah Saleh-e Azerbaijan*, vol. 2, 9th edition, Tehran, Amir Kabir, 1978, pp. 671–783.
63. *Ibid.*, p. 674.
64. Agahi, Abdolhoseyn, "Shast Sal az Tarikh-e Ta'sis-e Hezb-e Komonist Iran Gozasht", *Donya*, no. 3., 1980, pp. 48–9.
65. *Donya*, vol. 12, No. 2, Summer 1971, pp. 101–9.
66. *Ibid.*, p. 106.
67. *Proclamation and Irreversible Proposals of the Khorasan Provincial Committee*, for the English translation see: Atabaki, T., *op. cit.*, pp. 151–6.
68. Lenin, V., "The Right of Nations to Self-determination", in: *Selected Writings*, Moscow, Progress Publishers, 1966, p. 350.
69. Until quite recently, it was widely believed that the Second Congress of the Communist Party of Iran was held at Urumiyeh, a city in western Azerbaijan, but according to Ehsan Tabari, a veteran Communist and leader of the Tudeh Party whose memoirs were published recently, the location of the Congress was not Urumiyeh, but Rostov, a city close to the Sea of Azov in the Soviet Union. See: Tabari, E., *Kazh-Raheh*, Tehran, Amir Kabir, 1987, p. 17.
70. "Program of the Communist Party of Iran", *Donya*, vol. 1, no. 4, 1961, p. 118.

71. Lewis, B., *op. cit.*, p. 338.
72. Mehmet Amin, *Türkçe Şirler*, 1897, cited in Lewis, B., *op. cit.*, p. 337. The name Turk, in Turkish usage, as well as in Persian, had always connoted a barbarian, robber, plunderer, vagabond and an ignorant person. See: Steingass, F., *Persian-English Dictionary*, 6th impression, London, Routledge and Kegan Paul, 1977, p. 296.
73. Akçuroğlu, Y., *Üç Terz-i Siyaset*, Cairo, Matba'eh-i Qadr, 1909, pp. 11–12.
74. Akçuroğlu, Y., (ed.), *Türk Yılı, 1928*, Istanbul, Yeni Metba'a, 1928, p. 396.
75. Lewis, B., *op. cit.*, p. 343.
76. *Ibid.*, p. 344.
77. *Ibid.*, p. 345.
78. Gökalp, Z., *Türkçülük Esasları* (The Principles of Turkism), Leiden, Brill, 1968, p. 17.
79. *Ibid.*
80. Kasravi, A., *Tarikh-e Hejdah Saleh-e Azerbaijan*, vol. 2, *op. cit.*, p. 749.
81. *Ibid.*
82. Malekzadeh, M., *op. cit.*, p. 959.
83. Anonymous, *Sharh-e Hal-e Sheykh Mohammad Khiyabani*, Berlin, Iranshahr, 1926, pp. 23_9. See also: Azari, A., *Qiyam-e Sheykh Mohammad Khiyabani*, 4th edition, Tehran, Safi 'Alishah, 1975, p. 10.
84. Kasravi, A., *Tarikh-e Hejdah Saleh-e Azerbaijan*, *op. cit.*, pp. 675–6.
85. *Mozakerat-e Majles*, 23 February 1911.
86. *Ibid.*
87. Kasravi, A., *Tarikh-e Hejdah Saleh-e Azerbaijan*, *op. cit.*, p. 678.
88. *Ibid.*, pp. 686–704.
89. Dowlatabadi, Y., *Hayat-e Yahya*, 3rd edition, vol. 3, Tehran, Ferdowsi, 1982, p. 85.
90. Azari, A., *op. cit.*, p. 225.
91. Kasravi, A., *Tarikh-e Hejdah Saleh-e Azerbaijan*, *op. cit.*, p. 859.
92. F.O. 371/6440, Report on Azerbaijan during 1920.
93. Azari, A., *op. cit.*, p. 263.
94. F.O. 248/1278, Interview with Khiyabani, 1 May 1920.
95. Azari, A., *op. cit.*, p. 149.
96. Kasravi, A., *Tarikh-e Hejdah Saleh-e Azerbaijan*, *op. cit.*, p. 872.
97. Azari, A., *op. cit.*, p. 299.
98. F.O. 371/1278, 11–12 September 1920.
99. F.O. 371/4927, 20 September 1920.

100. Yaqikiyan, G., *Showravi va Jonbesh-e Jangal, Yaddasht-ha-ye Yek Shahed-e 'Eyni*, Tehran, Novin, 1984, p. 137.

101. The Cossack Brigade was formed in 1879 and composed of Iranian troops. Being under the command of Russian military officers, it soon came to enjoy a reputation for military discipline, rigidness and brutality. The most notorious example of its intervention occurred in 1907, when under the command of the Russian colonel Liakhov, the brigade bombarded the *Majles*. Following the collapse of the Tsarist Empire in 1917, Russian control over the Cossack Brigade ceased. The Cossack Brigade continued to exist and, indeed, provided Reza Khan with the military support necessary to launch his *coup d'état* in 1921. Reza Khan then merged the Brigade with the Gendarmerie as part of his reorganization of Iran's national army. F.O. 371/2762, Memorandum on the Persian Army, 1907.

102. F.O. 371/4927. In his memoirs, Mokhber os-Saltaneh denies the accusation that Khiyabani was murdered by the troops of the Cossack Brigade. He pretends that Khiyabani committed suicide in the cellar of his house when the troops surrounded the premises. See: Mokhber os-Saltaneh, M., *op. cit.*, p. 318. According to Bristow, however, a member of staff in the British Consulate at Tabriz: "The Sheykh was discovered in his hiding place and shot by Cossacks". See: F.O. 371/1278, 15 September 1920.

Chapter 3: The Reign of Reza Shah: one country, one nation

1. Taqieva, A., *Natsional'no-Osvoboditl'noye Dvizheniye v Iranskom Azerbaidzhane v 1917-1920*, Baku, 1956, p. 114. See also: "Zendegi-ye Yek Mobarez-e Kohansal", *Donya*, vol. 11, no. 4, 1974, pp. 54–5.

2. Ivanov, M., *Tarikh-e Novin-e Iran*, Stockholm, Tudeh, 1977, p. 52.

3. Banani, A., *The Modernization of Iran, 1921-1941*, California, Stanford University Press, 1961, p. 34.

4. *Ibid.*

5. "Türk Ocağınde Konfirans", *Yeni Mecmu'a*, no. 81, 2 August 1923, pp. 317–18.

6. *Iranshahr*, no. 2, 18 October 1923, pp. 95–103. Here loosely rendered in English.

7. Afshar, M., "Aghaz-nameh", *Ayandeh*, vol. 1, no. 1, 1925, p. 5.

8. *Ibid.*, p. 6.

9. *Ayandeh*, vol. 2, no. 8, 1926, pp. 560–61.

10. *Ibid.*, pp. 561–2.

11. *Ibid.*, p. 566.

12. Ganji, M., and Milani, A., "Iran: Developments During The Last Fifty Years", in Jacqz, J.W. (ed.), *Iran, Past and Future*, New York, Aspen Institute for Humanistic Studies, 1976, p. 45.
13. *Ibid.*
14. Makki, H., *Tarikh-e Bist Saleh-e Iran*, vol. 6, Tehran, Nasher, 1983. See also: Mokhber os-Saltaneh, M., *Khaterat va Khatarat, op. cit.*, p. 411.
15. For the Press in Reza Shah's era, see: Sadr-Hashemi, M., *Tarikh-e Jarayed va Matbu'at-e Iran*, vol. 1, Isfahan, Kamal, 1984, pp. 29–33.
16. Makki, H., *op. cit.*, pp. 412–13
17. Lambton, A.K.S., *Landlord and Peasant in Persia*, London, Oxford University Press, 1951, pp. 285–6. See also: Makki, H., *op. cit.*, pp. 66–80.
18. Banani, A., *op. cit.*, p. 130.
19. Floor, W., *Industrialization in Iran, 1900–1941*, Occasional Papers Series, no. 23, University of Durham Press, 1984, pp. 53–5.
20. *Ibid.*, pp. 58–63.
21. Millspaugh, A., *Americans in Persia*, New York, Da Capo Press, 1976, p. 36.

Chapter 4: The Rebirth of the Autonomous Movement in Azerbaijan

1. Anonymous, *Gozashteh Cheragh-e Rah-e Ayandeh Ast*, vol. 1, Tehran, Zebarjad, undated, p. 19.
2. *Ettela'at*, no. 4, July 1941.
3. Azimi, F., *Iran, The Crisis of Democracy*, London, Tauris, 1989, p. 35.
4. Abutorabiyan, H., *Matbu'at-e Iran az Shahrivar 1320 ta 1326*, Tehran, Ettela'at, 1987, p. 13.
5. Elwell Sutton, L.P., "Political Parties in Iran", *The Middle East Journal*, no. 1, 1949, pp. 45–62.
6. F.O. 371/40172, Russian Relations and Activities in Persia since 1941.
7. *Ibid.*
8. Khameh'i, A., *Forsat-e Bozorg-e az Dast Rafteh*, Tehran, Hafteh, 1984, p. 35.
9. For a detailed study of the Tudeh Party see: Abrahamian, E., *Social Bases of Iranian Politics, The Tudeh Party (1941–1953)*, Ph.D. thesis, Columbia University, 1969. In recent years, a number of memoirs have been published by leaders and ex-members of the Tudeh Party. Some of these memoirs contain first-hand information on the early history of the Tudeh Party. See: Eskandari, I., *Khaterat*, in four vols., Paris, Hezb-e

Demokratik-e Mardom-e Iran, 1988; Jahanshahlu Afshar, N., *Ma va Biganegan*, in two vols., Berlin, no publisher given, 1982; Khameh'i, A., *Khaterat*, in three vols.: *Panjah Nafar va Seh Nafar, Forsat-e Bozorg-e az Dast Rafteh , Az Enshe'ab ta Kudeta*, Tehran, Hafteh, 1984; Forutan, Gh., *Afsaneh-e Ma*, no publisher given, undated; Tabari, E., *Kazh Raheh*, Tehran, Amir Kabir, 1987; Maleki, K., *Khaterat-e Siyasi*, Tehran, Ravaq, 1981; Keshavarz, F., *Man Mottaham Mikonam*, Tehran, Ravaq, 1980.

10.   Among the veteran Communists was Ja'far Pishevari, Commissar of Foreign Affairs in the short-lived Republic of Gilan, which was set up by the *Jangalis* in 1920. Although Pishevari attended the gathering at Soleyman Mirza's house, he never joined the Tudeh Party. For more details about Pishevari, see Chapter 5.

11.   For a detailed study of "The Fifty-Three", see: Abrahamian, E., *Iran Between Two Revolutions*, op. cit., pp. 155–62. Also the following memoirs: Eskandari, I., op. cit., vol. 1; Khameh'i, A., *Panjah Nafar va Seh Nafar*, op. cit.; Jahanshahlu, N., op. cit.; Maleki, K., op. cit.

12.   *Siyasat*, no. 1, February 1942, in: *Gozashteh Cheragh-e Rah-e Ayandeh Ast*, op. cit., p. 135.

13.   For the text of the Treaty see Appendix.

14.   *Gozashteh Cheragh-e Rah-e Ayandeh Ast*, op. cit., p. 150.

15.   *Ibid.*, p. 153.

16.   *Foreign Relations of the United States*, 1942, vol. 4, p. 227, Dreyfus to the Secretary of State, 5 March 1942.

17.   Mosaddeq, M., *Mozakerat-e Majles*, 26 July 1945.

18.   Dreyfus to the Secretary of State, 5 March 1942, op. cit.

19.   Mokhber os-Saltaneh, M., op. cit. p. 351.

20.   Mehdinia, J., *Zendegi-ye Siyasi-ye Qavam os-Saltaneh*, Tehran, Pasargard, 1987, p. 46. Also Makki, H., op. cit., vol. 2, pp. 364–71.

21.   Dreyfus to the Secretary of State, 5 August 1942, op. cit., p. 152.

22.   *Ibid.*, p. 151.

23.   For detailed accounts of the two days of rioting, see: Kuhi Kermani, H., *Az Shahrivar-e 1320 ta Faje'eh-e Azerbaijan va Zanjan*, vol. 2, Tehran, Mazaheri, 1946, pp. 313–71; also McFarland, S.L., "Anatomy of an Iranian Political Crowd: The Tehran Bread Riot of December 1942", *International Journal of Middle East Studies*, no. 17, 1985, pp. 51–65.

24.   Khameh'i A., *Forsat-e Bozorg-e az Dast Rafteh*, op. cit., pp. 58–67.

25.   Dreyfus to the Secretary of State, 13 December 1942, op. cit., p. 219.

26.   Khameh'i, A., *Forsat-e Bozorg-e az Dast Rafteh*, op. cit., p. 59.

27.   F.O. 371/40172, Russian Relations and Activities in Persia Since 1941.

28.   Abrahamian, E., *Iran Between Two Revolutions*, op. cit., p. 186.

29.   F.O. 371/61993, The Tudeh Party and Iranian Trade Unions.

30. *Rahbar*, no. 281, 8 May 1944.
31. *Gozashteh Cheragh-e Rah-e Ayandeh Ast*, op. cit., p. 170.
32. *Ibid.*
33. *Azhir*, no. 157, 15 June 1944.
34. Abrahamian, E., *Iran-e Between Two Revolutions, op. cit.*, p. 200.
35. Key Ostovan, H., *Siyasat-e Movazeneh-e Manfi dar Majles-e Chahardahom*, vol. 1, Tehran, Taban, 1948, p. 128.
36. *Mozakerat-e Majles*, 22 June 1944.
37. *Mozakerat-e Majles*, 3 July 1944.
38. *Mozakerat-e Majles*, 13 July 1944.
39. Several deputies, including Mosaddeq, argued that for a bill to be passed by the *Majles*, it must receive a majority of half plus one of all votes cast. See: *Mozakerat-e Majles*, 13 July 1944.
40. *Azhir*, no. 169, 16 July 1944.
41. F.O. 371/40172, Russian Relations and Activities in Persia Since 1941.
42. F.O. 371/40177, Tabriz Diary of 1944, no. 1, 1–15 January 1944.
43. *Ibid.*
44. *Ibid.*
45. F.O. 371/40177, Tabriz Diary of 1944, no. 2, 16–31 January 1944.
46. F.O. 371/40177, Tabriz Diary for 1944, no. 4, 15 February–6 March 1944.
47. *Ibid.*
48. F.O. 371/40177, Tabriz Diary for 1944, no. 7, 20 April–4 May 1944.
49. *Mozakerat-e Majles*, 9 December 1944.
50. Key Ostovan, H., vol. 1, *op. cit.*, pp. 156–157.
51. *Ibid.*
52. *Mozakerat-e Majles*, 10 August 1944.
53. Fateh, M., *Panjah Sal Naft-e Iran*, 2nd edition, Tehran, Payam, 1979, p. 355.
54. *Azhir*, no. 205, 26 October 1944.
55. *Rahbar*, no. 402, 13 October 1944; no. 411, 24 October 1944.
56. The party's liaison with the Soviet authorities, Qazar Simoniyan, at first tried to reject the Soviets' request that a demonstration be organized in support of the oil concession. As a ploy to get the Soviets to change their mind, he referred to the possibility of the right-wing parties attacking the Tudeh demonstrators. Instead of backing off, the Soviet authorities insisted that they send troops to protect the demonstrators.
57. *Rahbar*, no. 380, 12 September 1944.
58. Al-e Ahmad, the outstanding Iranian essayist, some years later in a reflective article recalls how, on 27 October 1944, he left the ranks of the demonstrators in shame when he saw the first signs of the Soviet

military presence in the streets. Al-e Ahmad, J., *Dar Khedmat va Khiyanat-e Roshanfekran*, vol. 2, Tehran, Khwarazmi, 1978, p. 175.

59. Kambakhsh, A., *Nazar-i beh Jonbesh-e Kargari va Komonisti dar Iran*, Stassfurt, Tudeh, 1972, pp. 88–91.

60. Eskandari, I., *Khaterat, op. cit.*, vol. 2, pp. 84–6; Khameh'i, A., *Forsat-e Bozorg-e az Dast Rafteh, op. cit.*, pp. 130–45.

61. *Mozakerat-e Majles*, 29 October 1944.

62. Kuhi Kermani, H., *op. cit.*, p. 624.

63. F.O. 371/40241, Telegram From Foreign Office to Sir Reader Bullard, 3 October 1944.

64. F.O. 371/40243, Draft note for the Secretary of State (for Cabinet), 16 October 1944.

65. See for example:"*Sar-o-Tah Yek Karbas*", the editorial written by Khalil Maleki, *Rahbar*, no. 438, 10 December 1944.

66. *Azhir*, no. 250, 18 February 1945.

67. Parliamentary speeches by Fereydun Keshavarz, Ardashes Ovanessian and Iraj Eskandari on 17 January, 21 January and 28 May 1945, respectively, *Mozakerat-e Majles*.

68. Atabaki, T., "L'Organisation syndicale ouvrière en Iran, de 1941 à 1946", *Soual*, no. 8, Paris, February 1988, pp. 44–8.

69. Khameh'i, A., *Forsat-e Bozorg-e az Dast Rafteh, op. cit.*, pp. 152–3.

70. One such forceful measure Bayat undertook was to co-operate with certain deputies in the *Majles* such as Mosaddeq in order to end the second mission of Millspaugh, the American adviser to Iran's Department of Finance. Millspaugh's second mission began in 1943, seventeen years after his first engagement, but this time it came to an end in a more scandalous and destructive atmosphere. For instance, the latter's introduction of a new tax bill facilitated greater financial corruption in the country. Concerning the records of Millspaugh's second mission, see: *Gozashteh Cheragh-e Rah-e Ayandeh Ast, op. cit.*, pp. 160–69.

71. Khameh'i, A., *Forsat-e Bozorg-e az Dast Rafteh, op. cit.*, p. 162.

72. Parliamentary speech, *Mozakerat-e Majles*, 23 September 1945. Also Sadr, M., *Khaterat-e Sadr ol-Ashraf*, Tehran, Vahid, 1985, pp. 30–191.

73. *Bagh-e Shah* - The Shah's Garden, a government park now in the center of Tehran where the most prominent of the Constitutionalists were executed during the purges carried out by order of Mohammad 'Ali Shah.

74. Key Ostovan, H., *op. cit.*, vol. 2, p. 49.

75. *Rahbar*, no. 624, 7 August 1945.

76. *Rahbar*, no. 620, 1 August 1945.

77. For details on this legislative motion and the diverse reactions to it, see: Key Ostovan, H., *op. cit.*, vol. 2, pp. 118–59.

78. Years after the event, Ahmad Zanganeh, an Iranian officer, described the panic and disorder which the sudden Russian offensive caused to break out amidst the defending Iranian troops. For his account, see: Zanganeh, A., *Khaterat-i az Ma'muriyat-ha-ye Man dar Azerbaijan*, Tehran, Sharq, 1976, pp. 16–34.

79. Dutch Archive, Archief van de Nederlandse Legatie te Teheran, Verslag Over Iraanse Militaire Zaken, 8 March 1944.

80. Pakdaman, N., *Amar-nameh-e Eqtesad-e Iran dar Aghaz-e Jang-e Jahani-ye Dovvom*, vol. 1, Tehran University Press, 1976, p. 9.

81. Mosaddeq, M., Parliamentary speech, *Mozakerat-e Majles*, 20 April 1945.

82. *Ibid*. See also: *Faryad*, no. 21, 13 July 1942.

83. *Bank-e Markazi-ye Iran*, no. 208–9, Tehran, 1959.

84. F.O. 371/27192, Tabriz Diary for November 1940.

85. *Ibid*.

86. *Azhir*, no. 165, 4 July 1944.

87. *Azhir*, no. 155, 11 June 1944.

88. F.O. 371/31426, Tabriz Diary, 24 July 1942.

89. F.O. 371/35090, Tabriz Diary, 8–15 February 1943.

90. Aslan Daneshiyan, Gholam Yahya's son, very generously gave me a copy of his father's unpublished memoirs during my visit to Baku in October 1989. I am deeply grateful to him.

91. *Rahbar*, no. 565, 24 May 1945.

92. F.O. 371/31426, Tabriz Diary, 24 July 1942.

93. Chashm Azar, M.Q., *Azerbaijan Demokratik Partiyasinin Yarannasi va Fa'aliyyati*, Baku, Elm, 1986, p. 18.

94. *Ibid*.

95. *Ibid*. In the catalogue of Persian newspapers in the Library of Tehran University, Shabestari is recorded as the license holder of *Azerbaijan*, while Shams is mentioned as the editor-in-chief. See: Sadeqi Nasab, V.M., *Fehrest-e Ruznameh-ha-ye Farsi-ye Sal-e 1320-1332 Shamsi dar Majmu'eh-e Entesharat-e Ketabkhaneh-e Markazi va Markaz-e Asnad-e Daneshgah-e Tehran*, Tehran, Entesharat-e Daneshgah-e Tehran, 1981.

96. F.O. 371/31426, Consul Cook to Sir Reader Bullard, Tabriz, 8 April 1942.

97. Chashm Azar, M.Q., *op. cit.*, p. 19.

98. *Ibid*.

99. *Ibid.*, p. 24. It is interesting to note that most of the active members of the Tabriz anti-Fascist Committee were those whose names have already been mentioned as the architects of the other Societies. On the Tabriz anti-Fascist Committee were Badegan, Vela'i, Nunkrani and Shabestari, together with Asadi, Giverkiyan and Javidan.

100. F.O 371/31426, Consul Cook to Sir Reader Bullard, Tabriz, 26 January 1942. Shortly after publishing *Vatan Yolunda*, the Soviets began to publish their second newspaper, called *Qizil 'Askar* (The Red Soldier).

101. The Persian language press consisted of the following newspapers: *Ariya* (1941), *Akhtar-e Shomal* (1942-1945), *Faryad* (1942), *Ghoghay-e Zendegi* (1943-1944), *Goftar va Kerdar* (1942-1943), *Jodat* (1942-1946), *Kayvan* (1944-1945), *Kelid-e Nejat* (1944-1945), *Mahtab* (1941), *Neda-ye Haqq* (1944-1945), *Partow-e Eslam* (1944), *Seda-ye Azerbaijan* (1941), *Shahin* (1941-1945), *Tabriz* (1942-1944). The newspapers in Azerbaijani were: *Yumuruq* (Tabriz) (1943-1945), *Yumuruq* (Ardabil) (1943-1945), *Adabiyat Sahifasi* (Tabriz) (1943-1946) and the bilingual (Persian-Azerbaijani) newspapers were: *Azerbaijan* (1941-1942), *Khavar-e now* (the Tudeh Party's official provincial organ) (1943-1945), *Setareh-e Azerbaijan* (1944-1945). The one Armenian newspaper was: *Haga-Fashist* (1943-1945).

102. F.O. 371/31426, Consul Cook to Sir Reader Bullard, 20 May 1942.

103. *Ibid.*

104. Chashm Azar, M.Q., *op. cit.*, p. 20.

105. Ziba'i, A., *Komonizm dar Iran ya Tarikh-e Mokhtasar-e Komonist-ha dar Iran*, Tehran, no publisher given, 1964, p. 234. This book was published by the then head of SAVAK (Iranian Secret Police) and bears his name as the author. In truth it was mainly written by ex-Tudeh members who had been arrested after the 1953 *coup d'état* and were serving prison sentences at the time. They were provided with all SAVAK's secret documents concerning the Tudeh Party and the activities of Communists in Iran, and told to put together an antiCommunist propaganda book. Despite SAVAK's unhistorical motives, the book is an excellent source of information on the subjects it covers.

106. *Ibid.*

107. Chashm Azar does not mention Kalantari as one of the founders of the Provincial Committee. However, in an interview, Hoseyn Malek, who joined the Committee later on, told me that Kalantari was the only non-Communist member of the Provincial Committee and was removed after the first Provincial Conference.

108. *Rahbar*, no. 483, 6 February 1945.

109. According to the Soviet account, by the beginning of 1944, the total number of the Tudeh Party membership in Azerbaijan was 5,000. Archive of the Azerbaijan Institute of History, dos. 5, no. 12/5-9.

110. Maleki, K., *op. cit.*, p. 364.

111. Mir Ja'far Abbasovich Baqirov (1896-1956): First Secretary of the Central Committee of the Soviet Azerbaijan Communist Party and the Soviet Azerbaijan Council of the People's Commissars. As a *protégé* of

Stalin, Baqirov soon became a key figure during Stalin's era and actively participated in the extensive Stalinist purges. According to the Soviet historian Roy A. Medvedev, over 10,000 people were shot in Azerbaijan in 1937-8, "on the charge of attempting to murder Baqirov". After Stalin's death in 1953, Baqirov was removed from all his posts and was arrested the following year. He was tried in Baku on 12-26 April 1956, by the Military Collegium of the Supreme Court of the USSR and sentenced to death. Wieczynski, J.L., (ed.) *The Modern Encyclopedia of Russia and Soviet History*, Gulf Breeze (Florida), Academic International Press, 1976, pp. 238-40; Medvedev, R.A., *Let History Judge, The Origin and Consequences of Stalinism*, New York, Macmillan, 1972, p. 344.

112.   Maleki, K., "Speech at Tabriz", *Rahbar*, no. 591, 24 June 1945.

113.   *Rahbar*, no. 604, 12 July 1945.

114.   In his memoirs, Maleki describes the efforts he made to counter the propaganda activities of the rival faction. One example he gives is his replacing the portrait of Stalin in party headquarters with pictures of the early Azerbaijani Constitutionalists – such men as Sattar Khan and Baqer Khan. See: Maleki, K., *op. cit.*, pp. 365-74.

115.   According to Anvar Khameh'i, the constant pressure exerted by the "pro-Baqirov" tendency within the Provincial Committee eventually forced not only Khalil Maleki to leave Azerbaijan but other eminent party members as well: members such as Amir Khizi, the committee chairman; Ovanessian, a known leader of the Tudeh Party and deputy of the *Majles*; Zolun, a long-standing Jewish Communist; and Hoseyn Malek. See: Khameh'i, A., *Forsat-e Bozorg-e az Dast Rafteh, op. cit.*, pp. 193-4.

116.   Pakdaman, N., *op. cit.*, p. 13.

117.   Chashm Azar, M.Q., *op. cit.*, p. 22.

118.   F.O. 371/31426, Tabriz Diary, 21 September-31 October 1942.

119.   *Ibid.*

120.   Wash. Nat. Arch., 891.00/10-504, 12 December 1942.

121.   F.O. 371/45450, Visit of the Soviet Trade Union Delegation to Persia, 16 September 1945.

122.   F.O. 371/40178, Tabriz Diary, 28 July-10 August, 1944.

123.   *Ibid.*

124.   F.O. 371/40178, Tabriz Diary, 16-30 November, 1944.

125.   Maleki, K., *op. cit.*, p. 374.

126.   F.O. 371/40178, Tabriz Diary, 21 September-12 October, 1944.

127.   Wash. Nat. Arch., 891.00/10-2844, 29 October 1944.

128.   *Rahbar*, no. 572, 1 June 1945.

129. *Azhir*, no. 219, 10 December 1944; no. 234, 9 January 1945; no. 237, 16 January 1945; no. 239, 14 February 1945, *Rahbar*: no. 464, 14 January 1945; no. 523, 2 April 1945; no. 527, 8 April 1945; no. 628, 12 August 1945.
130. *Rahbar*, no. 597, 3 July 1945.
131. Wash. Nat. Arch. 891.00/6–145, 1 January 1945.
132. *Khavar-e Now*, no. 71, 9 July 1945.
133. *Mozakerat-e Majles*, 4 June 1945.
134. *Rahbar* reported several incidents in which Tudeh supporters were assaulted. See: *Rahbar*, no. 578, 8 June 1945; no. 581, 12 June 1945.
135. *Rahbar*, no. 518, 21 March 1945; no. 603, 11 July 1945.
136. *Rahbar*, no. 522, 1 April 1945.
137. Daneshiyan, Q.Y., Unpublished Memoirs.
138. *Rahbar*, no. 637, 23 August 1945.
139. The declaration published by the Ministry of Internal Affairs; *Rahbar*, no. 630, 14 August 1945. According to Anvar Khameh'i's account, the Soviets deplored the Liqvan incident, particularly since Hajj Ehtesham was one of the grain suppliers to the Red Army. Subsequently, they asked Ardashes Ovanessian, the representative in Azerbaijan of the Tudeh Party's Central Committee and a deputy in the *Majles*, to leave Azerbaijan. See: Khameh'i, A., *Forsat-e Bozorg-e az Dast Rafteh*, *op. cit.*, p. 174.
140. *Rahbar*, no. 633, 19 August 1945.
141. *Ibid.*
142. *Mozakerat-e Majles*, 11 August 1945.
143. *Iran-e Ma*, no. 440, 14 August 1945.

Chapter 5: The Democrat Party of Azerbaijan

1. For a detailed review of the Comintern policy see: Ulyanovsky, R.A. (ed.), *The Comintern and the East*, Moscow, Progress, 1979. For a case study of the Comintern policy see: Ulyanovsky, R.A. (ed.), *The Comintern and the East, A Critique of the Critique*, Moscow, Progress, 1978.
2. *Azhir*, no. 156, 13 June 1944.
3. *Ibid.*
4. *Azerbaijan*, no. 6, 18 September 1945.
5. Eskandari, I., *op. cit.*, vol. 4, p. 217.
6. *Shahrivarin On-Ikisi, Azerbaijan Demokrat Ferqehsinin Birinji Iyl Downemi Münasibatile*, Tabriz Markazi Tablighat Shubasinin Nashriyeh-si, 1946, p. 1.

7. Khameh'i, A., *Forsat-e Bozorg-e az Dast Rafteh*, *op. cit.*, pp. 194–5.
8. "Azerbaijan Demokrat Ferqehsinin Muraji'at-namehsi", in *Shahrivarin On-Ikisi*, *op. cit.*, pp. 5–7.
9. Chashm Azar, *op. cit.*, p. 56.
10. *Iran-e Ma*, no. 460, 9 December 1945.
11. *Ibid.*
12. *Azerbaijan*, no. 1, 5 September 1945.
13. Jahanshahlu Afshar, N., *op. cit.*, p. 306; see also: Eskandari, I., *op. cit.*, vol. 4, p. 213.
14. Keshavarz, F., *op. cit.*, p. 61.
15. Eskandari, I., *op. cit.*, vol. 1, p. 88.
16. Chashm Azar, M.Q., *op. cit.*, p. 53.
17. Eskandari, I., "Memorandum on the ADF's foundation", *op. cit.* vol. 4, p. 218. According to the Soviet account, on the eve of "fusion" the total number of the Tudeh Party's membership in Azerbaijan was 44,000, consisting of 72 per cent farmers, 11.1 per cent labourers, 10.2 per cent skilled workers, and the remainder 6.7 per cent white-collar workers, civil servants and intellectuals. Archive of the Azerbaijan Institute of History, doc. 5, no. 12/5–9.
18. Eskandari, I., *op. cit.*, p. 218.
19. *Ibid.*
20. Pesyan, N., *Marg Bud Bazgasht ham Bud*, Tehran, Emruz, 1949, p. 22.
21. Jahanshahlu Afshar, N., *op. cit.*, pp. 231–41.
22. *Azerbaijan*, no. 5, 17 September 1945.
23. F.O. 371/45478, Tabriz Diary, 7–21 September 1945.
24. Ferqeh-e Demokrat-e Azerbaijan, *Si Sal*, no place given, Tudeh, 1978, p. 17.
25. *Ibid.*
26. Pesyan. N., *op. cit.*, p. 23.
27. *Azerbaijan Demokrat Ferqehsinin Maram-namehsi va Nizam-namehsi*, Tabriz, Azerbaijan Matba'ehsi, 1945, pp. 5–20.
28. *Ayandeh*, nos. 9–10, 1945.
29. *Azerbaijan*, no. 22, 7 October 1945.
30. *Azerbaijan Demokrat Ferqehsinin Maram-nameh va Nizam-namehsi*, *op. cit.*, second part, pp. 1–9.
31. Chashm Azar, M.Q., *op. cit.*, p. 62.
32. Eskandari, I., "Memorandum on the ADF's Foundation", *op. cit.*, p. 219. According to Eskandari, of the five, Javid not only did not possess any office in the Congress' elected organs, but was not even present during its proceedings. Nevertheless, Javid's name has been mentioned by Chashm Azar as a member of the elected Central Committee. See: Chashm Azar, M.Q., *op. cit.*, p. 62.

33. *Azerbaijan*, no. 47, 11 November 1945.
34. Chashm Azar, M.Q., *op. cit.*, pp. 71–3.
35. *Ibid.*, pp. 77–8.
36. The rebellion, known by some of its participants as "Qiyam-e Afsaran-e Khorasan" (the Khorasani Officers' Insurrection) broke out in midAugust 1945, in Khorasan. Twenty-five officers and soldiers, led by 'Ali Akbar Eskandani, a major in the Iranian army, left their barracks in Mashhad, taking weapons and ammunition with them. The rebellion proved short-lived. After an early confrontation with the governmental forces and suffering seven casualties, including Eskandani himself, the rebels were dispersed. They eventually took refuge in the Soviet Union. The exiled officers were lodged in Shaholan, a village near Baku, and were soon joined by other officers who had fled Iran. After the Islamic Revolution, two of the officers who took part in the Khorasan Rebellion published their memoirs which are very informative. See Tafreshiyan, A., *Qiyam-e Afsaran-e Khorasan*, Tehran, 'Elm, 1980. Also: Shafa'i, A., *Qiyam-e Afsaran-e Khorasan va Si-o-haft Sal Zendegi dar Showravi*, Tehran, Ketabsara, 1987.
37. The first group of officers were: Azar, 'Azimi, Qazi 'Asadollahi, Mortazavi, Agahi, Musavi and Nazari. The second group included: Pirzadeh, Khal'atbari, Qamsariyan, Salimi, Qahreman and Shafa'i. See: Shafa'i, A., *op. cit.*, p. 134.
38. F.O. 371/45478, Tabriz Diary, 25 October–21 November 1945. Also: Jahanshahlu Afshar, N., *op. cit.*, p. 249.
39. A copy of the memorandum is presented in Pesyan, N., *op. cit.*, pp. 32–4.
40. Kuniholm, B.R., *The Origin of the Cold War in the Near East, Great Power Conflict and Diplomacy in Iran, Turkey, and Greece*, Princeton University Press, 1980, p. 279.
41. For the reports describing these rallies, see for example *Azerbaijan*, nos. 54, 56, 58, dated 14, 16, 19 November respectively.
42. Azerbaijan Demokrat Ferqehsi, *Shahrivarin On-Ikisi*, *op. cit.*, p. 21.
43. The election proceedings were by no means homogeneous. The city of Tabriz was represented by 256 delegates and therefore occupied 35 per cent of the seats at the assembly, whereas some districts had not held such election rallies. See: Chashm Azar, M.Q., *op. cit.*, p. 87.
44. *Azerbaijan*, no. 62, 23 November 1945.
45. *Ibid.*
46. "Azerbaijan Majlisi Mo'assesanin Qararlari", *Azerbaijan*, nos. 63, 26 November 1945
47. *Azerbaijan*, no. 69, 3 December 1945.
48. *Azerbaijan*, no. 73, 7 December 1945.

49. "Interview with Seyyed Ja'far Pishevari", *Khandani-ha*, no. 30, 3 December 1945.

50. Chashm Azar, M.Q., *op. cit.*, p. 88.

51. *Azerbaijan*, no. 69, 3 December 1945.

52. *Ibid.*

53. Abrahamian, E., *Iran Between Two Revolutions, op. cit.*, p. 289.

54. Abrahamian, E., "Communism and Communalism in Iran: the Tudeh and the Firqah-i Dimukrat", *International Journal of Middle Eastern Studies*, no. 1, 1970, pp. 291–316.

55. Pishevari, M.J., *Sechmish Asarlari*, Baku, Azerbaijan Nashriychsi, 1965, p. 6. In the modern history of Iran there can be no other figure whose identity has aroused so much controversy as Pishevari. Lenczowski holds that Pishevari is none other than Sultanzadeh, the distinguished leader of the Communist Party who was executed during the Stalinist purges of the late 1930s in the Soviet Union. According to Lenczowski, Sultanzadeh was not executed but managed to escape and, having changed his name, entered upon the political scene in Iran for the second time. Kuniholm maintains that Pishevari was a member of the Marxist group "The Fifty-Three" and was arrested in 1937. Cottam claims that Pishevari's first name was Mohammad, rather than Ja'far, whereas Hugh Thomas believes Pishevari's original name was Seijo Ja'far Badka Bayl, which he then changed to Sultanzadeh. Later still, according to Thomas: "Allowing it to be assumed that he had been a victim of Stalin's purges in 1938, he secretly returned to Persia under a new name and re-founded the Communist Party as the Tudeh, in 1941." Eagleton, too, in his book on the Kurdish rebellion of 1946, dates Pishevari's return to Iran as sometime "during the Second World War". It is interesting to note that none of the above mentioned authors cites his sources for these biographical "facts". See: Lenczowski, G., *Russia and the West in Iran 1918-1948*, Ithaca, Cornell University Press, 1949, p. 98; Kuniholm, B. R., *op. cit.*, p. 135. Cottam, R., *Nationalism in Iran*, Pittsburg University Press, 1964, p. 125; Thomas, H., *Armed Truce, The Beginning of the Cold War 1945-1946*, London, Sceptre, 1988, pp. 562-3; Eagleton, W.J.R., *The Kurdish Republic of 1946*, Oxford University Press, 1964, p. 41.

56. *Achiq Söz*, no. 458, 26 April 1917.

57. *Azerbaijan Joz'-e la-Yanfak-e Iran*, nos.1,3,7,9 28 January-28 February 1918.

58. *Hürriyat*, no. 72, 21 May 1920.

59. *Ibid.*

60. F.O. 371/1278, November 1920. See also: Manshur Garckani, M.A., *Siyasat-e Dowlat-e Showravi dar Iran az 1296 ta 1306*, vol. 1, Tehran, no publisher given, 1947, p. 55.

61.   Fakhra'i, I., *Sardar-e Jangal*, Tehran, 'Elmi, 1972, pp. 246–72.

62.   Rostamova, S., *Matbu'at-e Komonisti-ye Iran dar Mohajerat 1917–1932*, Baku, Azerbaijan, 1985, p. 43.

63.   For a documentary study of the Baku Congress, see: Pearce, B. (ed.), *Congress of the Peoples of the East*, London, New Park, 1977; Gruber, H., *Soviet Russia Masters the Comintern*, New York, Anchor Books, 1974.

64.   Institute of Marxism-Leninism, The Soviet Azerbaijan Communist Party's Central Archive, Fond 544, Cat. 2, vol. 8, pp. 1–43.

65.   Shahrokhi, K., *Azadeh-e Gomnam*, Tehran, no publisher given, 1955, p. 92. Fakhra'i, too, in his well researched study mentions Pishevari as a member of the Iranian delegation to the Baku Congress. See Fakhra'i. E., *op. cit.*, p. 274.

66.   Pishevari, M.J., *Sechmish Asarlari*, *op. cit.*, p. 10.

67.   According to Ovanessian, the newspaper *Haqiqat*, which was banned after its hundred and fourth issue, had a circulation of between 2000 and 2500. See: Ovanessian, A., *Safehat-i Chand az Jonbesh-e Kargari va Komonisti-ye Iran dar Dowran-e Reza Shah*, no place given, Tudeh, 1979, p. 11.

68.   Taqi Shahin, a member of the Central Committee of the ADF and Pishevari's Under-Secretary, in an interview with me claimed that Pishevari was indeed the Communist Party's First Secretary when he was arrested.

69.   United States Central Intelligence Agency, ORE 23–49, 18 July 1949, Significant Biographical Data, p. 25. Also: Pishevari, M.J., *Yaddasht-ha-ye Zendan*, no place given, no publisher given, undated, p. 9.

70.   Khameh'i, A., *Panjah Nafar va Seh Nafar*, *op. cit.*, p. 190.

71.   Wash. Nat. Arch., 891.00/6–2146, 21 June 1946.

72.   Khameh'i, A., *Forsat-e Bozorg-e az Dast Rafteh*, *op. cit*, p. 21.

73.   Eskandari, I., *op. cit.*, vol. 4, p. 216.

74.   It is worth noting that among those whom I interviewed concerning Pishevari's death, no one was able to present conclusive proof for or against the murder hypothesis. Those who believe that Pishevari was murdered claim that a personal conflict had developed between Pishevari and Baqirov after the fall of the autonomous government. According to some ADF leaders, the conflict came out in public during a banquet which Baqirov gave in 1947, on the anniversary of the founding of the Soviet Red Army. On this occasion Baqirov made a toast and praised the courageous efforts of the ADF leadership in "liberating Azerbaijan" but then he added some remarks about the party's shortcomings. He allegedly said that the cause of the fall of the autonomous government was "the low level of ties between north and south" and "the fact that

the ADF had not been closely enough linked to the Communist Party of Soviet Azerbaijan". Pishevari is said to have retorted bitterly to these remarks and to have surprised and angered Baqirov. According to eyewitness accounts: "From his (Pishevari's) point of view, the main reason for their failure, contrary to what Baqirov believed, was that they had depended too much on Soviet Azerbaijan, so that many observers characterized them as Soviet agents and co-ordinators." Baqirov's reaction was harsh and abrupt: "*Otur kishi!*" (Sit down, and shut up!) However, in an interview with me Rahim Qazi, who was present at the banquet in question, while corroborating the above account in detail, claims that it was Azar, a high-ranking general in the army of the autonomous government who quarrelled with Baqirov at the banquet, and not Pishevari.

75. *Azad Millat*, no. 3, 28 February 1946.
76. Jahanshahlu Afshar, N., *op. cit.*, p. 317.
77. *Rahbar*, no. 829, 2 October 1945.
78. Jahanshahlu Afshar, N., *op. cit.*, p. 318.
79. Javid, S., *Gusheh'i az Khaterat-e Nahzat-e Melli-ye Azerbaijan*, Tehran, no publisher given, 1979, pp. 33–4. See also: *Iran-e Ma*, no. 559, 18 June 1946.
80. Javid, S., *op. cit.*, p. 35.
81. Manshur Garekani, M.A., *op. cit.*, p. 165.
82. Wash. Nat. Arch. 891.00/7–1546, 15 July 1946. See also: *Iran-e Ma*, no. 559, 18 June 1946.
83. *Azerbaijan*, no. 82, 20 December 1945.
84. Agahi, A., "Shast Sal az Tarikh-e Ta'sis-e Hezb-e Komonist-e Iran Gozasht", *Donya*, no. 3, 1980, p. 54.
85. *Azerbaijan*, no. 82, 20 December 1945.
86. Jahanshahlu Afshar, N., *op. cit.*, p. 318.
87. Daneshiyan, G.Y., Unpublished Memoirs. See also: Taher, S., *Feda'i Zheneral*, Baku, Azerbaijan, 1987, pp. 6–11.
88. Daneshiyan, G.Y., *op. cit.* His involvement in these activities is confirmed by official Iranian Government records. See: Akhgar, I., *Marg Hast va Bazgasht Nist*, Tehran, Chehr, undated, p. 319.
89. Jahanshahlu Afshar, N., *op. cit.*, p. 319.
90. Sheyda, Y., *Biriya Ürek Sözlari*, Tabriz, Ark, 1981, p. 6.
91. *Rahbar*, no. 461, 10 January 1945.
92. Sheyda, Y., *op. cit.*
93. F.O. 371/40178, Tabriz Diary, 21 September–12 October 1944.
94. Jahanshahlu Afshar, N., *op. cit.*, p. 306.
95. Jahanshahlu Afshar, N., *op. cit.*, pp. 306–8.

96. Rossow, R., "The Battle of Azerbaijan 1946", *Middle East Journal*, no. 1, 1956, p. 30.

97. I would like to take the opportunity to thank Dr. Jahanshahlu Afshar, a former prominent leader in the Democrat Party of Azerbaijan, for the generous help he has given me with the preparation of this table.

98. Although every effort has been made to present accurate information on the personalities listed in this table, the data about class origins are bound to be somewhat imprecise and must be taken with a degree of reserve. Furthermore, it is worth mentioning that terminology to do with class distinctions in Western societies by no means fully corresponds to the prevalent social conditions in Iran.

99. As the years went by, the Tudeh Party gradually transformed its early political stance and came to be the orthodox Marxist-Leninist party in Iran. This, however, did not help to bring the ADF and the Tudeh Party closer together. In 1960, on the occasion of a plenum known as *Pelenom-e Vahdat* (the Plenum of Unity), the ADF was at least nominally merged with the Tudeh Party and renamed itself "the Provincial Committee of the Tudeh Party in Azerbaijan". None the less, as political developments in the following years clearly demonstrated, despite making some trivial concessions for the sake of apparent unity and pretending to accommodate the Tudeh Party's brand of Marxism, the ADF faction within the Tudeh Party retained its own network of power and its own distinct Leninist features.

Chapter 6: The Autonomous Government of Azerbaijan

1. Ferqeh-e Demokrat-e Azerbaijan, *Si Sal*, *op. cit.*, p. 49.

2. The members of the new chairing committee were: Shabestari, Badegan, Rafi'i, Jodat, Vela'i, 'Azima, Diba'iyan, Dilmaqani and Teymuri. *Azerbaijan*, no. 78, 12 December 1945. Also: Chashm Azar, M.Q., *op. cit.*, p. 90.

3. "Azerbaijan Milli Majlisinin Dakhili Nizam-namehsi", *Azerbaijan*, no. 79, 14 December 1945.

4. *Ibid.*

5. Wash. Nat. Arch. 891.00/12–1845, 23 January 1946.

6. *Azerbaijan*, no. 78, 12 December 1945. Until a minister of labour was designated, the prime minister exercised the functions of the ministry of labour.

7. *Ibid.*

8. F.O. 371/52663, 12 January 1946.

9. *Azerbaijan*, no. 78, 14 December 1945.

10. Wash. Nat. Arch. 891.00/3-2346, 23 March 1946.
11. *Azerbaijan*, no. 79, 14 December 1945.
12. F.O. 371/52663, 12 January 1946.
13. For the original text, see: Pesyan, N., *op. cit.*, p. 98. According to a report published in the *New York Times*, following the Derakhshani-Pishevari agreement, there were only fourteen officers who decided not to stay in Azerbaijan. *New York Times*, 17 December 1945.
14. F.O. 371/52661, 26 December 1945.
15. F.O. 371/52661, 26 December 1945, also: Zanganeh, A., *op. cit.*, pp. 66-138.
16. Wash. Nat. Arch. 891.00/2-2047, 21 February 1946.
17. Wash. Nat. Arch. 891.00/12-1845, 23 January 1946.
18. *Ibid.*
19. *Ibid.*
20. Chashm Azar, M.Q., *op. cit.*, pp. 89-90.
21. Wash. Nat. Arch. 891.00/12-1845, 18 December 1945.
22. Kuniholm, B.R. , *op. cit.*, p. 304.
23. According to Article 6 of the Treaty: "If a third party should attempt to carry out a policy of usurpation by means of armed intervention in Persia or if such a power should desire to use Persian territory as a base of operations against Russia or if a foreign power should threaten the frontiers of Federal Russia or those of its allies, and if the Persian Government should not be able to put a stop to such a menace after having been once called upon to do so by Russia, Russia shall have the right to advance her troops into the Persian interior for the purpose of carrying out the military operation necessary for its defence. Russia undertakes, however, to withdraw her troops from Persian territory as soon as the danger has been removed." For the text of the treaty see: Hurewitz, J.C., *Diplomacy in the Near and Middle East*, New Jersey, Van Nostrand, 1956, vol. 2., pp. 90-94.
24. Kuniholm, B.R., *op. cit.*, p. 304.
25. *Iran-e Ma*, no. 465, 18 December 1945.
26. Key Ostovan, H., *op. cit.*, vol. 2, p. 214.
27. *Mozakerat-e Majles*, 26 January 1946.
28. *Mozakerat-e Majles*, 2, 11, and 15 December 1945.
29. Maleki, K., *op. cit.*, p. 392.
30. *Iran-e Ma*, no. 462, 12 December 1945.
31. *Iran-e Ma*, no. 467, 20 December 1945.
32. *Azhir*, no. 157, 15 June 1944.
33. *Mozakerat-e Majles*, 15 December 1945.
34. Wash. Nat. Arch. 891.00/6-646, 6 June 1946.
35. Thomas, H., *Armed Truce*, *op. cit.*, p. 156.

36. *Izvestia*, 18 December 1945, cited in Thomas, J.R., *The Rise and Fall of the Azerbaijan People's Republic [sic] as Reflected in Izvestia, 1945–1947*, Certificate Essay, Columbia University, 1953, p. 53.

37. *Rahbar*, no. 671, 13 March 1946.

38. For a detailed account of these events and the measures taken by the Tudeh Party and Seyyed Zia Tabataba'i's group, see: Khameh'i, A., *Forsat-e Bozorg-e az Dast Rafteh*, *op. cit.*, pp. 278–86.

39. Mas'udi, Q., *Jariyan-e Mosaferat-e Misiyun-e E'zami-ye Iran beh Mosko*, Tehran, Chap, 1946, p. 17.

40. *Ibid.*, pp. 67–8.

41. *Ibid.*, p. 70.

42. For the text of the Tripartite Treaty, signed by Britain, USSR and Iran, see: Hurewitz, J.C., *Diplomacy in the Middle East, 1914–1956*, vol. 2, Princeton, Van Nostrand, 1956, pp. 233–4.

43. Vail Motter, T.H., *The Persian Corridor and Aid to Russia*, Washington, Office of the Chief of Military History, Department of Army, 1952, pp. 281–3. For a more detailed account of the Allied Military withdrawal from Iran, see Gobad Irani, R., "American Diplomacy: An Option Analysis of the Azerbaijan Crisis, 1945–1946", *International Studies*, 1978, pp. 25–34.

44. Khan Malek Yazdi, *Ghogha-ye Takhliyeh-e Iran*, Tehran, Selseleh, 1983, p. 114.

45. *Mozakerat-e Majles*, 3 March 1946.

46. Key Ostovan, H., *op. cit.*, vol. 2, pp. 279–80.

47. Relations between Qavam and 'Ala were hostile enough to influence the manoeuvres Qavam adopted in dealing with the United Nations. As a *protégé* of the Shah, 'Ala was more committed to the Court than to the policies of the government. In a few instances, he therefore acted as an "envoy of the Court" rather than in co-ordination with the government. For more details about 'Ala's independent actions in the United Nations with regard to the Azerbaijan question, see Taqizadeh's recently published memoirs: Afshar, I. (ed.) *Zendegi-ye Tufani, Khaterat-e Seyyed Hasan Taqizadeh*, Tehran, 'Elmi, 1989, pp. 276–8.

48. Gromyko, A., *Memoirs, from Stalin to Gorbachev*, London, Arrow Books, 1989, pp. 303–4.

49. Mas'udi, Q., *op. cit.*, p. 200.

50. *Jebheh*, no. 119, 6 April 1946.

51. *Jebheh*, no. 133, 23 April 1946.

52. The Azerbaijan delegation was made up of Pishevari, Badegan, Jahanshahlu Afshar, Ebrahimi, Dilmaqani, Shahin and Seyf Qazi. And the following persons were designated by the Central Government to

carry out negotiations with the Democrats: Mostashar od-Dowleh, Farmanfarma'iyan, Ipakchiyan, Sepehr, Lankarani and Firuz.

53. *Zafar*, no. 241, 24 April 1946.

54. *Rahbar*, no. 700, 23 April 1946.

55. *Rahbar*, no. 703, 26 April 1946. Ten years later as the leader of the dissident faction which left the Tudeh Party, Maleki changed his attitude and criticized the Tudeh Party for supporting the autonomous movement in Azerbaijan. See: Maleki K. and Khameh'i, A., *Pas az Dah Sal Enshe'abiyun-e Hezb-e Tudeh Sokhan Miguyand*, no publisher given, 1957, pp. 19–20.

56. *Jebheh*, no. 135, 25 April 1946.

57. *Jebheh*, no. 144, 7 May 1946.

58. *Azerbaijan* no. 172, 14 April 1946.

59. *Azerbaijan*, no. 178, 21 April 1946.

60. *Azerbaijan*, no. 179, 22 April 1946.

61. *Azerbaijan*, no. 180, 23 April 1946.

62. Ferqeh-e Demokrat-e Azerbaijan, *Si Sal, op. cit.*, p. 66.

63. Azerbaijan Demokrat Ferqehsi Markaz Komitehsi, *Azerbaijan Milli Majlisi va Azerbaijan Milli Hükumatinin Qarar va Qanunlar Majmu'ahsi, Azerbaijan Milli Majlisinin Musadere Haqqinda Tasvib olunmush Qanuni*, Baku, Azerbaijan, 1980, pp. 10–12.

64. *Ibid.*, p. 12.

65. Ferqeh-e Demokrat-e Azerbaijan, *Si Sal, op. cit.*, p. 67.

66. "Azerbaijan Milli Majlisinin Felahat Bahrehsinin Malek ile Akinji Arasinda Bulunmasi Qanuni", *Azad Millat*, no. 12, 16 April 1946.

67. *Azerbaijan*, no. 96, 9 January 1946.

68. *Azerbaijan*, no. 84, 23 December 1945.

69. The qualifications for candidates and voters were the same as those concerning the elections for the National Assembly, except that the age limits were different. Every Azerbaijani, including women, who was over nineteen years old was eligible to vote, and everyone between the age of twenty-five and seventy-five was qualified to stand for office. See *Azerbaijan*, no. 97, 10 January 1946.

70. Elections for the Tabriz Municipal Council were held on 15–20 January 1946, and elections for the District and Municipal Councils for outlying regions were held 9–14 February. See *Azerbaijan* nos. 103, 107, and 115, 17, 22 January and 1 February 1946 respectively.

71. Wash. Nat. Arch., 891.00/2-1946, 19 February 1946.

72. *Ibid.*

73. Wash. Nat. Arch. 891.00/12-1845, 23 January 1946.

74. *Azerbaijan*, no. 2, 8 September 1945.

75. On the history of the Kurdish autonomous movement in the post-World War II period, the best study available in English is still William Eagleton's book: Eagleton, W., *The Kurdish Republic of 1946*, London, Oxford University Press, 1963. See also: Roosevelt, A., "The Kurdish Republic of Mahabad", *Middle East Journal*, no. 1, July 1947, pp. 247–69. For an eyewitness account see: Tafreshiyan, A., *op. cit.*, pp. 77–114. For the Iranian government's point of view, see: Pesyan, N., *Az Mahabad-e Khunin ta Keraneh-ha-ye Aras*, Tehran, Chap, 1949.

76. Chashm Azar, M.Q., *op. cit.*, p. 46. Eagleton gives "September 1945" as the date for the formation of the Party; Eagleton, W., *op. cit.*, p. 56. However, the date given by Chashm Azar was confirmed by Rahim Qazi in an interview I had with the latter.

77. Eagleton, W., *op. cit.*, p. 57.

78. *Ibid.*

79. *Ibid.*, p. 60.

80. Although the Kurdish Democrats officially called their regime in Mahabad the Republic of Kurdistan, in a press interview of 11 January 1946, the President of the Republic stressed their commitment to the Iranian Constitutional Code and their wish to remain as an autonomous region within the national boundaries of Iran. For the reprinted text of this interview, see: *Kurdistan*, no. 223, 13 January 1989.

81. Wash. Nat. Arch. 891.00/2–2846, 28 February 1946.

82. *Ibid.*

83. *Azerbaijan*, no. 190, 5 May 1946.

84. *Ibid.*

85. *Azerbaijan*, no. 185, 29 April 1946.

86. For the full text of the Democrats' early proposal, see: *Shahrivarin On-Ikisi*, *op. cit.*, pp. 106–10.

87. The Atlantic Charter was a declaration of fundamental political principles for the post-War world issued by Roosevelt and Churchill at Placentia Bay, Newfoundland, in August 1941. Among the principles guaranteed by the Charter was the "right of people to choose their own forms of government and to live free from fear and want".

88. Wash. Nat. Arch., 891.00/5–146, 1 May 1946.

89. *Azerbaijan*, no. 199, 15 May 1946.

90. For a more detailed review of the disputed issues see: *Shahrivarin On-Ikisi*, *op. cit.*, pp. 110–15. Also, *Gozashteh Cheragh-e Rah-e Ayandeh Ast*, *op. cit.*, pp. 368–75.

91. F.O. 371/52679, 16 July 1946.

92. Tafreshiyan, A., *op. cit.*, p. 76.

93. F.O. 371/56831, 20 March 1946.

94. *Azerbaijan*, no. 223, 11 June 1946.

95. The text of the Agreement is given in the Appendix.

96. *Azerbaijan*, no. 228, 18 June 1946. According to a report from the US Consulate in Tabriz, Pishevari's negotiations with the Central Government caused disputes and even violent reactions among some Democrats. The report, however, is not confirmed by other sources. See: Wash. Nat. Arch., 891.00/6–2446, 24 June 1946.

97. *Azerbaijan*, no. 223, 24 June 1946.

98. *Ibid.*

99. *Iran-e Ma*, no. 562, 21 June 1946.

100. *Iran-e Ma*, no. 568, 30 June 1946.

101. *Ibid.*

102. *Iran-e Ma*, no. 566, 26 June 1946.

103. Abrahamian, E., *Iran Between Two Revolutions*, *op. cit.*, p. 231.

104. The labour bill prohibited child labour, limited the work day to eight hours, established that salaries would be paid over the weekend, that there would be six days of holiday a year with pay, that 1 May would be a holiday, that workers had the right to strike, and that the minimum wage must be regularly adjusted in accordance with the cost of living. See: Atabaki, T., "L'Organisation syndicale ouvrière en Iran", *op. cit.*, p. 51.

105. Eskandari, I., *op. cit.*, vol. 2., p. 141.

106. *Rahbar*, no. 795, 22 August 1946.

107. Wash. Nat. Arch. 891.00/8–1346, 13 August 1946.

108. *Ibid.*

109. Wash. Nat. Arch. 891.00/12-3046, 30 December 1946. *Azerbaijan*, no. 355, 22 November 1946.

110. Eskandari, I., *op. cit.*, vol. 2., pp. 143–4.

111. *Kayhan*, no. 984, 18 June 1946.

112. Khameh'i, A., *op. cit.*, p. 307.

113. Wash. Nat. Arch., 891.00/15–2246, 22 May 1946.

114. *Iran-e Ma*, no. 636, 24 September 1946.

115. Solat Qashqa'i, M.N., *Sal-ha-ye Bohran*, Tehran, Rasa, 1987, p. 26.

116. *Jebheh*, no. 274, 18 October 1946.

117. *Rahbar*, no. 703, 26 April 1946.

118. *Aras*, no. 42, 20 February 1946.

119. *Dad*, no. 774, 27 June 1946.

120. Eskandari, I., *op. cit.*, vol. 2, p. 147.

121. Wash. Nat. Arch. 891.00/6–646, 6 June 1946.

122. Wash. Nat. Arch. 891.00/1–1146, 11 January 1946. F.O. 371/52661, 29 December 1945.

123. Wash. Nat. Arch., 891.00/12–1845, 23 January 1946.

124. Chashm Azar, M.Q., *op. cit.*, p. 121.

125. *Khandani-ha*, no. 30, 3 November 1946.
126. During the year from 1945 to 1946, the following Azerbaijani-language newspapers were being published: *Azerbaijan* (the ADF's official organ), *Azad Millat* (the official organ of the National Assembly of Azerbaijan), *Yeni Sharq, Ghalabeh, Jodat, Urumiyeh, Javanlar* (the official organ of the Democratic Youth Organization of Azerbaijan), *Azar, Azerbaijan, Ulduzi, Adabiyat Sahifahsi, Sha'irlar Majlisi, Ma'arif, Vatan, Feda'i, Demokrat, Günesh.*
127. Iran is actually mentioned once in the fourth volume of *Vatan Dili*, and on that occasion only in a geographical context. See: *Vatan Dili*, Dördunji Kitab, p. 113.
128. Tafreshiyan, A., *op. cit.*, pp. 71–2.
129. *Ibid.*
130. *Rahbar*, no. 755, 30 June 1946. *Iran-e Ma*, no. 666, 30 October 1946.
131. *Azerbaijan*, no. 331, 23 October 1946.
132. *Azerbaijan*, no. 355, 22 November 1946.
133. *Zafar*, no. 400, 17 November 1946.
134. *Rahbar*, no. 868, 4 December 1946.
135. *Iran-e Ma*, no. 674, 12 November 1946. *Jebheh*, no. 294, 17 November 1946.
136. *Jebheh*, no. 298, 21 November 1946.
137. *Nabard-e Emruz* (in place of *Jebheh*), no. 1, 22 November 1946.
138. *Azerbaijan*, no. 357, 25 November 1946.
139. Wash. Nat. Arch., 891.00/12–3046, 30 December 1946.
140. *Ibid.*
141. *Ibid.*
142. *Azad Millet*, no. 118, 26 November 1946.
143. *Nabard-e Emruz*, no. 1, 22 November 1946.
144. *Iran-e Ma*, no. 684, 25 November 1946.
145. *Nabard-e Emruz*, no. 3, 25 November 1946.
146. *Azerbaijan*, no. 357, 26 November 1946.
147. *Ibid.*
148. *Zafar*, no. 413, 2 December 1946.
149. *Nabard-e Emruz*, no. 3, 25 November 1946.
150. *Azerbaijan*, no. 366, 7 December 1946. For the Persian text, see *Iran-e Ma*, no. 693, 8 December 1946.
151. Wash. Nat. Arch. 891.00/12–3046, 30 December 1946.
152. *Ibid.*
153. *Ibid.*
154. *Iran-e Ma*, no. 696, 11 December 1946.
155. Jahanshahlu Afshar, N., *op. cit.*, p. 308.
156. *Ibid.*, p. 358.

157. *Azerbaijan*, no. 371, 12 December 1946.
158. Wash. Nat. Arch., 891.00/12-2346, 23 December 1946.
159. Among such minor cases was the vague resistance organized by the *Komiteh-e Enteqam* (the Revenge Committee) which took place in a suburb of Tabriz: Ruzegar M., *Khaterat* (unpublished memoirs). In an interview with me, Mohammad Ruzegar described the resistance as "purely unprompted" and denied any possible link between the above mentioned group and the ADF leadership.
160. Douglas, W.O., *Strange Land and Friendly People*, New York, Harper and Brothers, 1951, p. 45.
161 In accounts of the Democrats, reference is made to more than 10,000 casualties, whereas semi-official reports of the Iranian government estimate the number of dead at 800. On the other hand, a British source cited by the US Embassy in Tehran gives the number of killed Democrats as 421. For the Democrats' account, see: Azerbaijan Demokrat Ferqehsi, *Azadliq Yolunun Mubarizlari*, vol. 2, Baku, Azerbaijan, 1969, p. 5. The Iranian government estimation has been reported in *Khandani-ha*, no. 36, 24 December 1946. The American Embassy's report has been classified under Wash. Nat. Arch. 891.00/1-1547, 15 January 1947.
162. The international dimensions of the Azerbaijan "crisis" have been the subject of several books, articles and university theses. The most recent study to appear which particularly focuses on international power politics as a backdrop to the events in Azerbaijan is: L'Estrange Fawcett, L., *The Struggle for Persia, the Azerbaijan Crisis of 1946*, D. Phil. thesis, St Antony's College, University of Oxford, 1988.
163. For a detailed study on this subject see: Atabaki, T., "Afsaneh-e Yek Oltimatom", *Chashmandaz*, no. 3, Autumn 1987, pp. 54-68; Thorpe, J.A., "Truman's Ultimatum to Stalin on the 1946 Azerbaijan Crisis", *The Society for Iranian Studies Newsletters*, vol. 7, no. 3, October 1972, pp. 8-10.
164. *New York Times*, 25 April 1952.
165. United States, Department of State, *Foreign Relations of the United States, 1946*, vol. 7, Washington, 1969, p. 348.
166. Keshavarz, F., *op. cit.*, p. 67; Fateh, M., *op. cit.*, p. 375; Khameh'i, A., *op. cit.*, p. 235; Maleki, K., *op. cit.*, pp. 426-7; Ladjevardi, H., *op. cit.*, p. 287.
167. Wash. Nat. Arch., 891.00/12-2346, 23 December 1946.
168. Wash. Nat. Arch., 891.00/12-3046, 30 December 1946.
169. *Azerbaijan*, no. 1, 5 September 1945.
170, *Azerbaijan*, no. 8, 20 September 1945.

Chapter 7: Epilogue

1. Eckart Ehlers, "Capitals and Spatial Organization in Iran, Esfahan, Shiraz, Tehran, in: C. Adle and B. Hourcade (Ed), *Tèhèran Capitale bicentenaire,* Paris, Diffusion, 1992, pp. 155–156.
2. Eckart Ehlers , op.cit., p. 156.
3. Op.cit, p. 161.
4. Ibid.
5. Ibid.
6. Gellner, E., op.cit, p. 140.
7. The Caucasus and Central Asian Chronicle, vol. 8, no. 4, 1989, pp. 7–10.
8. *Newsweek*, May 26, 1997, p. 31.

Bibliography

Unpublished Sources

A. Interviews

Chashm Azar, Mir Qasem: Chief Adviser to the Prime Minister in the Azerbaijan National Government, Chairman of the ADF in exile, Baku, Republic of Azerbaijan, October 1989.

Firuz, Mozaffar: Under-Secretary to the Iranian Prime Minister, Qavam, Paris, April 1986.

Malek, Hoseyn: sociologist, ex-member of Tudeh Party. Paris/Utrecht, April 1986/May 1989.

Nazari, Hasan: leading member of ADF. Köln, May 1986, December 1989.

Qazi, Rahim: leading member of the Democrat Party of Kurdistan. Baku, Republic of Azerbaijan, October 1989.

Ruzegar, Mohammad: member of the ADF. Dushanbeh, Republic of Tajikistan, October 1989.

Shahin, Taqi: Chief Secretary to the Prime Minister in the Azerbaijan National Government. Baku, Republic of Azerbaijan, October 1989.

Shamideh, Ali: leading member of the ADF. Baku, Republic of Azerbaijan, October 1989.

Shandermani, Akbar: leading member of the Tudeh Party. Dushanbeh, Republic of Tajikistan, October 1989.

B. Archives

Washington National Archive, Washington, D.C.

General Records of the Department of State: Iran, Decimal File, Record Group 59, 1940–47. Reference: Wash. Nat. Arch. 891.00/:

229

1-1146, 1-1547, 2-1946, 2-2047, 2-2846, 3-2346, 5-146, 6-145, 6-646, 6-2146, 6-2446, 7-1546, 8-1346, 10-504, 10-2844, 12-1845, 12-2346, 12-3046.

Library of Congress, Washington, D.C. Declassified Documents: United States Central Intelligence Agency. Iran, ORE 23-49.

Institute of Marxism-Leninism, Communist Party's Central Archive, Baku, Republic of Azerbaijan. Reference: Fond 544, Cat. 2, vol. 8.

Archive of the Azerbaijan Institute of History, Baku, Republic of Azerbaijan. Reference: Dos. 5, no. 12/5-9.

Public Record Office, London. Foreign Office Papers of the Eastern Department: Persia, Legation and Consular Correspondence 1940-47. Reference: F.O. 371/: 301, 956, 1278, 4927, 6440, 27192, 31426, 35090, 40172, 40177, 40178, 40241, 40243, 45450, 45478, 52661, 52663, 52679, 52740, 56831, 61993.

Ministry of Foreign Affairs, the Hague. Archief van de Nederlandse Legatie te Teheran, Politieke Zaken, 1903-45. Reference: 36/523. Dos. 19.

C. Unpublished Memoirs
Daneshiyan, Q.Y.
Ruzegar, M.

Published Sources

A. Documents
Azerbaijan Demokrat Ferqehsinin Maram-namehsi va Nizam-namehsi, Tabriz, Azerbaijan Matba'ehsi, 1945.

Azerbaijan Milli Majlis va Azerbaijan Milli Hükumatinin Qarar va Qanunlar Majmu'ehsi (1945-1946), Baku, Azerbaijan, 1980.

Ferqeh-e Demokrat-e Azerbaijan, *Si Sal,* no place given, Tudeh, 1978.

Maram-nameh-e Ferqeh-e Siyasi-ye Demokrat-e Iran ('Amiyun), 4th edition, Tehran, Matba'eh-e Dowlati, 1911.

Mozakerat-e Majles-e Showra-ye Melli, 1911, 1941-6.

Maram-nameh-e Jam'iyat-e Sosyal-Revolusiyoner-e Iran, Tehran,

Matba'eh-e Dowlati, undated.
Shahrivarin On-Ikisi, Azerbaijan Demokrat Ferqehsinin Birinji Iyl Downemi Münasibatile, Tabriz, Markazi Tablighat Shubasinin Nashriyehsi, 1946.
US Department of State, *Foreign Relations of the United States*, Washington, D.C., Government Printing Office, 1941–7.

B. Books and Articles

Abrahamian, E., *Iran Between Two Revolutions*, Princeton University Press, 1982.

———— "Communist and Communalism in Iran: the Tudeh Party and the Firqah-i Dimukrat", *International Journal of Middle Eastern Studies*, vol. 1, no. 4, October 1970.

Abutorabiyan, H., *Matbu'at-e Iran az Shahrivar 1320 ta 1326*, Tehran, Ettela'at, 1987.

Adamiyat, F., *Fekr-e Azadi va Moqaddameh-e Nahzat-e Mashrutiyat*, Tehran, Sokhan, 1961.

———— *Fekr-e Demokrasi-ye Ejtema'i dar Nahzat-e Mashrutiyat-e Iran*, Tehran, Payam, 1975.

Afshar, I., *Owraq-e Tazeh-yab-e Mashrutiyat*, Tehran, Javidan, 1980.

Agahi, 'Abdolhoseyn, "Shast Sal az Tarikh Ta'sis-e Hezb-e Komonist-e Iran Gozasht", *Donya*, no. 3, 1980.

Akçuroğlu, Y., *Üç Terz-i Siyaset*, Cairo, Matba'eh-i Qadr, 1909.

———— (ed.), *Türk Yili*, Istanbul, Yeni Matba'a, 1928.

Akhgar, I., *Marg Hast va Bazgasht Nist*, Tehran, Chehr, undated.

Alter, P., *Nationalism*, London, Edward Arnold, 1989.

Altstadt, A., *The Azerbaijani Turks, Power and Identity under Russian Rule*, Stanford, Hoover Institute Press, 1992.

Al-e Ahmad, J., *Dar Khedmat va Khiyanat-e Roshanfekran*, vol. 2, Tehran, Khwarazmi, 1978.

Amuzegar, S.H., *Naft va Havades-e Azerbaijan*, Tehran, Matbu'at, 1947.

Anderson, B., *Imagined Communities, Reflection on the Origin and Spread of Nationalism*, 3rd print, London, Verso, 1986.

Andrews, P., *Ethnic Groups in the Republic of Turkey*, Wiesbaden, Ludwig Reichert Verlag, 1989.

Anonymous, *Gozashteh Cheragh-e Rah-e Ayandeh Ast*, vol. 1, Tehran, Zebarjad, undated.

Anonymous, *Hodud al-'Alam men al-Mashreq ela al-Maghreb*, Sotudeh, M. (ed.), Tehran, Daneshgah-e Tehran Press, 1962.

Anonymous, *Haqq-e Daf'-e Sharr va Qiyam bar Zedd-e Zolm*, no publisher given, undated.

Anonymous, "Sanad-i Nashenakhteh dar Bareh-e Hezb-e Sosyal-Demokrat-e Iran", *Donya*, vol. 7, no. 2., Summer 1966.

Anonymous, *Sharh-e Hal-e Sheykh Mohammad Khiyabani*, Berlin, Iranshahr, 1926.

Atabaki, T., "Two Programmes of the Communist Movement in Khorasan in the early 1920s", *Utrecht Papers on Central Asia*, Utrecht, University of Utrecht, 1987.

——————— "L'Organisation syndicale ouvrière en Iran, de 1941 à 1946", *Soual*, no. 8, Paris, February 1988.

——————— "Afsaneh-e Yek Oltimatom", *Chashmandaz*, no. 3, Autumn, 1987.

Avery, P., Hambly, G., Melville, C., (eds.), *The Cambridge History of Iran*, vol. 7, Cambridge, Cambridge University Press, 1991.

Azerbaijan Demokrat Ferqehsi, *Azadliq Yolunun Mubarizlari*, Baku, Azerbaijan, 1969.

Azari, A., *Qiyam-e Sheykh Mohammad Khiyabani*, 4th edition, Tehran, 1975.

Azimi, F., *Iran, The Crisis of Democracy*, London, Tauris, 1989.

Bahar, M., *Tarikh-e Mokhtasar-e Ahzab-e Siyasi-ye Iran*, vol. 1, Tehran, Jibi, 1978.

Banani, A., *The Modernization of Iran, 1921–1941*, California, Stanford University Press, 1961.

Berkes, N., *The Development of Secularism in Turkey*, Montreal, McGill University Press, 1964.

Blucher, W.V., *Zeitenwende*, Persian Translation: *Safar-nameh-e Blucher*, Tehran, Khwarazmi, 1984.

Boyle, J.A., (ed.), *The Cambridge History of Iran*, vol. 5, Cambridge, Cambridge University Press, 1968.

Browne, E.G., *The Press and Poetry of Modern Persia*, Cambridge, Cambridge University Press, 1914.

Carr, E.H., *The Bolshevik Revolution 1917–1923*, vol. 1, London, Macmillan, 1950.

Chashm Azar, M.Q., *Azerbaijan Demokratik Partiyasinin Yaranmasi va Fa'aliyyati*, Baku, Elm, 1986.

Connor, W., "A Nation is a Nation, is a State, is an Ethnic Group ...", *Ethnic and Racial Studies*, vol 1, no. 4, 1978.

——————— *The National Question in Marxist-Leninist Theory and Strategy*, New Jersey, Princeton University Press, 1984.

Cottam, R., *Nationalism in Iran*, Pittsburg University Press, 1964.

Douglas, W.O., *Strange Land and Friendly People*, New York, Harper and Brothers, 1951.

Dowlatabadi, Y., *Hayat-e Yahya*, 3rd edition, vol. 3, Tehran, Ferdowsi, 1982.

Eagleton, W., *The Kurdish Republic of 1946*, London, Oxford University Press, 1963.

Ehtesham ol-Saltaneh, *Khaterat*, 2nd edition, Tehran, Zavvar, 1988.

Elias, N., *The Court Society*, New York, Pantheon Books, 1984.

Elwell Sutton, L.P., "The Political Parties in Iran", *The Middle East Journal*, no. 1, 1949.

Eskandari, I., *Khaterat*, in 4 vols., Paris, Hezb-e Demokratik-e Mardom-e Iran, 1988.

Ibn Faqih, Abu Bakr Ahmad b. Mohammad b. Eshaq Hamedani, *al-Buldan*, Tehran, Bonyad-e Farhang-e Iran, 1970.

Fakhra'i, I., *Sardar-e Jangal*, Tehran, 'Elmi, 1972.

Fateh, M., *Panjah Sal Naft-e Iran*, 2nd edition, Tehran, Payam, 1979.

Floor, W., *Industrialization in Iran, 1900–1941*, Occasional Paper Series, no. 23, University of Durham Press, 1984.

Forutan, Gh., *Afsaneh-e Ma*, no publisher given, undated.

Frye, R.N. (ed.), *The Cambridge History of Iran*, vol. 4, Cambridge, Cambridge University Press, 1975.

Gellner, E., *Nations and Nationalism*, Oxford, Basil Blackwell, 1983.

Ghobad Irani, R., "American Diplomacy: An Option Analysis of the Azerbaijan Crisis, 1945–1946", *International Studies*, 1978.

Gökalp, Z., *Türkçülük Esasları (The Principles of Turkism)*, Leiden, Brill, 1968.

Gromyko, A., *Memoirs, from Stalin to Gorbachev*, London, Arrow Books, 1989.

Gruber, H., *Soviet Russia Masters the Comintern*, New York, Anchor Books, 1974.

Haddad, W.W. and Coshenwald, W. (eds.), *Nationalism in a Non-National State*, Columbus, Ohio State University Press, 1977.

Ibn Hawqal, *Surat al-Arz*, Sho'ar, J. (ed.), Tehran, Bonyad-e Farhang-e Iran, 1966.

Hess, G.R., "The Iranian Crisis of 1945–46 and the Cold War", *Political Science Quarterly*, March 1974.

Hobsbawm, E.J., *Nations and Nationalism since 1780, Programme, Myth, Reality*, Cambridge, Cambridge University Press, 1990.

Hovanissian, R.G., *The Republic of Armenia*, vol. 1, Berkeley, University of California Press, 1971.

Hurewitz, J.C., *Diplomacy in the Near and Middle East*, New Jersey, Van Nostrand, 1956.

Al-Istakhri, Abu Ishaq al-Farsi, *Kitab al-Masalik wa-l-Mamalik*, de Goeje, M.J. (ed.), Leiden, Brill, 1927.

Ivanov, M., *Tarikh-e Novin-e Iran*, Stockholm, Tudeh, 1977.

Jackson, P. (ed.), *The Cambridge History of Iran*, vol. 6, Cambridge, Cambridge University Press, 1986.

Jacqs, J.W. (ed.), *Iran, Past and Future*, New York, Aspen Institute for Humanistic Studies, 1976.

Javid, S., *Gusheh'i az Khaterat-e Nahzat-e Melli-ye Azerbaijan*, Tehran, no publisher given, 1979.

Jahanshahlu Afshar, N., *Ma va Biganegan*, in 2 vols., Berlin, no publisher given, 1982.

Kambakhsh, 'A., *Nazar-i beh Jonbesh-e Kargari va Komonisti dar Iran*, Stassfurt, Tudeh , 1972.

———————— "Dar Bareh-e Sosiyal-Demokrasi-ye Enqelabi", *Donya*, vol. 4, no. 3, Summer 1962.

Kasravi, A., *Azari ya Zaban-e Bastan-e Azerbaijan*, 2nd edition, Tehran, Taban, 1938.

———————— *Tarikh-e Mashruteh-e Iran*, 14th edition, Tehran, Amir Kabir, 1978.

———————— *Tarikh-e Hejdah Saleh-e Azerbaijan*, 9th edition, Tehran, Amir Kabir, 1978.

Kazemzadeh, F., *The Struggle for Transcaucasus (1917–1921)*, New York, Philosophical Library, 1951.

Keshavarz, F., *Man Mottaham Mikonam*, Tehran, Ravaq, 1980.

Key Ostovan, H., *Siyasat-e Movazeneh-e Manfi dar Majles-e Chahardahom*, Tehran, Taban, 1948.

Khameh'i, A., *Panjah Nafar va Seh Nafar*, Tehran, Hafteh, 1984.

———————— *Forsat-e Bozorg-e az Dast Rafteh*, Tehran, Hafteh, 1983.

————————— *Az Enshe'ab ta Kudeta*, Tehran, Hafteh, 1984.

Khan Malek Yazdi, *Ghogha-ye Takhliyeh-e Iran*, Tehran, Selseleh, 1983.

Kuhi Kermani, H., *Az Shahrivar-e 1320 ta Faje'eh-e Azerbaijan va Zanjan*, vol. 2, Tehran, Mazaheri, 1946.

Kuniholm, B., *The Origin of the Cold War in the Near East, Great Power Conflict and Diplomacy in Iran, Turkey, and Greece*, Princeton University Press, 1980.

Ladjevardi, H., *Labour Unions and Autocracy in Iran*, Syracuse University Press, 1985.

Lambton, A.K.S., *Landlord and Peasant in Persia*, London, Oxford University Press, 1951.

Lenczowski, G., *Russia and the West in Iran, 1918-1948, A Study in Big-Power Rivalry*, Ithaca, Cornell University Press, 1949.

Lenin, V., "The Right of Nations to Self-Determination", *Selected Writings*, Moscow, Progress Publishers, 1966.

Lewis, B., *The Emergence of Modern Turkey*, London, Oxford University Press, 1962.

Louis, W.L., *The British Empire in the Middle East 1945-51*, Oxford, 1984.

Makki, H., *Tarikh-e Bist Saleh-e Iran*, Tehran, Nasher, 1983.

Maleki, K., *Khaterat-e Siyasi*, Tehran, Ravaq, 1981.

Malekzadeh, M., *Tarikh-e Enqelab-e Mashrutiyat-e Iran*, 2nd edition, Tehran, 'Elmi, 1984.

Manshur Garekani, M.A., *Siyasat-e Dowlat-e Showravi dar Iran az 1296 ta 1306*, Tehran, no publisher given, 1947.

Mark, E.M., "Allied Relations in Iran 1941-1947", *Wisconsin Magazine of History*, Fall 1975.

Markaz-e Amar-e Iran, *Iran dar Ayeneh-e Amar*, no. 6, Tehran, 1988.

Al-Mas'udi, *Kitab al-Tanbih wa-l-Ishraf*, de Goeje, M.J. (ed.), Leiden, Brill, 1894.

Mas'udi, Q., *Jariyan-e Mosaferat-e Misiyun-e E'zami-ye Iran beh Mosko*, Tehran, Chap, 1946.

McFarland, S.L., "A Peripheral View of the Origin of the Cold War: The Crisis in Iran 1941-1947", *Diplomatic History*, vol. 4, no. 4, 1980.

Mehdinia, J., *Zendegi-ye Siyasi-ye Qavam os-Saltaneh*, Tehran, Pasargard, 1987.

Millspaugh, A., *Americans in Persia*, New York, Da Capo Press, 1976.

Mokhber os-Saltaneh Hedayat, M., *Khaterat va Khatarat*, 3rd edition, Tehran, Zavvar, 1982.

Moshiri, M., *Sharh-e Ma'muriyat-e Ajudanbashi*, Tehran, Ashrafi, 1977.

Mostashar od-Dowleh, Y., *Resaleh-e Mosumeh beh Yek Kalemeh*, Paris, no publisher given, undated.

Al-Muqaddasi, Shams al-Din b. Abi 'Abdollah Mohammad b. Abi Bakr al-Banna al-Sami al-ma'ruf beh al-Beshari, *Ahsan al-Taqasim fi Ma'rifat al-Aqalim*, de Goeje, M.J. (ed.), Leiden, Brill, 1906.

Nateq, H., *Iran dar Rah-yabi-ye Farhangi, 1834–1848*, London, Payam, 1988.

——————— "Anjoman-ha-ye Showra'i dar Enqelab-e Mashrutiyat", *Alefba*, no. 4., Paris, 1983.

Nazem ol-Eslam Kermani, *Tarikh-e Bidari-ye Iraniyan*, New Edition, Tehran, Agah and Novin, 1983.

Ovanessian, A., *Safehat-i Chand az Jonbesh-e Kargari va Komonisti-ye Iran dar Dowran-e Reza Shah*, no place given, Tudeh, 1979.

Pakdaman, N., *Amar-nameh-e Eqtesad-e Iran dar Aghaz-e Jang-e Jahani-ye Dovvom*, vol. 1, Tehran University Press, 1976.

Pearce, B. (ed.), *Congress of the Peoples of the East*, London, New Park, 1977.

Pesyan, N., *Marg Bud Bazgasht ham Bud*, Tehran, Emruz, 1949.

Pesyan, N., *Az Mahabad-e Khunin ta Keraneh-ha-ye Aras*, Tehran, Chap, 1949.

Phau, R., "Containment in Iran 1946: The Shift to an Active Policy", *Diplomatic History*, vol. 1, no. 4, 1977.

Pishevari, M.J., *Yaddasht-ha-ye Zendan*, no publisher given, undated.

——————— *Sechmish Asarlari*, Baku, Azerbaijan Nashriyehsi, 1965.

Ra'in, I., *Heydar Khan 'Amoghlu*, vol. 2., Tehran, no publisher given, 1979.

Rahimi, M., *Qanun-e Asasi-ye Iran va Osul-e Demokrasi*, 3rd Edition, Tehran Amir Kabir, 1978.

Ramazani, R., *The Foreign Policy of Iran*, University Press of Virginia, 1966.

——————— "The Autonomous Republic of Azerbaijan and the Kurdish People's Republic, Their Rise and Fall", *Studies on the Soviet Union 11*, no. 4, 1971.

Ravasani, S., *Sowjetrepublik Gilan: Die sozialistische Bewegung in Iran seit Ende des 19JH. bis 1922*, Berlin, no publisher given, undated.

Rasulzadeh, M.A., *Tanqid-e Ferqeh-e E'tedaliyun ya Ejtema'iyun E'tedaliyun*, Tehran, Farus, 1910.

Rezazadeh Malek, R., *Heydar Khan 'Amoghlu*, Tehran, Ruzbeh, undated.

Roosevelt, A., "The Kurdish Republic of Mahabad", *Middle East Journal*, no. 1, July 1947.

Rossow, R., "The Battle of Azerbaijan 1946", *The Middle East Journal*, no. 1, winter 1956.

Rostamova, S., *Matbu'at-e Komonisti-ye Iran dar Mohajerat 1917–1932*, Baku, Azerbaijan, 1985.

Rumlu, Hasan Beg, *Ahsan al-Tavarikh*, Nava'i, A. (ed.), Tehran, Babak, 1978.

Sadeqi Nasab, V.M., *Fehrest-e Ruznameh-ha-ye Farsi Sal-e 1320–1332 Shamsi dar Majmu'eh-e Entesharat-e Ketab Khaneh-e Markazi va Markaz-e Asnad-e Daneshgah-e Tehran*, Tehran, Entesharat-e Daneshgah, 1981.

Sadr Hashemi, M., *Tarikh-e Jarayed va Matbu'at-e Iran*, Isfahan, Kamal, 1984.

Sadr, M., *Khaterat-e Sadr ol-Ashraf*, Tehran, Vahid, 1985.

Safa'i, E., *Rahbaran-e Mashruteh: Sani' od-Dowleh*, Tehran, no publisher given, 1964.

Sani' od-Dowleh, *Rah-e Nejat*, Tehran, Farus, 1907.

Seton-Watson, H., *Nation and States, An Enquiry into the Origins of Nations and the Politics of Nationalism*, Boulder, Westview Press, 1977.

Shafa'i, A., *Qiyam-e Afsaran-e Khorasan va Si-o-haft Sal Zendegi dar Showravi*, Tehran, Ketabsara, 1987.

Sharif Kashani, M.M., *Vaqe'at-e Ettefaqiyyeh dar Ruzegar*, Tehran, Nashr-e Tarikh-e Iran, 1983.

Shahrokhi, K., *Azadeh-e Gomnam*, Tehran, no publisher given, 1955.

Sheyda, Y., *Biriya Ürek Sözlari*, Tabriz, Ark, 1981.

Solat Qashqa'i, M.N., *Sal-ha-ye Bohran*, Tehran, Rasa, 1987.

Stalin, J., *Marxism and the National Question*, New York, International Publishers, 1935.

Sumbatzadeh, A.S., *Azerbaidzhanskaia Istoriografia XIX–XX vekov*, Baku, 'Elm, 1987.

Swietochowski, T., *Russian Azerbaijan 1905-1920, The Shaping of National Identity in a Muslim Community*, Cambridge, Cambridge University Press, 1985.

Tabari, E., *Kazh-Raheh*, Tehran, Amir Kabir, 1987.

Tafreshiyan, A., *Qiyam-e Afsaran-e Khorasan*, Tehran, 'Elm, 1980.

Taher, S., *Feda'i Zheneral*, Baku, Azerbaijan, 1987.

Taherzadeh Behzad, K., *Qiyam-e Azerbaijan dar Enqelab-e Mashrutiyat-e Iran*, Tehran, Eqbal, 1963.

Taqieva, A., *Natsional'no-Osvoboditl'noye Dvizheniye v Iranskom Azerbaidzhane 1917-1920*, Baku, 1956.

Taqizadeh, H., *Khetabeh, Tarikh-e Ava'el-e Enqelab va Mashrutiyat-e Iran*, Tehran, Bashgah-e Mehregan, 1959.

——————— *Zendegi-ye Tufani, Khaterat-e Seyyed Hasan Taqizadeh*, Afshar, I. (ed.), Tehran, 'Elmi, 1989.

Thomas, H., *Armed Truce, The Beginnings of the Cold War 1945-1946*, London, Sceptre, 1988.

Ulyanovsky, R.A. (ed.), *The Comintern and the East*, Moscow, Progress, 1979.

Ulyanovsky, R.A. (ed.), *The Comintern and the East, A Critique of the Critique*, Moscow, Progress, 1978.

Vail Motter, T.H., *The Persian Corridor and Aid to Russia*, Washington, Office of the Chief of Military History, Department of the Army, 1952.

Yaqikiyan, G., *Showravi va Jonbesh-e Jangal, Yaddasht-ha-ye Yek Shahed-e 'Eyni*, Tehran, Novin, 1984.

Yaqut al-Hamavi, *Kitab Mu'jam al-Buldan*, Wüstenfeld, F. (ed.), Leipzig, Brockhaus, 1866.

Zanganeh, A., *Khaterat-i az Ma'muriyat-ha-ye Man dar Azerbaijan*, Tehran, Sharq , 1976.

Ziba'i, A., *Komonizm dar Iran ya Tarikh-e Mokhtasar-e Komonist-ha dar Iran*, Tehran, no publisher given, 1964.

C. Theses and Dissertations

Abrahamian, E., *Social Bases of Iranian Politics, The Tudeh Party, 1941-1953*, Ph.D. thesis, Columbia University, 1969.

Alpern, S.B., *Iran, 1941-1946, A Case Study in the Soviet Theory of Colonial Revolution*, Certificate essay, Russian Institute, Columbia, 1953.

L'Estrange Fawcett, L., *The Struggle for Persia: The Azerbaijan Crisis of 1946*, D. Phil. thesis, St Antony's College, University of Oxford, 1988.

Ghobad Irani, R., *The Azerbaijan Crisis 1945–6, An Option Analysis of US Policy*, Ph.D. thesis, Maryland University, 1973.

Hetrick, K.L., *The United Nations as a National Foreign Policy Instrument, The Iranian Case of 1946*, Ph.D. thesis, Rutgers University, 1979.

Kovac, J.E., *Iran and the Beginning of the Cold War: A Case Study in the Dynamics of International Politics*, Ph.D. thesis, University of Utah, 1970.

Ladjevardi, H., *Politics and Labour in Iran: 1941–1949*, D. Phil. thesis, St. Antony's College, University of Oxford, 1980.

Schumann, M.L., *The Autonomous Republic of Azerbaijan and Kurdistan in Iran, November 1945 to December 1946*, Certificate essay, Russian Institute, Columbia, 1953.

Modjtehedi, M., *La Question d'Azerbaidjan: Le Mouvement des Democrates et les efforts de l'ONU*, Ph.D. thesis, University of Paris, 1952.

Thomas, J.R., *The Rise and Fall of the Azerbaijan People's Republic as Reflected in Izvestia, 1945–1946*, Certificate essay, Russian Institute, Columbia, 1953.

Vahdat, M., *The Soviet Union and the Movement to Establish Autonomy in Iranian Azerbaijan*, Ph.D. thesis, University of Indiana, 1958.

D. Newspapers and periodicals

Achiq Söz
Anjoman
Aras
Azad Millat
Azerbaijan
Azerbaijan Joz'-e la-Yanfak-e Iran
Azhir
Dad
Donya
Ettela'at
Faryad
Haqiqat

Hürriyat
Iran-e Ma
Iran-e Now
Iranshahr
Jarideh-e Melli
Javanlar
Jebheh
Kaveh
Kayhan
Khandani-ha
Kurdustan
Nabard-e Emruz (in place of *Jebheh*)
New York Times
Rahbar
Yeni Mecmu'a
Zafar

Index

241